A Verilog® HDL Primer

Third Edition

A Verilog® HDL Primer

Third Edition

J. Bhasker

eSilicon Corporation

BSP BS Publications

An Imprint of **BSP Books Pvt., Ltd.**

4-4-309/316, Giriraj Lane,

Sultan Bazar, Hyderabad - 500 095

A Verilog HDL Primer, Third Edition
by **J. Bhaskar**
First Indian Ed. 2008
17th Reprint 2026

Published by :

BSP BS Publications
An Imptint of **BSP Books Pvt., Ltd.**
4-4-309/316, Giriraj Lane, Sultan Bazar,
Hyderabad - 500 095
Phone: 040 - 23445688
e-mail: info@bspbooks.net
www.bspbooks.net

In arrangement with
Star Galaxy Publishing
1058 Treeline Drive, Allentown, PA 18103
Phone : 610-391-7296

For sale in India, Pakistan, Srilanka, Bangladesh, Nepal, Maldives and Maynmar only.

Original English language edition published by Star Galaxy Publishing

WARNING - DISCLAIMER

The author and publisher have used their best efforts in preparing this book and the examples contained in it. They make no representation, however, that the examples are error-free or are suitable for every application to which a reader may attempt to apply them. The author and the publisher make no warranty of any kind, expressed or implied, with regard to these examples, documentation or theory contained in this book, all of which is provided "as is". The author and the publisher shall not be liable for any direct or indirect damages arising from any use, direct or indirect, of the examples provided in this book.

Verilong® is a registered trademark of Cadence Design Systems, Inc.
VeriBest® is a registered trademark of Mentor Graphics Corporation.
Material in Appendix A is reprinted with permission fromIEEE Std 1364-2001 "IEEE Standard Hardware Description Language Based on the Verilog Hardware Description Language", Copyright © 2001 by the IEEE. The IEEE disclaims any responsibility or liability resulting from the placement and use in the described manner.

Price: Rs. 895.00
ISBN: 978-81-7800-142-5 (Paperback)

Other books by the same author:

- A VHDL Synthesis Primer, Second Edition, BS Publications, ISBN 81-7800-014-8, Indian Reprint 2001 **(for Indian subcontinent)**.
- A SystemC Primer, Second Edition, BS Publications, ISBN 978-81-7800-141-8, Indian Reprint 2008 **(for Indian subcontinent)**.
- Verilog HDL Synthesis, A Practical Primer, BS Publications, ISBN 81-7800-011-3, Indian Reprint 2001 **(for Indian subcontinent)**.

To my wife, Geetha

Contents

Preface xv

CHAPTER 1

Introduction 1

1.1. What is Verilog HDL?, 1
1.2. History, 2
1.3. Major Capabilities, 3
1.4. Exercises, 5

CHAPTER 2

A Tutorial 6

2.1. A Module, 6
2.2. Delays, 8
2.3. Describing in Dataflow Style, 9
2.4. Describing in Behavioral Style, 11
2.5. Describing in Structural Style, 15
2.6. Describing in Mixed-design Style, 17
2.7. Simulating a Design, 18
2.8. Exercises, 23

CHAPTER 3

Language Elements 25

3.1. Identifiers, 25
3.2. Comments, 26
3.3. Format, 26
3.4. System Tasks and Functions, 27
3.5. Compiler Directives, 27
3.5.1. `define and `undef, 28
3.5.2. `ifdef, `ifndef, `else, `elsif and `endif, 29
3.5.3. `default_nettype, 29
3.5.4. `include, 30
3.5.5. `resetall, 30
3.5.6. `timescale, 30
3.5.7. `unconnected_drive and `nounconnected_drive, 32
3.5.8. `celldefine and `endcelldefine, 33
3.5.9. `line, 33
3.6. Value Set, 33
3.6.1. Integers, 34
Simple Decimal Form, 34
Base Format Notation, 35
3.6.2. Reals, 37
3.6.3. Strings, 37
3.7. Data Types, 38
3.7.1. Net Types, 39
Wire and Tri Nets, 40
Wor and Trior Nets, 41
Wand and Triand Nets, 41
Trireg Net, 42
Tri0 and Tri1 Nets, 42
Supply0 and Supply1 Nets, 43
3.7.2. Undeclared Nets, 43
3.7.3. Vectored and Scalared Nets, 44
3.7.4. Variable Types, 44
Reg Variable, 45
Memories, 45
Integer Variable, 48
Time Variable, 50
Real and Realtime Variable, 51
3.7.5. Arrays, 51
3.7.6. Difference between Reg and Wire, 52
3.8. Parameters, 53

3.8.1. *Local Parameters,* 54
3.9. Exercises, 54

CHAPTER 4
Expressions 56
4.1. Operands, 56
4.1.1. *Constant,* 57
4.1.2. *Parameter,* 58
4.1.3. *Net,* 58
4.1.4. *Variable,* 59
4.1.5. *Bit-select,* 59
4.1.6. *Part-select,* 60
4.1.7. *Memory and Array Element,* 61
4.1.8. *Function Call,* 62
4.1.9. *Signedness,* 62
4.2. Operators, 63
4.2.1. *Arithmetic Operators,* 65
Result Size, 66
Unsigned and Signed, 67
4.2.2. *Relational Operators,* 69
4.2.3. *Equality Operators,* 71
4.2.4. *Logical Operators,* 72
4.2.5. *Bit-wise Operators,* 73
4.2.6. *Reduction Operators,* 75
4.2.7. *Shift Operators,* 77
4.2.8. *Conditional Operator,* 78
4.2.9. *Concatenation and Replication,* 79
4.3. Kinds of Expressions, 81
4.4. Exercises, 82

CHAPTER 5
Gate-level Modeling 83
5.1. The Built-in Primitive Gates, 83
5.2. Multiple-input Gates, 84
5.3. Multiple-output Gates, 87
5.4. Tristate Gates, 88
5.5. Pull Gates, 90
5.6. MOS Switches, 90
5.7. Bidirectional Switches, 93
5.8. Gate Delays, 93
5.8.1. *Min:typ:max Delay Form,* 95

5.9. Array of Instances, 96
5.10. Implicit Nets, 97
5.11. A Simple Example, 97
5.12. A 2-to-4 Decoder Example, 99
5.13. A Master-slave Flip-flop Example, 100
5.14. A Parity Circuit, 101
5.15. Exercises, 102

CHAPTER 6

User-Defined Primitives **103**

6.1. Defining a UDP, 103
6.2. Combinational UDP, 104
6.3. Sequential UDP, 106
6.3.1. Initializing the State Variable, 106
6.3.2. Level-sensitive Sequential UDP, 107
6.3.3. Edge-triggered Sequential UDP, 107
6.3.4. Mixing Edge-triggered and Level-sensitive Behavior, 108
6.4. Another Example, 109
6.5. Summary of Table Entries, 110
6.6. Exercises, 110

CHAPTER 7

Dataflow Modeling **112**

7.1. Continuous Assignment, 112
7.2. An Example, 115
7.3. Net Declaration Assignment, 115
7.4. Delays, 116
7.5. Net Delays, 118
7.6. Examples, 120
7.6.1. Master-slave Flip-flop, 120
7.6.2. Magnitude Comparator, 120
7.7. Exercises, 121

CHAPTER 8

Behavioral Modeling **122**

8.1. Procedural Constructs, 122
8.1.1. Initial Statement, 123
8.1.2. Always Statement, 125
8.1.3. In One Module, 128
8.2. Timing Controls, 130

8.2.1. Delay Control, 130
8.2.2. Event Control, 132
Edge-triggered Event Control, 132
Level-sensitive Event Control, 135
8.3. Block Statement, 136
8.3.1. Sequential Block, 137
8.3.2. Parallel Block, 138
8.4. Procedural Assignments, 141
8.4.1. Intra-statement Delay, 142
8.4.2. Blocking Procedural Assignment, 144
8.4.3. Nonblocking Procedural Assignment, 145
8.4.4. Continuous Assignment vs Procedural Assignment, 149
8.5. Conditional Statement, 150
8.6. Case Statement, 152
8.6.1. Don't-cares in Case, 154
8.7. Loop Statement, 155
8.7.1. Forever-loop Statement, 155
8.7.2. Repeat-loop Statement, 156
8.7.3. While-loop Statement, 157
8.7.4. For-loop Statement, 157
8.8. Procedural Continuous Assignment, 158
8.8.1. Assign - deassign, 158
8.8.2. Force - release, 160
8.9. A Handshake Example, 161
8.10. Exercises, 163

CHAPTER 9
Structural Modeling **166**
9.1. Module, 166
9.2. Ports, 167
9.2.1. Parameter Ports, 168
9.3. Module Instantiation, 169
9.3.1. Unconnected Ports, 171
9.3.2. Different Port Lengths, 172
9.3.3. Module Parameter Values, 173
Defparam Statement, 173
Module Instance Parameter Value Assignment, 174
9.4. External Ports, 177
9.5. Examples, 182
9.6. Generate Statement, 185
9.6.1. Generate-loop, 186

9.6.2. Generate-conditional, 188
9.6.3. Generate-case, 191
9.7. Configurations, 192
9.8. Exercises, 196

CHAPTER 10

Other Topics 198

10.1. Tasks, 198
10.1.1. Task Definition, 198
10.1.2. Task Calling, 201
10.2. Functions, 204
10.2.1. Function Definition, 205
10.2.2. Function Call, 208
10.2.3. Constant Functions, 209
10.3. System Tasks and Functions, 210
10.3.1. Display Tasks, 211
Display and Write Tasks, 211
Strobe Tasks, 213
Monitor Tasks, 214
10.3.2. File I/O Tasks, 215
Opening and Closing Files, 215
Writing out to a File, 217
Reading from a File, 218
Annotating from a SDF file, 219
10.3.3. Timescale Tasks, 220
10.3.4. Simulation Control Tasks, 221
10.3.5. Simulation Time Functions, 222
10.3.6. Conversion Functions, 223
10.3.7. Probabilistic Distribution Functions, 223
10.3.8. String Formatting, 225
10.4. Disable Statement, 226
10.5. Named Events, 228
10.6. Mixing Structure with Behavior, 231
10.7. Hierarchical Path Name, 232
10.8. Sharing Tasks and Functions, 235
10.9. Attributes, 237
10.10. Value Change Dump (VCD) File, 238
10.10.1. Four-state VCD File, 238
10.10.2. Extended VCD File, 240
10.10.3. An Example, 241
10.10.4. Format of VCD File, 243

10.11. Specify Block, 243
10.12. Strengths, 253
10.12.1. Drive Strength, 253
10.12.2. Charge Strength, 254
10.13. Race Condition, 255
10.14. Command Line Arguments, 257
10.15. Exercises, 258

CHAPTER 11

Verification **260**

11.1. Writing a Test Bench, 260
11.2. Waveform Generation, 261
11.2.1. A Sequence of Values, 261
11.2.2. Repetitive Patterns, 263
11.3. Testbench Examples, 270
11.3.1. A Decoder, 270
11.3.2. A Flip-flop, 271
11.4. Reading Vectors from a Text File, 273
11.5. Writing Vectors to a Text File, 276
11.6. Some More Examples, 277
11.6.1. A Clock Divider, 277
11.6.2. A Factorial Design, 279
11.6.3. A Sequence Detector, 283
11.6.4. A LED Sequencer, 285
11.7. Utilities, 287
11.7.1. Checking for x, 287
11.7.2. Passing a File to a Task, 288
11.7.3. Debugging Opcodes, 289
11.7.4. Check No Missing Clock, 289
11.7.5. Clock Burst Generator, 290
11.8. Exercises, 291

CHAPTER 12

Modeling Examples **294**

12.1. Modeling Simple Elements, 294
12.2. Different Styles of Modeling, 299
12.3. Modeling Delays, 301
Transport Delays, 304
12.4. Modeling a Truth Table, 305
12.5. Modeling Conditional Operations, 307

12.6. Modeling Synchronous Logic, 309
12.7. A Generic Shift Register, 313
12.8. A Gray Counter, 314
12.9. A Decade Counter, 315
12.10. Parallel to Serial Converter, 316
12.11. State Machine Modeling, 316
12.12. Interacting State Machines, 319
12.13. Modeling a Moore FSM, 323
12.14. Modeling a Mealy FSM, 325
12.15. A Simplified Blackjack Program, 327
12.16. A Scan Cell, 330
12.17. A BCD to 7-segment Decoder, 331
12.18. Utilities, 332
12.18.1. Default Value on a Bus, 332
12.19. Exercises, 333

APPENDIX A

Syntax Reference **335**

A.1. Keywords, 335
A.2. Syntax Conventions, 337
A.3. The Syntax, 337

Bibliography **369**

Index **370**

❑

Preface

Here is a neat and concise book that explains the basics of the Verilog hardware description language. The Verilog hardware description language, commonly and henceforth referred to as Verilog HDL, can be used to model digital designs at multiple levels of abstraction, ranging from the switch-level to the algorithmic-level. The language offers a powerful set of primitives, including logic gates and user-defined primitives, and a wide range of constructs that can be used to model not only the concurrent behavior of hardware but also its sequential nature and its structural composition. The language is also extensible via a programming language interface (PLI). Verilog HDL is a simple language to use but strong enough to model multiple levels of abstraction. The Verilog HDL language was standardized by the IEEE in 1995, called the IEEE Std 1364-1995. An updated version of the language was standardized in 2001 as IEEE Std 1364-2001. The new standard includes many new features such as multi-dimensional arrays, generate statements, configurations, amongst others. This edition is based on the latest standard.

The purpose of this book is to introduce the Verilog hardware description language to the reader by explaining its basic and important constructs through examples. It is a primer. Each aspect of the language is described using clear, concise English so that it is easy to understand and not intimidating for a beginner. My hope is that this book can provide the very first step in learning Verilog HDL.

The book provides a thorough understanding of the basics of the Verilog language, both from the features point of view and its usage in modeling. A number of examples for each language construct is provided; in addition, examples are provided to illustrate how constructs can be used collectively to model hardware. The various modeling styles supported by Verilog HDL are described in detail. The book also explains how stimulus and control can be described using the same Verilog language, including response monitoring and verification. The syntax of many of the constructs are shown in an easy to read manner, sometimes although not complete. This is done purposely to help explain the construct. The complete syntax of constructs of the Verilog language is provided in an appendix for reference.

The book is not theoretical in nature. Rather than using the technical jargon of the formal definition of the language, it introduces the syntax and semantics of the language using common terms. No attempt has been made to address the entire language, for example, features such as the programming language interface, switch-level modeling, and stochastic modeling are not described in this book. The book restricts itself to the most useful and common features of the language that are enough to model simple as well as complex devices.

This book is intended for hardware designers as well as circuit and system designers, software tool developers, and those interested in learning to model hardware using Verilog HDL. The book can also be used as an introductory text in a first university course on computer-aided design, hardware modeling, or synthesis. It is well suited for working professionals as well as for undergraduate and graduate study. Designers can use this book as a way to get to know Verilog HDL and as a reference for work with Verilog HDL. Students and professors will find this book useful as a teaching tool for hardware design and for hardware description languages.

The book assumes a basic knowledge of digital hardware design as well as familiarity with a high-level programming language such as C.

RTL: Register Transfer Level.

This book is a language book and therefore does not stress any domain-specific modeling styles, such as the RTL modeling style. For RTL synthesis modeling, consult the companion book "*Verilog HDL Synthesis, A Practical Primer*".

Finally, I would like to comment that it is impractical to learn a language by reading alone. Typing out examples from this book and compiling and simulating them on a Verilog simulator is the best way to gain a complete and thorough understanding of the language. Once you have mastered this book, look at the IEEE Standard Language Reference Manual (LRM) for complete information on the Verilog HDL standard.

Book Organization

Chapter 1 provides a brief history of the language, describing its major capabilities.

Chapter 2 provides a quick overview of the language, by demonstrating the three main styles of describing a design: dataflow, behavioral, and structural style.

Chapter 3 describes the basic elements, that is, the nuts and bolts, of the language. It describes identifiers, comments, system tasks, compiler directives and data types, amongst others.

Chapter 4 is devoted solely to expressions. An expression can be used in many different places in a Verilog description, including delays. The chapter also describes the various kinds of operators and operands that can be used to form an expression.

Chapter 5 describes gate-level modeling, that is, modeling a design using built-in primitive gates. Gate delays, the concept of time and delay scaling, MOS switches and bidirectional switches are introduced and described.

Verilog HDL provides the capability of creating user-defined primitives, that is, new primitives in addition to the built-in primitives. This is the topic of Chapter 6. Combinational and sequential user-defined primitives are easily understood with given examples.

In Verilog HDL, the dataflow modeling style is modeled using the continuous assignments. Chapter 7 describes this assignment and explains its execution semantics. Two kinds of delay, assignment delay and net delay, are described.

Chapter 8 describes the behavioral modeling style. It describes the two main procedural constructs: the initial statement and the always statement. The chapter also describes procedural assignments in detail. Sequential and parallel blocks are explained in detail with examples. High-level programming constructs such as conditional statement and loop statement are described in this chapter.

The structural style of modeling is elaborated in Chapter 9. The concept of hierarchy and matching of ports is examined in this chapter. Also included in this chapter is how modules connect with each other via port associations.

Advanced topics such as specify blocks, value change dump file, signal strengths are presented in Chapter 10. This chapter also describes tasks and functions, and strategies on how tasks and functions can be shared. Named events are introduced in this chapter.

Chapter 11 and 12 are the most practical chapters since they talk about verification and modeling. Chapter 11 shows a number of test bench examples that show waveform generation and response monitoring. Chapter 12 shows a number of modeling examples that demonstrate the collective usage of Verilog language constructs.

Finally, Appendix A contains a complete syntax reference of the Verilog language. The grammar is described in Backus-Naur Form (BNF) and the constructs are all arranged alphabetically for easier search.

Exercises have been included for each and every chapter making the book more useful in an university course.

In all the Verilog HDL descriptions that appear in this book, reserved words, system tasks and system functions, and compiler directives are in **boldface**. In syntax descriptions, operators and punctuation marks that are part of the syntax are in boldface. Optional items in a grammar rule are indicated by using non-bold square brackets ([...]). Non-bold curly braces ({...}) identify items that are repeated zero or more times. Occasionally ellipsis (. . .) is used in Verilog HDL source to indicate code that is not relevant to that discussion. Certain words are written in `Courier` font to identify its Verilog meaning rather than its English meaning such as in `and` gate.

All the examples have been tested on ModelSim SE 5.8a simulator.

What's New in Third Edition

Much has changed since the second edition was published over five years ago. A new version of the Verilog HDL language has become an IEEE standard, IEEE Std 1364-2001. In this text, the new features of the language have been merged into the existing chapters without explicitly demarcating the new additions to the language. In Chapter 3, the new compiler directives, the variable types and local parameters have been introduced. Multi-dimensional arrays, indexed part select, signed expressions and arithmetic shift have been added to Chapter 4. Event controls and procedural assignments have been elaborated in Chapter 8. Chapter 9 describes generate statements, configurations and the alternate style of writing port and parameter declarations. Chapter 10 explains the new and powerful input-output functions that make file reading and writing much easier. Verification utilities have been added to Chapter 11. Additional models have been included in Chapter 12. Finally the appendix has been updated with the IEEE 1364-2001 syntax grammar.

The new language has introduced alternate styles for writing many features of the language. In this book, I have used both the styles just to show the versatility of the language. The preferred style is identified as a guideline in the side bar. I have also used the side bars to provide or suggest a number of other guidelines. In some cases, I do not follow these guidelines in this text. This is done purposely so that I can continue to demonstrate the rich variety of the language. However, I do follow these guidelines in my day-to-day work when writing Verilog models.

Acknowledgments

It is my pleasure to acknowledge the assistance of the following individuals who offered their valuable time and energy to review drafts of this and earlier edition manuscript despite their very busy schedule.

1. Shalom Bresticker at Motorola Semiconductor.
2. Steven Sharp at Cadence Design Systems.

3. Michael McNamara at Verisity.
4. Vincent Zeyak Jr. at Agere Systems.
5. Brett Graves, Gabe Moretti and Doug Smith at VeriBest.
6. Stephanie Alter, Danny Johnson, Sanjana Nair, Carlos Roman, Mourad Takla, Jenjen Tiao and Sriram Tyagarajan at Bell Labs, Lucent Technologies.
7. Maqsoodul Mannan at National Semiconductor Corp.

This book owes a lot to their detailed comments and constructive criticism. I am gratefully indebted to them. Thank you very much!

I would like to thank Jean Dussault and Hao Nham for their continuous support and for providing a stimulating work atmosphere at Bell Labs during the development of previous editions.

I would like to thank Prasad Subramaniam and Hao Nham in continuing to support me in my adventures in writing books.

Last, but not least, I would like to thank my wife, Geetha, and my three sons who gave me lots of emotional support, without which I would never have succeeded.

J. Bhasker
Allentown, PA
January 2005

❑

1

Introduction

This chapter describes the history of the Verilog HDL language and it's major capabilities.

1.1 *What is Verilog HDL?*

Verilog HDL is a hardware description language that can be used to model a digital system at many levels of abstraction ranging from the algorithmic-level to the gate-level to the switch-level. The complexity of the digital system being modeled could vary from that of a simple gate to a complete electronic digital system, or anything in between. The digital system can be described hierarchically and timing can be explicitly modeled within the same description.

The Verilog HDL language includes capabilities to describe the behavioral nature of a design, the dataflow nature of a design, a design's structural composition, delays and a waveform generation mechanism including aspects of response monitoring and verification, all modeled using one single language. In addition, the language provides a programming language interface through which the internals of a design can be accessed during simulation including the control of a simulation run.

The language not only defines the syntax but also defines very clear simulation semantics for each language construct. Therefore, models written in this language can be verified using a Verilog simulator. The language inherits many of its operator symbols and constructs from the C programming language. Verilog HDL provides an extensive range of modeling capabilities, some of which are quite difficult to comprehend initially. However, a core subset of the language is quite easy to learn and use. This is sufficient to model most applications. The complete language, however, has sufficient capabilities to capture the descriptions from the most complex chips to a complete electronic system.

1.2 History

The Verilog HDL language was first developed by Gateway Design Automation[1] in 1983 as a hardware modeling language for their simulator product. At that time it was a proprietary language. Because of the popularity of their simulator product, Verilog HDL gained acceptance as a usable and practical language by a number of designers. In an effort to increase the popularity of the language, the language was placed in the public domain in 1990. Open Verilog International (OVI) was formed to promote Verilog. In 1992, OVI decided to pursue standardization of Verilog HDL as an IEEE standard. This effort was successful and the language became an IEEE standard in 1995. The complete standard is described in the Verilog Hardware Description Language Reference Manual. The standard is called IEEE Std 1364-1995.

A new revision of the language was standardized in 2001, called IEEE Std 1364-2001. This revision included many new features, including alternate port and argument declaration styles, generate statements and configurations.

1. Gateway Design Automation has since been acquired by Cadence Design Systems.

1.3 *Major Capabilities*

Listed below are the major capabilities of the Verilog hardware description language:

- Primitive logic gates, such as **and**, **or** and **nand**, are built-in into the language.
- Flexibility of creating a user-defined primitive (UDP). Such a primitive could either be a combinational logic primitive or a sequential logic primitive.
- Switch-level modeling primitive gates, such as **pmos** and **nmos**, are also built-in into the language.
- Explicit language constructs are provided for specifying pin-to-pin delays, path delays and timing checks of a design.
- A design can be modeled in three different styles or in a mixed style. These styles are: behavioral style - modeled using procedural constructs; dataflow style - modeled using continuous assignments; and structural style - modeled using gate and module instantiations.
- There are two data types in Verilog HDL; the net data type and the variable data type. The net type represents a physical connection between structural elements while a variable type may represent an abstract data storage element.
- Hierarchical designs can be described, up to any level, using the module instantiation construct.
- A design can be of arbitrary size; the language does not impose a limit.
- Verilog HDL is non-proprietary and is an IEEE standard.
- It is human and machine readable. Thus it can be used as an exchange language between tools and designers.
- The capabilities of the Verilog HDL language can be further extended by using the programming language interface (PLI) mechanism. PLI is a collection of routines that allow foreign functions to access information within a Verilog module and allows for designer interaction with the simulator.

- A design can be described in a wide range of levels, ranging from switch-level, gate-level, register-transfer-level (RTL) to algorithmic-level, including process and queuing-level.
- A design can be modeled entirely at the switch-level using the built-in switch-level primitives.
- The same single language can be used to generate stimulus for the design and for specifying test constraints, such as specifying the values of inputs.
- Verilog HDL can be used to perform response monitoring of the design under test, that is, the values of a design under test can be monitored and displayed. These values can also be compared with expected values, and in case of a mismatch, a report message can be printed.
- At the behavioral-level, Verilog HDL can be used to describe a design not only at the RTL-level, but also at the architectural-level and its algorithmic-level behavior.
- At the structural-level, gate and module instantiations can be used.
- Figure 1-1 shows the mixed-level modeling capability of Verilog HDL, that is, in one design, each module may be modeled at a different level.

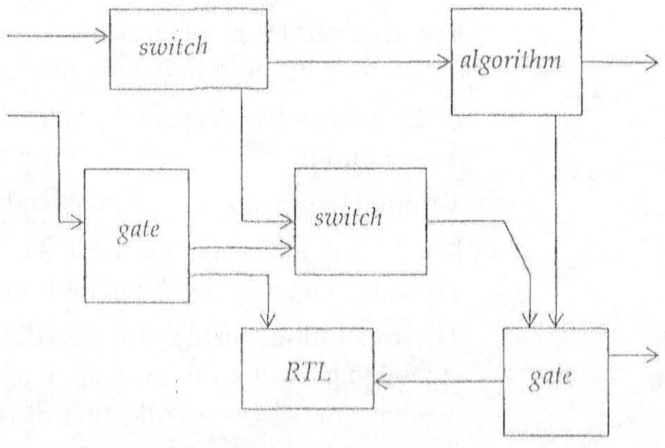

Figure 1-1 Mixed-level modeling.

- Verilog HDL also has built-in logic functions such as & (bitwise-and) and | (bitwise-or).
- High-level programming language constructs such as conditionals, case statements, and loops are available in the language.
- Notion of concurrency and time can be explicitly modeled.
- Powerful file read and write capabilities are provided.
- The language is non-deterministic under certain situations, that is, a model may produce different results on different simulators; for example, the ordering of events on an event queue is not defined by the standard.

1.4 Exercises

1. In which year was Verilog HDL first standardized by the IEEE?
2. What are the three basic description styles supported by Verilog HDL?
3. Can timing of a design be described using Verilog HDL?
4. What feature in the language can be used to describe parameterized designs?
5. Can a test bench be written using Verilog HDL?
6. Verilog HDL was first developed by which company?
7. What are the two main data types in Verilog HDL?
8. What does UDP stand for?
9. Name two switch-level modeling primitive gates.
10. Name two logic primitive gates.

❑

2

A Tutorial

This chapter provides a quick tutorial of the language.

2.1 A Module

The basic unit of description in Verilog is the *module*. A module describes the functionality or structure of a design and also describes the ports through which it communicates externally with other modules. The structure of a design is described using switch-level primitives, gate-level primitives and user-defined primitives; dataflow behavior of a design is described using continuous assignments; sequential behavior is described using procedural constructs. A module can also be instantiated inside another module.

Here is the basic syntax of a module.

```
module module_name ( port_list ) ;
  Declarations:
    reg, wire, parameter,
    input, output, inout,
    function, task, . . .
```

```
    Statements:
        Initial statement
        Always statement
        Module instantiation
        Gate instantiation
        UDP instantiation
        Continuous assignment
        Generate statement
endmodule
```

Declarations are used to define the various items, such as variables and parameters, used within the module. Statements are used to define the functionality or structure of the design. Declarations and statements can be interspersed within a module; however, a declaration must appear before its use. For clarity and readability it is best to put all declarations before any statements, and this convention is followed in all examples in this book.

Here is a simple example of a module that models the half-adder circuit shown in Figure 2-1.

```
module half_adder (a, b, sum, carry);
  input a, b;
  output sum, carry;

  assign #2 sum = a ^ b;
  assign #5 carry = a & b;
endmodule
```

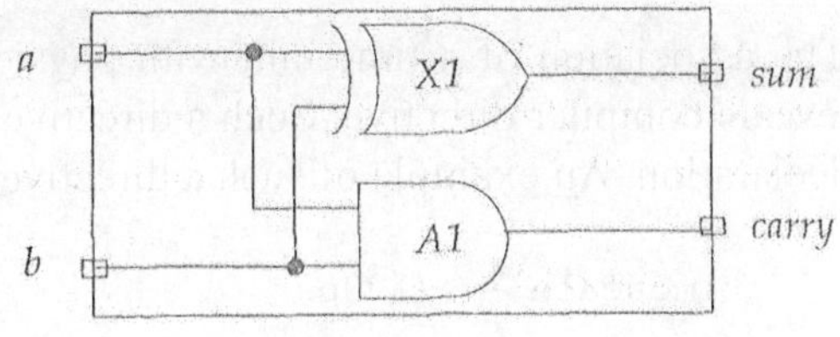

Figure 2-1 A half-adder circuit.

The name of the module is `half_adder`. It has four ports; two input ports `a` and `b`, and two output ports `sum` and `carry`. All ports are of size 1-bit since no range has been specified. Also, these four ports are of the net data type since no declaration has been specified.

The module contains two continuous assignment statements that describe the dataflow behavior of the half-adder. The statements are concurrent in the sense that their order of appearance within the module is not important. Execution of each statement occurs based on events occurring on nets `a` and `b`.

Within a module, a design can be described in the following styles:

i. Dataflow style
ii. Behavioral style
iii. Structural style
iv. Any mix of above

The following sections describe these design styles with examples. But first, a little explanation about delays in Verilog HDL.

2.2 Delays

All delays in a Verilog HDL model are specified in terms of time units. Here is an example of a continuous assignment with a delay.

```
assign #2 sum = a ^ b;
```

The #2 refers to 2 time units.

The association of a time unit with physical time is made using the **`timescale** compiler directive. Such a directive is specified before a module declaration. An example of such a directive is:

```
`timescale 1ns/100ps
```

which says that one time unit is to be treated as 1ns and that the time precision is to be 100ps (the time precision says that all delays must be rounded to 0.1ns). If this compiler directive is present in the module containing the above continuous assignment, the #2 refers to 2ns.

If no such compiler directive is specified, a Verilog HDL simulator may default to a certain time unit; this default time unit is unspecified by the IEEE Verilog HDL standard.

2.3 *Describing in Dataflow Style*

The basic mechanism used to model a design in the dataflow style is the continuous assignment. In a continuous assignment, a value is assigned to a net. The syntax of a continuous assignment is:

```
assign [ delay ] LHS_net = RHS_expression;
```

Anytime the value of an operand used in the right-hand side expression changes, the right-hand side expression is evaluated, and the value is assigned to the left-hand side net after the specified delay. The delay specifies the time duration between a change of operand on the right-hand side and the assignment to the left-hand side. If no delay value is specified, the default is zero delay.

Here is an example of a 2-to-4 decoder circuit, shown in Figure 2-2, modeled using the dataflow style.

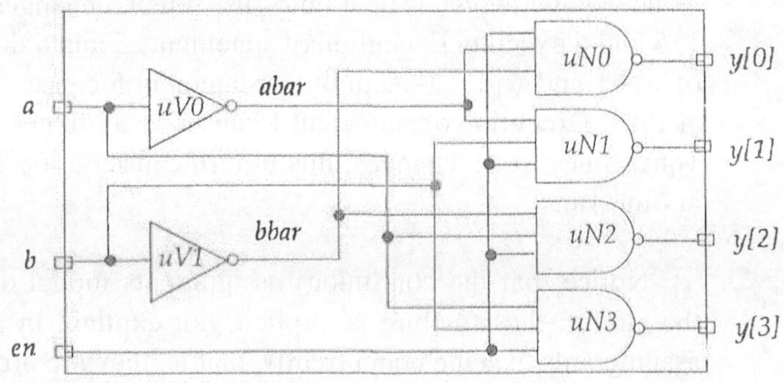

Figure 2-2 A 2-to-4 decoder circuit.

```
`timescale 1ns/1ns
module decoder2x4 (a, b, en, y);
  input a, b, en;
  output [0:3] y;
  wire abar, bbar;
```

```
    assign #1 abar = ~ a;                          // Stmt 1.
    assign #1 bbar = ~ b;                          // Stmt 2.
    assign #2 y[0] = ~ (abar & bbar & en);  // Stmt 3.
    assign #2 y[1] = ~ (abar & b & en);        // Stmt 4.
    assign #2 y[2] = ~ (a & bbar & en);        // Stmt 5.
    assign #2 y[3] = ~ (a & b & en);             // Stmt 6.
endmodule
```

The first statement, the one that begins with a backquote, is an example of a compiler directive. The compiler directive **`timescale** sets the time unit in the module for all delays to be 1ns and the time precision to be 1ns. For example, the delay values #1 and #2 in the continuous assignments correspond to delay values of 1ns and 2ns respectively.

The module decoder2x4 has three input ports and one 4-bit output port. A net declaration declares the two wires abar and bbar (a wire is one of the net types). In addition, the module contains six continuous assignment statements.

See the waveforms in Figure 2-3. When en changes at 5ns, statements 3, 4, 5, and 6 are executed; this is because en is an operand on the right-hand side of each of these continuous assignments. y[0] gets assigned to its new value, which is 0, at time 7ns. When a changes at 15ns, statements 1, 5 and 6 execute. Execution of statements 5 and 6 do not affect the value of y[0] and y[1]. Execution of statement 5 causes y[2] to change to 0 at 17ns. Execution of statement 1 causes abar to get its new value at time 16ns. Since abar changes, this in turn causes y[0] to change value to 1 at time 18ns.

Notice that the continuous assignments model dataflow behavior of the circuit; the structure is implicit, not explicit. In addition, continuous assignments execute concurrently, that is, they are order-independent.

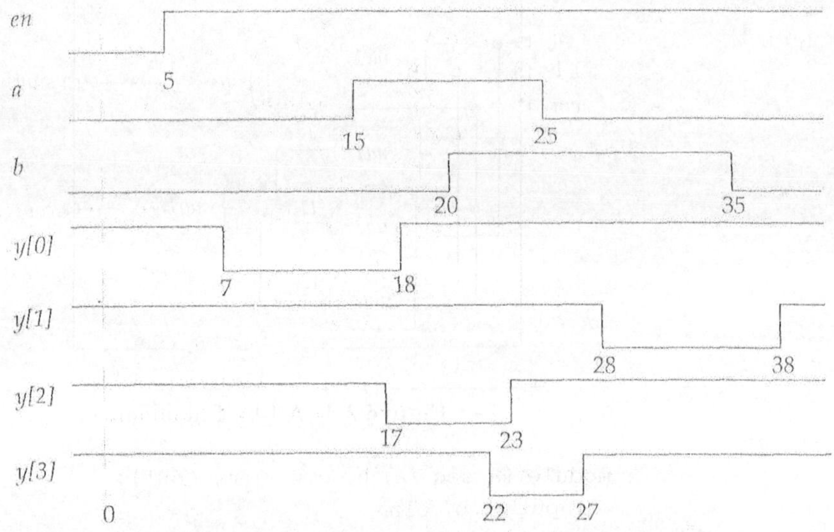

Figure 2-3 Example of continuous assignments.

2.4 Describing in Behavioral Style

The behavior of a design is described using procedural constructs. These are:

i. Initial statement: This statement executes only once.

ii. Always statement: This statement always executes in a loop, that is, the statement is executed repeatedly.

Only a variable data type can be assigned a value in either of these statements. Such a data type retains its value until a new value is assigned. All initial statements and always statements begin execution at time 0 concurrently.

Here is an example of an always statement used to model the behavior of a 1-bit full-adder circuit shown in Figure 2-4.

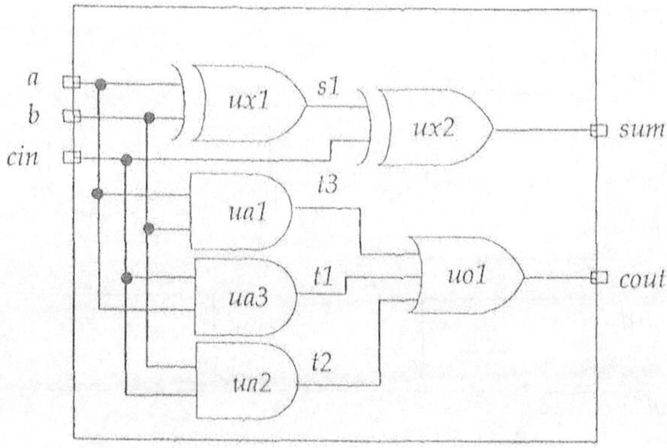

Figure 2-4 A 1-bit full-adder.

```
module fa_seq (a, b, cin, sum, cout);
  input a, b, cin;
  output reg sum, cout;
  reg t1, t2, t3;

  always
    @(a or b or cin) begin
      sum <= (a ^ b) ^ cin;
      t1 = a & cin;
      t2 = b & cin;
      t3 = a & b;
      cout <= (t1 | t2) | t3;
    end
endmodule
```

The module `fa_seq` has three inputs and two outputs. `sum`, `cout`, `t1`, `t2` and `t3` are declared to be of type **reg** (**reg** is one of the variable data types) because these are assigned values within the always statement. The always statement has a *sequential block* (**begin-end** pair) associated with an event control (the expression following the @ character). This means that whenever an event occurs on `a`, `b` or `cin`, the sequential block is executed. Statements within a sequential block execute sequentially and the execution suspends after the last statement in the sequential block has executed. After the sequential block completes execution, the always statement again waits for an event to occur on `a`, `b`, or `cin`.

The statements that appear within the sequential block are examples of *procedural assignments*. There are two kinds of procedural assignments: the blocking procedural assignment (with the "=") and the nonblocking procedural assignment (with the "<="). A blocking procedural assignment completes execution before the next statement executes. A nonblocking assignment schedules the value to be assigned to the target at a future time and continues execution, that is, it does not wait until the target has been assigned its value. A blocking assignment waits until the target gets its new value. A procedural assignment may optionally have a delay.

Delays can be specified in two different forms:

i. Inter-statement delay: This is the delay by which a statement's execution is delayed.

ii. Intra-statement delay: This is the delay between computing the value of the right-hand side expression and its assignment to the left-hand side.

Here is an example of an inter-statement delay.

```
sum = (a ^ b) ^ cin;
#4 t1 = a & cin;
```

The delay in the second statement specifies that the execution of the assignment is to be delayed by 4 time units. That is, after the first statement executes, wait for 4 time units, and then execute the second assignment. Here is an example of intra-statement delay.

```
sum = #3 (a ^ b) ^ cin;
```

The delay in this assignment means that the value of the right-hand side expression is to be computed first, wait for 3 time units, and then assign the value to `sum`.

Chapter 8 provides guidelines on when to use blocking and nonblocking assignments.

If no delays are specified in a blocking procedural assignment, zero delay is the default, that is, assignment occurs instantaneously. If no delay is specified in a nonblocking assignment, the assignment occurs at the end of the time step, that is, after all events that occur at that time have been completed. More on this and other forms of statements that can be specified in an always statement are discussed in Chapter 8.

Here is an example of an initial statement.

```
`timescale 1ns/1ns
module generate_waves (mclr, wren);
  output reg mclr, wren;

  initial
    begin
      mclr = 0;          // Stmt 1
      wren = 0;          // Stmt 2
      mclr = #5 1;       // Stmt 3
      wren = #3 1;       // Stmt 4
      mclr = #6 0;       // Stmt 5
      wren = #2 0;       // Stmt 6
    end
endmodule
```

This module generates the waveforms shown in Figure 2-5. The initial statement contains a sequential block which starts execution at time 0ns and after it completes executing all statements within the sequential block, the initial statement suspends forever. This sequential block contains examples of blocking procedural assignments with intra-statement delays specified. Statements 1 and 2 execute at time 0ns. The execution of the third statement, also at time 0, causes `mclr` to get assigned a value at time 5ns. Statement 4 executes at 5ns, and `wren` gets assigned the value at 8ns. Similarly, `mclr` gets the value 0 at 14ns and `wren` gets the value 0 at 16ns. After statement 6 executes, the initial statement suspends forever. Chapter 8 describes initial statement in more detail.

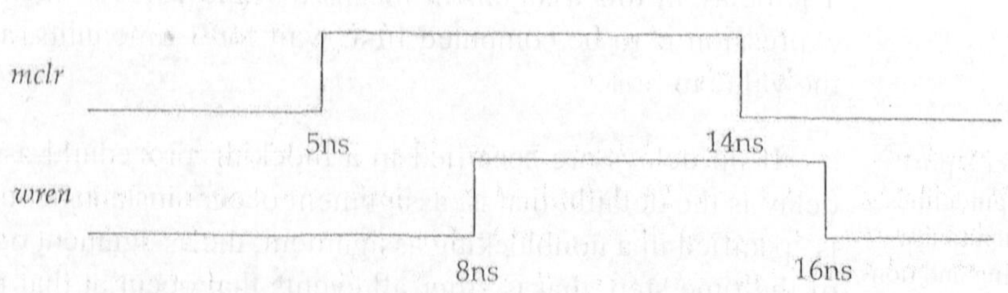

Figure 2-5 Output of module `generate_waves`.

2.5 Describing in Structural Style

Structure can be described in Verilog HDL using:

i. Built-in gate primitives (at the gate-level)
ii. Switch-level primitives (at the transistor-level)
iii. User-defined primitives (at the gate-level)
iv. Module instances (to create hierarchy)

Interconnections are specified by using nets. Here is an example of a full-adder circuit described in a structural fashion using built-in gate primitives and based on the logic diagram shown in Figure 2-4.

```
module fa_str (a, b, cin, sum, cout);
  input a, b, cin;
  output sum, cout;
  wire s1, t1, t2, t3;

  xor
    ux1 (s1, a, b),
    ux2 (sum, s1, cin);

  and
    ua1 (t3, a, b),
    ua2 (t2, b, cin),
    ua3 (t1, a, cin);

  or
    uo1 (cout, t1, t2, t3);
endmodule
```

In this example, the module contains gate instantiations, that is, instances of built-in gates **xor, and**, and **or**. The gate instances are interconnected by nets `s1`, `t1`, `t2`, and `t3`. The gate instantiations can appear in any order since no sequentiality is implied; pure structure is being shown; **xor**, **and** and **or** are built-in gate primitives; `ux1`, `ux2`, `ua1`, etc. are the instance names. The list of signals following each gate are its interconnections; the first one is the output of the gate and the rest are its inputs. For example, `s1` is connected to the output of the `xor` gate instance `ux1` while `a` and `b` are connected to its inputs.

A 4-bit full-adder can be described by instantiating four 1-bit full-adder modules, the logic diagram of which is shown in Figure 2-6. The model of this 4-bit full-adder is shown next.

```
module four_bit_fa (fa, fb, fcin, fsum, fcout);
  parameter SIZE = 4;
  input [SIZE:1] fa, fb;
  output [SIZE:1] fsum;
  input fcin;
  output fcout;
  wire [SIZE-1:1] ftemp;

  fa_str
    ufa1 (    // Named association
      .a(fa[1]), .b(fb[1]), .cin(fcin),
      .sum(fsum[1]), .cout(ftemp[1])
    ),
    ufa2 (    // Named association
      .a(fa[2]), .b(fb[2]), .cin(ftemp[1]),
      .sum(fsum[2]), .cout(ftemp[2])
    ),
    ufa3 (    // Positional association
      fa[3], fb[3], ftemp[2], fsum[3], ftemp[3]
    ),
    ufa4 (    // Positional association
      fa[4], fb[4], ftemp[3],fsum[4], fcout
    );
endmodule
```

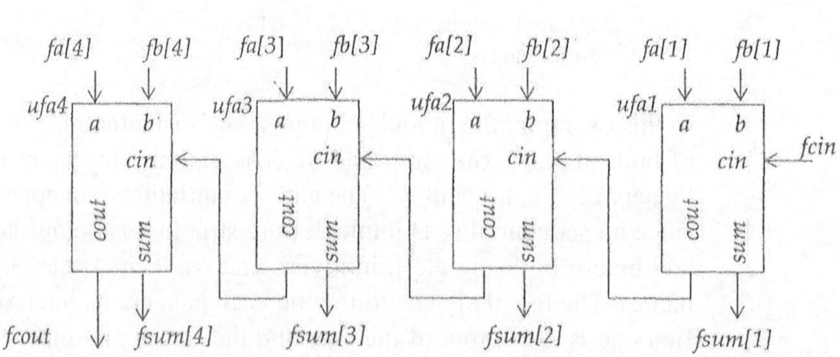

Figure 2-6 A 4-bit full-adder.

In this example, module instantiations are used to model a 4-bit full-adder. In a module instantiation, the ports can be associated by name or by position. The first two instantiations `ufa1` and `ufa2` use named associations, that is, the name of the port and the net to which it is connected to are explicitly described (each is of the form ". `port_name ( net_name`)"). The last two instantiations, instances `ufa3` and `ufa4`, associate ports with nets using positional association. The order of the associations is important here, for example, in instance `ufa4`, the first net `fa[4]` is connected to port `a` of `fa_str`, the second net `fb[4]` is connected to port `b` of `fa_str`, and so on.

2.6 *Describing in Mixed-design Style*

Within a module, structural and behavioral constructs can be mixed freely, that is, a module can contain a mixture of gate instantiations, module instantiations, continuous assignments, and always and initial statements, amongst others. Values from always statements and initial statements (remember only a variable data type can be assigned a value within these statements) can drive gates or switches, while values from gates or continuous assignments (can only drive nets) can in turn be used to trigger always statements and initial statements.

Here is an example of a 1-bit full-adder in a mixed-design style. In addition, the ports have been described using the *module port declaration style* - in this style, the declarations are merged with the port list itself. In the previous examples, the *module port list style* was used - in this style, a port list is specified in the module declaration and the port declarations appear later in the module body.

Note that a comma separates the different kinds of port declarations.

```
module fa_mix (
   input a, b, cin,
   output sum,
   output reg cout
);
reg t1, t2, t3;
wire s1;

xor ux1 (s1, a, b);           // Gate instantiation.
```

```
always
  @(a or b or cin) begin      // Always statement.
    t1 = a & cin;             // Blocking assignment.
    t2 = b & cin;
    t3 = a & b;
    cout <= (t1 | t2) | t3; // Nonblocking assignment.
  end

  assign sum = s1 ^ cin;      // Continuous assignment.
endmodule
```

Execution of the gate instantiation occurs whenever an event occurs on a or b. The always statement executes whenever there is an event on a, b or cin, and the continuous assignment executes whenever there is an event on s1 or cin.

2.7 *Simulating a Design*

Verilog HDL provides capabilities not only to describe a design but also to model stimulus, control, storing responses and verification, all using the same language. Stimulus and control can be generated using initial statements. Responses from the design under test can be saved as "save on change" or as strobed data. Finally, verification can be performed by automatically comparing with expected responses by writing appropriate statements in an initial statement.

Here is an example of a test module fa_top that tests the module fa_seq described earlier in Section 2.4.

A module can have an empty port list.

```
`timescale 1ns/1ns
module fa_top;
  reg pa, pb, pci;
  wire pco, psum;

  // Instantiate module under test:
  fa_seq uf1 (
    pa, pb, pci, psum, pco
                                    // Positional association.
```

```
initial
  begin: blk_only_once
   reg [3:0] pal;
    // Need 4 bits so that pal can have the value 8.

   for (pal = 0; pal < 8; pal = pal + 1)
     begin
       {pa, pb, pci} <= pal;
       #5 $display ("pa, pb, pci=%b%b%b", pa, pb, pci,
                    " ::: pco, psum=%b%b", pco, psum);
     end
  end
endmodule
```

The signals in the module instantiation are linked to the ports of the module under test using positional association, that is, `pa` is connected to port `a` of module `fa_seq`, `pb` is connected to port `b` of module `fa_seq`, and so on. Notice that a for-loop statement has been used in the initial statement to generate a waveform on `pa`, `pb` and `pci`. The target of the first assignment statement within the for-loop represents a concatenated target. The appropriate bits on the right-hand side are assigned to the left-hand side argument from right to left. The initial statement also contains an example of a predefined system task. The **$display** system task prints the specified argument values in the specified format to the output.

The delay control in the **$display** system task call specifies that the **$display** task is to be executed after 5 time units. This 5 time units basically represents the settling time for the logic, that is, the delay time between the application of a vector and observing the module-under-test's response.

There is yet another nuance to this model. `pal` is declared locally within the initial statement. To do this, the sequential block (**begin-end**) in the initial statement has to be labeled. `blk_only_once` is the block label in this case. The block label is not necessary if there are no variables declared locally within the block. Figure 2-7 shows the waveforms produced. Here is the output produced by the test module.

```
pa, pb, pci =000 ::: pco, psum =00
pa, pb, pci =001 ::: pco, psum =01
pa, pb, pci =010 ::: pco, psum =01
pa, pb, pci =011 ::: pco, psum =10
```

```
pa, pb, pci =100 ::: pco, psum =01
pa, pb, pci =101 ::: pco, psum =10
pa, pb, pci =110 ::: pco, psum =10
pa, pb, pci =111 ::: pco, psum =11
```

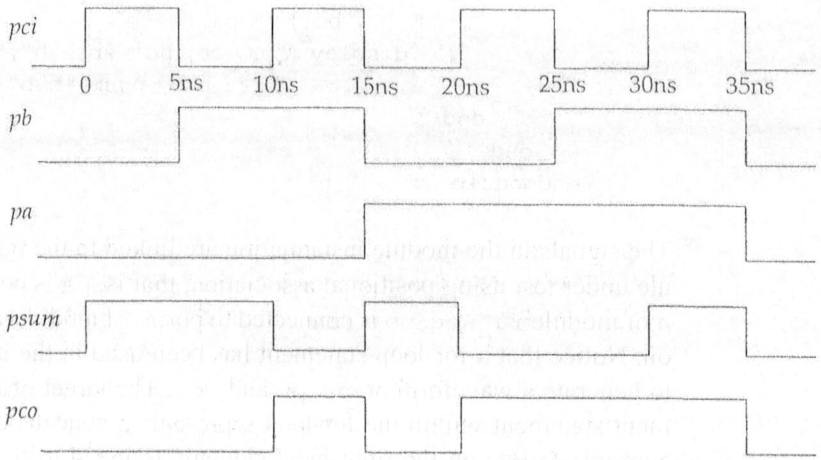

Figure 2-7 Waveforms produced by executing test bench `fa_top`.

Here is another example of a test module that exercises the cross-coupled nand gate module `rs_flipflop` shown in Figure 2-8.

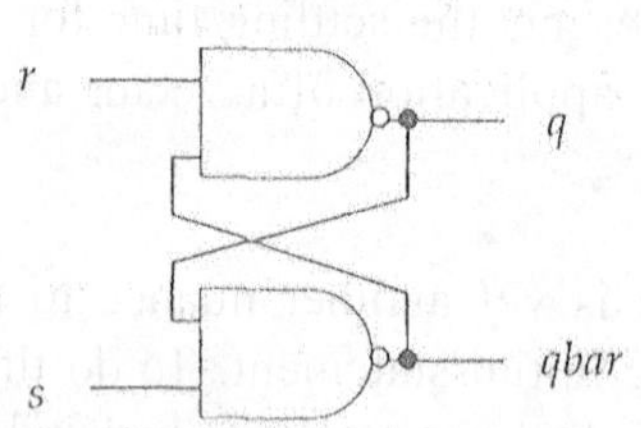

Figure 2-8 Cross-coupled nand gates.

```
`timescale 10ns/1ns
module rs_flipflop (q, qbar, r, s);
  output q, qbar;
  input r, s;

  nand #1 (q, r, qbar);
  nand #1 (qbar, s, q);
endmodule

module test_rs_flipflop;
  reg ts, tr;
  wire tq, tqb;

    // Instantiate module under test:
    rs_flipflop u_rsff (
      .q(tq), .s(ts), .r(tr), .qbar(qb)
    );                              // Using named association.

    // Apply stimulus:
    initial
      begin
        tr = 0;
        ts = 0;
        #5 ts = 1;
        #5 ts = 0;
        tr = 1;
        #5 ts = 1;
        tr = 0;
        #5 ts = 0;
        #5 tr = 1;
      end

    // Display output:
    initial
      $monitor ( "At time %t,", $time,
                "tr = %b, ts = %b, tq = %b, tqb = %b",
               tr, ts, tq, tqb);
endmodule
```

Instance names are optional in gate instantiations.

Module `rs_flipflop` describes the structure of the design. Gate delays are used in gate instantiations; for example, the gate delay for the first instantiation is 1 time unit. This gate delay implies that if `r` or `qbar` changes at say time `T`, then `q` gets the computed value at time `T+1`.

The module `test_rs_flipflop` is the test module. The design under test `rs_flipflop` is instantiated and its ports are connected using named association. There are two initial statements in this module. The first initial statement simply generates the waveform on `ts` and `tr`. This initial statement contains blocking procedural assignments with inter-statement delays.

The second initial statement is used to call the system task **$monitor**. This task when called causes the specified string to be printed whenever a change occurs in the specified variables in the argument list. Figure 2-9 shows the waveforms produced. Here is the output produced by the test module. Notice the effect produced by the **`timescale** directive on the delays.

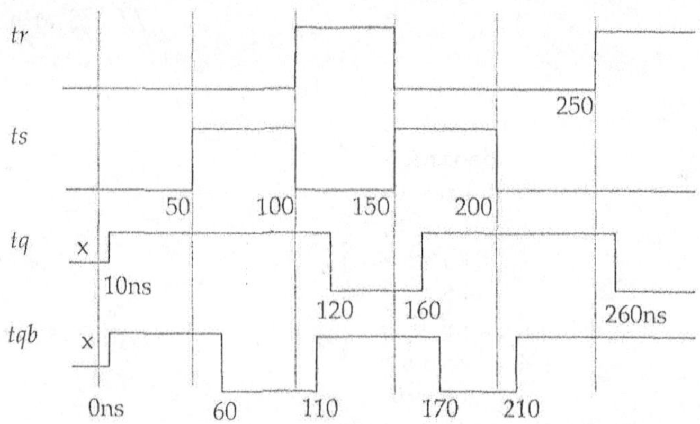

Figure 2-9 Waveforms produced by module `test_rs_flipflop`.

```
At time      0, tr = 0, ts = 0, tq = x, tqb = x
At time     10, tr = 0, ts = 0, tq = 1, tqb = 1
At time     50, tr = 0, ts = 1, tq = 1, tqb = 1
At time     60, tr = 0, ts = 1, tq = 1, tqb = 0
At time    100, tr = 1, ts = 0, tq = 1, tqb = 0
At time    110, tr = 1, ts = 0, tq = 1, tqb = 1
At time    120, tr = 1, ts = 0, tq = 0, tqb = 1
At time    150, tr = 0, ts = 1, tq = 0, tqb = 1
At time    160, tr = 0, ts = 1, tq = 1, tqb = 1
At time    170, tr = 0, ts = 1, tq = 1, tqb = 0
At time    200, tr = 0, ts = 0, tq = 1, tqb = 0
At time    210, tr = 0, ts = 0, tq = 1, tqb = 1
```

```
At time        250, tr = 1, ts = 0, tq = 1, tqb = 1
At time        260, tr = 1, ts = 0, tq = 0, tqb = 1
```

The following chapters elaborate on these topics and more in greater detail.

2.8 Exercises

1. What statement is primarily used to describe a design in the dataflow style?
2. What is the purpose of the **`timescale** compiler directive? Give an example.
3. What are the two kinds of delays that can be specified in a procedural assignment statement? Elaborate using an example.
4. Describe the 1-bit full-adder shown in Figure 2-4 using the dataflow style.
5. What is the key difference between an initial statement and an always statement?
6. Generate the waveform shown in Figure 2-10 on a variable `peg_tsi` using an initial statement.

Figure 2-10 A waveform on variable `peg_tsi`.

7. Write a model, in structural style, for the 2-to-4 decoder shown in Figure 2-2.
8. Write a test bench to test the module `decoder2x4` described in Section 2.3.
9. Name two kinds of assignment statements that you can have in a Verilog HDL model.
10. When is a label required to be specified in a sequential block?

11. Using the dataflow description style, write a Verilog HDL model for the exclusive-or logic shown in Figure 2-11. Use the specified delays.

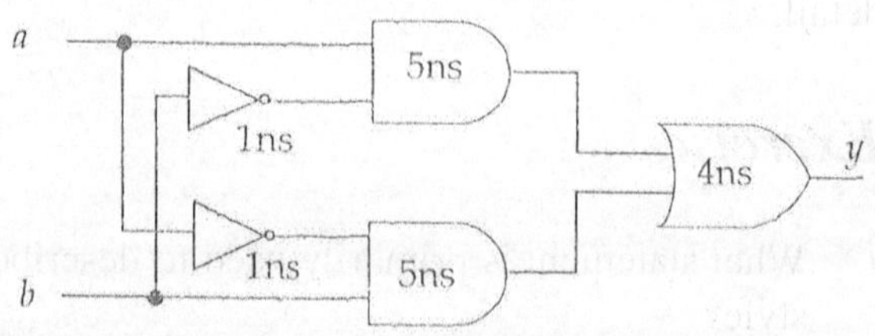

Figure 2-11 Exclusive-or logic.

12. What is wrong with the following continuous assignment?

```
assign reset = #2 ^ hwrite_bus;
```

❑

3

Language Elements

This chapter describes the basic elements of Verilog HDL. It introduces identifiers, comments, numbers, compiler directives, system tasks and system functions. In addition, it introduces the two data types in the language.

3.1 *Identifiers*

An *identifier* in Verilog HDL is any sequence of letters, digits, the $ character, and the _ (underscore) character, with the restriction that the first character must be a letter or an underscore. In addition, *identifiers are case-sensitive.* Here are some examples of identifiers.

```
Count
COUNT          // Distinct from Count.
_R2_D2
R56_68
FIVE$
```

An *escaped identifier* provides a way of including any of the printable ASCII characters in an identifier. An escaped identifier starts with a \ (backslash) character and ends with a white space (a *white space* is a space, tab or a newline). Here are some examples of escaped identifiers.

```
\7400
\.*.$
\{******}
\~Q
\OutGate                    // is same as OutGate
```

The last example explains the fact that, in an escaped identifier, the backslash and the terminating space are not part of the identifier. Thus, identifier `\OutGate` is identical to identifier `OutGate`.

Verilog HDL defines a list of reserved identifiers, called *keywords*, that can only be used in certain contexts. Appendix A lists all the reserved words in the language. Note that only the lower case keywords are reserved words. For example, identifier **always** (which is a keyword) is distinct from the identifier `ALWAYS` (which is not a keyword).

Guideline: Do not use keywords with different case or escaped keywords as identifiers.

In addition, an escaped keyword is not treated the same as the keyword. Thus, identifier \initial is distinct from the identifier **initial** (which is a keyword). Note that this convention is different from those of escaped identifiers.

3.2 *Comments*

There are two forms of comments in Verilog HDL.

```
/* First form: Can
  extend across
  many
  lines */

// Second form: Ends at the end of this line.
```

3.3 *Format*

Verilog HDL is case-sensitive. That is, identifiers differing only in their case are distinct. In addition, Verilog HDL is free-format, that is, constructs may be written across multiple lines, or on one line. White space (newline, tab, and space characters) have no special significance. Here is an example that illustrates this.

```
initial begin gre_sel = 3'b001; #2 gre_sel = 3'b011; end
```

Guideline: Keep line length less than 132 characters.

is same as:

```
initial
  begin
    gre_sel = 3'b001;
    #2 gre_sel = 3'b011;
  end
```

3.4 System Tasks and Functions

An identifier beginning with a $ character is interpreted as a system task or as a system function. A task provides a mechanism to encapsulate a behavior that can be invoked from different parts of a design. A task can return zero or more values. A function is like a task except that it can return only one value. In addition, a function executes in zero time, that is, no delays are allowed, while a task can have delays; however, a system task cannot have any delays.

```
$display ("Hi, you have reached LT today");
/* The $display system task displays the specified
   message to output with a newline character. */

$time
// This system function returns the current
// simulation time.
```

Tasks and functions are described in Chapter 10.

3.5 Compiler Directives

Certain identifiers that start with the ` (backquote) character are compiler directives. A compiler directive, when compiled, remains in effect through the entire compilation process (which could span multiple files) until a different compiler directive specifies otherwise. Here is a complete list of standard compiler directives.

- **`define, `undef**
- **`ifdef, `ifndef, `else, `elsif, `endif**

- **`default_nettype**
- **`include**
- **`resetall**
- **`timescale**
- **`unconnected_drive, `nounconnected_drive**
- **`celldefine, `endcelldefine**
- **`line**

3.5.1 `define and `undef

The **`define** directive defines a macro with its definition. It is used for text substitution and is very much like the #define in the C programming language. Here is an example of this directive.

Guideline: Use all uppercase characters in a macro name.

```
`define MAX_BUS_SIZE 32
`define RESULT_SIZE (AWIDTH * BWIDTH)
. . .
reg [`MAX_BUS_SIZE-1:0] add_reg;
```

Once the **`define** directive is compiled, the definition stays in effect through the entire compilation. For example the usage of MAX_BUS_SIZE could be across many different files with the **`define** directive in another file.

The **`undef** directive removes the definition of a previously defined text macro. Here is an example.

```
// Create a macro for text substitution:
`define WORD 16
. . .
wire [`WORD:1] siob_rdy;
. . .
`undef WORD
// The definition of WORD is no longer available
// after this `undef directive.
```

3.5.2 `ifdef, `ifndef, `else, `elsif and `endif

These compiler directives are used for conditional compilation. There are two forms of the directives - the **`ifdef** and the **`ifndef** forms. The **`ifdef** form checks for the existence of the definition of the macro, whereas the **`ifndef** form checks for the lack of definition of the macro. Here is an example.

```
`ifdef WINDOWS
  parameter WORD_SIZE = 16;
`else
  parameter WORD_SIZE = 32;
`endif
```

During compilation, if the text macro name WINDOWS is defined, the first parameter declaration is selected, otherwise the second parameter declaration is selected.

The **`else** directive is optional with the **`ifdef** directive.

The **`ifndef** directive is the opposite of **`ifdef**, which says "do something if macro is not defined". The **`elsif** directive is equivalent to **`else** followed by a **`ifdef** directive.

```
// If RTL_SYNTHESIS macro is not defined:
`ifndef RTL_SYNTHESIS
   assign #(PERIOD/2) core_clock = ~ core_clock;
`endif
```

@(a, b) is identical to @(a or b).

```
`ifdef ALWAYS_FORM
  always @(a, b) y <= a | b;
`elsif ASSIGN_FORM
  assign y = a | b;
`else
  or ulor (y, a, b);
`endif
```

3.5.3 `default_nettype

This directive is used to specify the net type for implicit net declarations, that is, for nets that are not declared.

```
`default_nettype wand
```

This directive must appear outside of a module.

This example specifies the default net type to be a wand net. Therefore, if a net is not declared in any module following this directive, the net is assumed to be a wand net. A value of **none** can also be specified as a default net type; this indicates that no implicit nets are allowed.

3.5.4 `include

Guideline: Keep multiple **`define** directives in a separate file `<design>_defines.v` and include the file in your design using the **`include** directive.

The **`include** compiler directive can be used to include the contents of any file in-line. The file can be specified either with a relative path name or with a full path name.

```
`include "../../primitives.v"
```

Upon compilation, this line is replaced with the contents of the file "../../primitives.v".

3.5.5 `resetall

This compiler directive resets all compiler directives to their default value.

```
`resetall
```

For example, this directive causes the default net type to be wire.

3.5.6 `timescale

In a Verilog HDL model, all delays are expressed in terms of time units. The association of time units with actual time is done using the **`timescale** compiler directive. This directive is used to specify the time unit and time precision. The directive is of the form:

```
`timescale time_unit / time_precision
```

where the *time_unit* and *time_precision* is made up of values from 1, 10, and 100 and units from *s*, *ms*, *us*, *ns*, *ps* and *fs*. Here is an example.

```
`timescale 1ns/100ps
```

indicates a time unit of 1ns and a time precision of 100ps. The **`timescale** directive appears outside of a module declaration and affects all delay values that follow it. Here is an example.

```
`timescale 1ns/100ps
module and_function (y, a, b);
  output y;
  input a, b;

  and #(5.22, 6.17) u1and (y, a, b);
    // Rise and fall delay specified.
endmodule
```

The directive specifies all delays to be in nanoseconds (ns) and delays are rounded to one-tenth of a nanosecond (100ps). Therefore, the delay value 5.22 becomes 5.2ns and the delay value 6.17 becomes 6.2ns. If instead the following **`timescale** directive is used in the above module,

```
`timescale 10ns/1ns
```

then 5.22 becomes 52ns, and 6.17 becomes 62ns.

The **`timescale** directive affects all delays in modules that follow this directive in a compilation until another **`timescale** directive or **`resetall** directive is found. What happens if there is more than one module in a design each having its own **`timescale** directive? In such a case, simulation always takes place in the smallest time precision of all the modules and all delays are appropriately scaled to this smallest time precision. Here is an example.

```
`timescale 1ns/100ps
module and_function (y, a, b);
  output y;
  input a, b;

  and #(5.22, 6.17) u1and (y, a, b);
endmodule

`timescale 10ns/1ns
module tb_and;
  reg put_a, put_b;
  wire get_y;
```

```
    initial
      begin
        put_a = 0;
        put_b = 0;
        #5.21 put_b = 1;
        #10.4 put_a = 1;
        #15 put_b = 0;
      end

    and_function u_and_function (get_y, put_a, put_b);
  endmodule
```

In this example, each module has its own **`timescale** directive. The **`timescale** directive is first applied to the delays. Therefore in the first module, 5.22 is 5.2ns, 6.17 is 6.2ns, and in the second module, 5.21 is 52ns, 10.4 is 104ns, and 15 is 150ns. If module `tb_and` were simulated, the smallest time precision of all modules in this design is 100ps. Therefore, all delays (especially the delays in module `tb_and`) will be scaled to a precision of 100ps. Delay 52ns now becomes 520*100ps, 104ns becomes 1040*100ps, and 150ns becomes 1500*100ps. More importantly, simulation occurs using a time precision of 100ps. If module `and_function` were simulated, the **`timescale** directive of module `tb_and` has no effect since module `tb_and` is not a child module of module `and_function`.

3.5.7 `unconnected_drive and `nounconnected_drive

Any unconnected input ports in module instantiations that appear between these two directives are either pulled up or pulled down.

```
`unconnected_drive pull1
. . .
/* All unconnected input ports between these two
  directives are pulled up (connected to 1). */
`nounconnected_drive

`unconnected_drive pull0
. . .
/* All unconnected input ports between these two
  directives are pulled down (connected to 0). */
`nounconnected_drive
```

Both these directives must appear outside of a module.

3.5.8 `celldefine and `endcelldefine

These two directives are used to mark a module as a cell module. They typically encompass a module definition, as shown in the following example.

Guideline: Module name and port names of a cell are typically all in uppercase characters.

```
`celldefine
module FD1S3AX (D, CK, Q);
  input D, CK;
  output Q;
  . . .
endmodule
`endcelldefine
```

Cell modules are used by some PLI routines. A cell module typically has a specify block that specifies the delays of the block. PLI routines can use this information to perform delay calculation for such cells.

3.5.9 line

The `**line** directive resets the line number and file name in a Verilog HDL compiler to that as specified.

```
`line 52 "reset_map.vg"
```

This directive is useful for Verilog writer tools such as preprocessors. When an automatically generated Verilog HDL file (with these directives) is compiled, the directive values are used to issue messages as it relates to the original file. An user would typically not use this directive directly.

3.6 *Value Set*

Verilog HDL has the following four basic values.

i. **0** : logic-0 or false

ii. **1** : logic-1 or true

iii. **x** : unknown

iv. **z** : high-impedance

Note that the interpretations of these four values are built-in into the language. A z in a value always means a high-impedance, a 0 always means a logic-0, and so on.

A z value at the input of a gate or in an expression is usually interpreted as an x. Furthermore, the values x and z are case-insensitive, that is, the value 0x1z is same as 0X1Z. A constant in Verilog HDL is made up of the above four basic values.

There are three types of constants in Verilog HDL.

i. Integer
ii. Real
iii. String

An underscore (_) character can be used in an integer constant or a real constant freely; they are ignored in the number itself. They can be used to improve readability; the only restriction is that the underscore character cannot be the first character.

3.6.1 Integers

An integer number can be written in the following two forms.

i. Simple decimal
ii. Base format

Simple Decimal Form

An integer in this form is specified as a sequence of digits with an optional + (unary) or a – (unary) operator. Here are some examples of integers in the simple decimal form.

```
32          is decimal 32
- 15        is decimal -15
```

An integer value in this form represents a signed number. A negative number is represented in two's complement form. Thus 32 is 100000 in a

6-bit binary, 0100000 in 7-bit binary; –15 is 10001 in 5-bit binary, and is 110001 in a 6-bit binary.

The number of bits in an integer of this form is at least 32 bits.

Base Format Notation

The format of an integer in this form is:

```
[ size ] ' [ signed ] base value
```

where the *size* specifies the size of the constant in number of bits, *signed* is one of s or S, *base* is one of o or O (for octal), b or B (for binary), d or D (for decimal), h or H (for hexadecimal) and *value* is a sequence of digits that are values from the *base*. The values x and z and the hexadecimal values a through f are case-insensitive. The integer is a signed integer when the signed qualifier is present, else it is an unsigned integer.

Here are some examples.

```
5'O37       5-bit octal
4'D2        4-bit decimal
4'B1x_01    4-bit binary
7'Hx        7-bit x (x extended), that is, xxxxxxx
4'hZ        4-bit z (z extended), that is, zzzz
8 'h 2A     Spaces are allowed between size and
            character and between base and value
8'sh51      8-bit signed number 01010001
6'so72      6-bit signed number 111010 which is
            decimal -6 which is same as 6'sh3A

// Examples of not legal integers:
4'd-4       Not legal: value cannot be negative
3' b001   Not legal: no space allowed between ' and base b
(2+3)'d10 Not legal; size cannot be an expression
```

Note that an x (or z) in a hexadecimal value represents four bits of x (or z), x (or z) in octal represents three bits of x (or z), and x (or z) in binary represents one bit of x (or z).

The size specification is optional in an integer of this form. If no size is specified in an integer, the size of the number is at least 32 bits. Here are some examples.

```
'o721      32-bit octal, unsigned
'hAF       32-bit hex, unsigned
'sb1011    32-bit binary, signed -5
```

If the size specified is larger than the number of bits specified for the constant, the number is padded to the left with 0's for unsigned numbers and with the leftmost bit for signed numbers. For the case where the leftmost bit is a x or a z, a x or a z respectively is used to pad to the left. For example,

```
10'b10      Padded with 0 to the left, 0000000010
10'bx0x1    Padded with x to the left, xxxxxxx0x1
8'sb101101  Padded with sign bit (1) to the
            left, 11101101
```

If the size specified is smaller than the number of bits specified for the constant, then the leftmost bits are appropriately truncated. For example,

The sign bit is not preserved during truncation.

```
3'b1001_0011       is same as 3'b011
5'HOFFF            is same as 5'H1F
3'sb10100          is same as 3'sb100
```

Similarly, when no size is specified and the target size required is larger, then the number is padded with 0's for unsigned numbers and with the leftmost bit for signed numbers. For the case when the leftmost bit is a x or a z, a x or a z respectively is used to pad to the left.

```
reg [15:0] pbus_select;

pbus_select = 'h5;    // Pads 0 to the left and
                      // assigns 0000 0000 0000 0101.
pbus_select = 'hx11;  // Pads x to the left and
                      // assigns xxxx xxxx 0001 0001.
pbus_select = 'hz51;  // Pads z to the left and
                      // assigns zzzz zzzz 0101 0001.
```

The ? character can be used as an alternate for value z in a number. It may be used to improve readability in cases where the value z is interpreted as a don't-care value (see Chapter 8).

3.6.2 Reals

A real number can be specified in one of the following two forms.

i. Decimal notation: Examples of numbers in this form are:

```
2.0
5.678
11572.12
0.1
2.        // Not legal: must have a digit
          // on either side of decimal.
```

ii. Scientific notation: Examples of numbers in this form are:

```
23_5.1e2  The value 23510.0; underscores are ignored
3.6E2     360.0 (e is same as E)
5E-4      0.0005
```

Implicit conversion to integer is defined by the language. Real numbers are converted to integers by rounding to the nearest integer.

```
42.446, 42.45   When converted to integer yields 42
92.5, 92.699    Yield 93 when converted into integer
-15.62          To integer gives -16
-26.22          To integer gives -26
```

3.6.3 Strings

A string is a sequence of characters within double quotes. A string may not be split across lines. Here are examples of strings.

```
"INTERNAL ERROR"
"REACHED->HERE"
```

A character is represented by an 8-bit ASCII value which is treated as an unsigned integer. Therefore a string is a sequence of 8-bit ASCII values. To store the string "INTERNAL ERROR", a variable of size 8*14 is needed.

```
reg [ 1 : 8*14 ] message;
. . .
message = "INTERNAL ERROR";
```

The \ (backslash) character can be used to escape certain special characters.

```
\n      newline character
\t      tab
\\      the \ character itself
\"      the " character
\206    character with octal value 206
```

3.7 Data Types

Verilog HDL has two groups of data types.

i. **Net type:**
A *net type* represents a physical connection between structural elements. Its value is determined from the value of its drivers such as a continuous assignment or a gate output. If no driver is connected to a net, the net defaults to a value of z.

ii. **Variable[1] type:**
A *variable type* represents an abstract data storage element. It is assigned values only within an always statement or an initial statement, and its value is saved from one assignment to the next. A variable type has a default value of x.

1. Prior to the IEEE Std 1364-2001, this used to be called a register type.

3.7.1 Net Types

Here are the different kinds of nets that belong to the net data type.

- wire
- tri
- wor
- trior
- wand
- triand
- trireg
- tri1
- tri0
- supply0
- supply1

A simple syntax for a net declaration is:

```
net_kind [ signed ] [ [ msb : lsb ] ] net1, net2 , . . . , netN;
```

Guideline: Use all lower case characters in a net name.

where *net_kind* is one of the nets listed above. Use the keyword **signed** to declare a net that holds a signed value; by default, a net holds an unsigned value. *msb* and *lsb* are constant expressions that specify the range of the net; the range specification is optional; if no range is specified, a net defaults to a size of one bit. Here are some examples of net declarations.

Guideline: Express range in a descending order with the least significant bit having index 0.

```
wire bist_ready, cnt_start;          // Two 1-bit wire nets.
wand [2:0] haddr;     // haddr is a 3-bit vector wand net.

`define SIZE 16
wire signed [7:0] pwdata, prdata; // pwdata and prdata
  // nets hold signed values in two's complement form.
wire signed [`SIZE-1:0] usb_data; // usb_data holds
  // signed value in two's complement form.
```

The various nets behave differently when there exists more than one driver for a net, that is, when there are multiple assignments to a net. For example,

```
wor qma_ready;
wire kbl_clear, kbl_enable;
. . .
assign qma_ready = bist_ready & cnt_start;
. . .
assign qma_ready = kbl_clear | kbl_enable;
```

In this example, qma_ready has two drivers, one from each of the continuous assignments. Since it is a wor net, the effective value of qma_ready is determined from a wor table (see following section on wor nets) using the values of the drivers (the values of the right-hand side expressions).

Wire and Tri Nets

This is the most common type of net which is used to connect elements. A wire net and a tri net are identical in syntax and semantics; the tri net may be used to describe a net where multiple drivers drive a net, and has no other special significance.

```
wire reset;
wire [3:1] mode_enable, clk_enable, clk_mode;
parameter MSB = 8, LSB = 0;
tri [MSB-1:LSB+1] rtc_status;
```

If multiple drivers drive a wire (or a tri) net, the effective value of the net is determined by using the following table.

wire (or tri)	0	1	x	z
0	0	x	x	0
1	x	1	x	1
x	x	x	x	x
z	0	1	x	z

Here is an example.

```
assign mode_enable = clk_enable & clk_mode;
. . .
assign mode_enable = clk_enable ^ clk_mode;
```

In this example, `mode_enable` has two drivers. The values of the two drivers (the values of the right-hand side expressions) are used to index in the above table to determine the effective value of `mode_enable`. Since `mode_enable` is a vector, each bit position is evaluated independently. For example, if the first right-hand side expression (`clk_enable`) has the value **01x** and the second right-hand side expression (`clk_mode`) has the value **11z**, the effective value of `mode_enable` is **x1x** (the first bits 0 and 1 index into the table to give an x, the second bits 1 and 1 index into the table to give a 1, the third bits x and z index into the table to give an x).

Wor and Trior Nets

This is a wired-or net, that is, if any one of the drivers is a 1, the value on the net is also a 1. Both wor and trior nets are identical in their syntax and functionality.

```
wor [MSB:LSB] ctrl_reg;
localparam MAX = 32, MIN = 1;
trior [MAX-1:MIN-1] mode_reg, next_data, load_reg;
```

If multiple drivers drive this net, the effective value of the net is determined by using the following table.

wor (or trior)	0	1	x	z
0	0	1	x	0
1	1	1	1	1
x	x	1	x	x
z	0	1	x	z

Wand and Triand Nets

This net is a wired-and net, that is, if any of the drivers is a 0, the value of the net is a 0. Both wand and triand nets are identical in their syntax and functionality.

```
wand [-7:0] paddress;
triand preset, pwrite;
```

If multiple drivers drive a wand net, the following table is used to determine the effective value.

wand (or triand)	0	1	x	z
0	0	0	0	0
1	0	1	x	1
x	0	x	x	x
z	0	1	x	z

Trireg Net

This net stores a value (like a variable) and is used to model a capacitive node. When all drivers to a trireg net are at high-impedance, that is, have the value z, the trireg net retains the last value on the net. In addition, the default initial value for a trireg net is an x.

```
trireg [1:8] bmc_datain, bmc_dataout;
```

Tri0 and Tri1 Nets

These nets also model wired-logic nets, that is, a net with more than one driver. The particular characteristic of a tri0 (tri1) net is that if no driver is driving this net, its value is 0 (1 for tri1).

Range indices can be negative.

```
tri0 [-3:3] ground_bus;
tri1 [0:-5] otp_bus, itp_bus;
```

The following table shows the effective value for a tri0 or a tri1 net that has more than one driver.

tri0 (tri1)	0	1	x	z
0	0	x	x	0
1	x	1	x	1
x	x	x	x	x
z	0	1	x	0(1)

Supply0 and Supply1 Nets

The supply0 net is used to model ground, that is, the value 0, and the supply1 net is used to model a power net, that is, the value 1.

```
`define RANGE [2:0]

supply0 logic_0, clk_ground, VSS;
supply1 `RANGE logic_1, VDD;
```

3.7.2 Undeclared Nets

In Verilog HDL, it is possible not to declare a net. In such a case, the net defaults to a 1-bit wire net.

This implicit net declaration can be changed by using the **`default_nettype** compiler directive. It is of the form:

```
`default_nettype net_kind
```

For example, with the compiler directive:

```
`default_nettype wand
```

any undeclared net defaults to a 1-bit wand net.

To enforce all nets to be explicitly declared, the value of **none** can be used with this directive.

```
`default_nettype none
```

In such a case, any undeclared net will be a syntax error. This is often useful to prevent hard-to-debug errors caused by a mistyped name.

3.7.3 Vectored and Scalared Nets

The keywords, **scalared** or **vectored**, can optionally be specified for a vector net. If a net is declared with the keyword **vectored**, then bit-selects and part-selects of this vector net are not allowed; in other words, the entire net has to be assigned (bit-selects and part-selects are described in the next chapter). Here is an example of such a declaration.

```
wire vectored [3:1] grb_count;
  // Bit-select grb_count[2] and part-select
  // grb_count[3:2] are NOT allowed.

wor scalared [4:0] bst_addr;
  // Same as:
  // wor [4:0] bst_addr;
  // Bit-select bst_addr[2] and part-select
  // bst_addr[3:1] are allowed.
```

If no such keyword is specified, then the default is **scalared**.

3.7.4 Variable Types

There are five different kinds of variable types.

- reg
- integer
- time
- real
- realtime

Guideline: Use all lowercase characters in a variable name.

A variable can be initialized to a constant value using the variable declaration assignment statement (described in 8.1.1).

Reg Variable

The reg kind of variable data type is the one most commonly used. A reg is declared by using a reg declaration, which is of the form:

```
reg [ signed ] [ [ msb : lsb ] ] reg1 , reg2 , . . . , regN ;
```

Guideline: Use parameters to specify size of range, e.g [SIZE-1:0].

where *msb* and *lsb* specify the range and are constant-valued expressions. The range specification is optional; if no range is specified, it defaults to a 1-bit reg variable. Here are some examples.

```
reg [3:0] ext_bus;          // ext_bus is a 4-bit variable.
reg test_reqa;              // A 1-bit variable.
reg [1:32] sm_datain, sm_address, tc_bus;
```

A reg variable can be of any size. A value in a reg variable is interpreted as an unsigned number, unless the keyword **signed** is used, in which case, the variable holds signed values (in two's complement form).

```
reg signed [1:4] xfer_rsp;

xfer_rsp = -2; // xfer_rsp has 14 (1110), the two's
                // complement of 2.
xfer_rsp = 5; // xfer_rsp has 5 (0101).

parameter MSB = 16, LSB = 1;
reg signed [MSB : LSB] usim_counter; // usim_counter
  // holds signed data in two's complement form.
```

An uninitialized reg variable has a default value of x.

Memories

A *memory* is an array of reg variables. It is declared using a reg declaration of the form:

```
reg [ [ msb : lsb ] ] memory1 [upper1 : lower1 ],
                      memory2 [upper2 : lower2 ], . . . ;
```

Here is an example of a memory declaration.

```
reg [0:3] ebi_mem [0:63]; // ebi_mem is an array of
  // sixty-four 4-bit reg variables.
reg gnt_rfile[1:5];
  // gnt_rfile is an array of five 1-bit reg variables.
```

ebi_mem and gnt_rfile are memories. A memory belongs to the variable data type. Arrays with more than two dimensions and arrays of nets are allowed; see later section on "Arrays".

A single reg declaration can be used to declare both variables and memories.

```
parameter ADDR_SIZE = 16, WORD_SIZE = 8;
reg [1:WORD_SIZE] par_ram [ADDR_SIZE-1 : 0], dburst_reg;
```

par_ram is a memory, an array of sixteen 8-bit reg variables, while dburst_reg is a 8-bit reg variable.

A word of caution in assignments. A memory cannot be assigned a value in one assignment, but a reg can. Therefore an index needs to be specified for a memory when it is being assigned. Let's look at this difference. In the following assignment,

```
reg [1:5] qburst; // qburst is a 5-bit reg variable.
. . .
qburst = 5'b11011;
```

is okay, but the following assignment:

```
reg hold_gnt [1:5]; // hold_gnt is a memory of
  // five 1-bit reg variables.
. . .
hold_gnt = 5'b11011;
```

is not. One way to assign to a memory is to assign a value to each word of a memory individually. For example,

```
reg [0:3] xp_rom [1:4];
```

```
xp_rom[1] = 4'hA;
xp_rom[2] = 4'h8;
xp_rom[3] = 4'hF;
xp_rom[4] = 4'h2;
```

To copy the contents of one memory to another memory, use a for loop and copy one word at a time. This is shown in the next example.

```
parameter WORD_LENGTH = 8, NUM_WORDS = 64;
reg [WORD_LENGTH-1:0]
  mem_a [NUM_WORDS-1:0],
  mem_b [NUM_WORDS-1:0];
integer i;

// mem_a = mem_b : not allowed.

for (i = 0; i < NUM_WORDS; i = i + 1)
  mem_a[i] = mem_b[i];
```

An alternate way to assign values to a memory is by using the system tasks:

i. **$readmem**: loads binary values.

ii. **$readmemh**: loads hexadecimal values.

These system tasks read and load data from a specified text file into a memory. The text file must contain the appropriate form of numbers, either binary or hexadecimal. Here is an example.

```
reg [1:4] cdn_rom [7:1];
$readmemb ("ram.patt", cdn_rom);
```

`cdn_rom` is a memory. The file `ram.patt` must contain binary values. The file may also contain white spaces and comments. Here is an example of what may be in the file.

```
1101
1100
1000
0111
0000
```

```
1001
0011
```

The system task **$readmemb** causes the values to be read in starting from index 7, the leftmost word index of cdn_rom. If only a part of the memory is to be loaded, the range can be explicitly specified in the **$readmemb** task, such as:

```
$readmemb ("ram.patt", cdn_rom, 5, 3);
```

in which case only cdn_rom[5], cdn_rom[4], and cdn_rom[3] words are read from the file beginning at the top. The values read are 1101, 1100 and 1000.

The file may also contain explicit addresses of the form:

```
@hex_address  value
```

such as in this example:

```
@5   11001
@2   11010
```

in which case the values are read into the specified addresses of the memory.

When only a start value is specified, read continues until the right-hand index bound of the memory is reached. For example,

```
$readmemb ("ram.patt", cdn_rom, 6);
   // Starts from address 6 and continues until 1.
$readmemb ("ram.patt", cdn_rom, 6, 4);
   // Reads from addresses 6 through 4.
```

Integer Variable

An integer variable contains integer values. It can be used as a general purpose variable, typically for modeling high-level behavior. It is declared using an integer declaration of the form:

```
integer integer1 , integer2, . . . , integerN [ msb : lsb ];
```

msb and *lsb* are constant-valued expressions that specify the range of an integer array; the array range specification is optional. Notice that no bit range is allowed. An integer holds a minimum of 32 bits; however, an implementation may provide more. Here are some examples of integer declarations.

```
integer a, b, c;      // Three integer variables.
integer hist[3:6]; // An array of four integers.
```

An integer variable holds signed quantities and arithmetic operations provide two's complement arithmetic results.

An integer can be accessed as a bit-vector. An integer variable is treated as a signed reg variable with the least significant bit index of 0. For example, given the above declaration for integer b, b[6] and b[20:10] are allowed. Here is an example.

```
reg [31:0] sel_reg;
integer sel_int;
. . .
// sel_int[6] and sel_int[20:10] are allowed.
. . .
sel_reg = sel_int;
```

This example shows that converting an integer to a bit-vector can be accomplished by simply using an assignment. Type conversion is automatic. No special functions are necessary. Converting from a bit-vector to an integer can also be accomplished by using an assignment. Here are some examples.

```
integer j;
reg [3:0] bcq;

j = 6;             // j has the value 32'b0000...00110.
bcq = j;           // bcq has the value 4'b0110.

bcq = 4'b0101;
j = bcq;           /// j has value 32'b0000...00101.

j = -6;            // j has the value 32'b1111...11010.
bcq = j;           // bcq has the value 4'b1010.
```

Note that the assignment always takes place from the rightmost bit to the leftmost bit; any extra bits are truncated. It is easy to think of type conversion if you can remember that integers are represented as two's complement bit-vectors.

Here is an example of an array of integers, showing the declaration, assignments and its usage.

```
module mod_int_array;
  localparam ARRAY_SIZE = 8;
  integer int_array [0:ARRAY_SIZE-1];

  initial
    begin
      int_array[0] = 56;
      int_array[1] = 12;
      int_array[2] = int_array[0] / 2;
      $display ("int_array[2] is %d ", int_array[2]);
    end
endmodule
```

Time Variable

A time variable is used to store and manipulate time values. It is declared using a time declaration of the form:

```
time time_id1 , time_id2 , . . ., time_idN [ msb : lsb ];
```

where *msb* and *lsb* are constant-valued expressions that indicate the range of indices. If no range is specified, each identifier stores one time value which is at least 64 bits. A time variable holds only an unsigned quantity. Here are examples of time declarations.

```
time events [0:31];   // Array of time values.
time curr_time;       // curr_time holds one time value.
```

Real and Realtime Variable

A real variable (or a realtime variable) can be declared using the following form.

```
// Real declaration:
real real_reg1 , real_reg2 , . . . , real_regN ;
// Realtime declaration:
realtime realtime_reg1 , realtime_reg2 , . . . ,
          realtime_regN ;
```

A realtime variable is exactly identical to a real variable. Here are some examples.

```
real swing_margin, top_mark;
realtime curr_time_in_real;
```

The default value of a real variable is 0. No range, bit range or word range, is allowed for declaring a real variable.

When assigning values x and z to a real variable, these values are treated as a 0.

```
real amr_count;
. . .
amr_count = 'b01x1Z;
```

`amr_count` has the value 'b01010 after the assignment.

3.7.5 Arrays

A multi-dimensional array of a net or a variable can be declared using an array declaration. An element of an array can be a scalar value or a vector value. Here are some examples.

```
wire push_bus [0:4]; // An array of 5 elements, where
  // each element is a scalar element: a 1-bit wire.
reg [0:7] smc_fifo [0:63], req_stack [0:63]; // Array of
  // 64 elements, each element being a 8-bit vector.
```

```
tri [0:31] biq_addr [0:1][0:3]; // Two-dimensional array
  // of tri wires, each element being 32 bits wide.

integer run_stats [0:15] [0:15]; // Array of 16-by-16
  // integer variables.
```

Guideline: Avoid writing names that differ in only the trailing digits, such as `ram_addr0` and `ram_addr`.

The vector size specifies the number of bits in each element of the vector, while the ranges on the right of the variable specify the number of elements in each dimension of the array. Note that a one-dimensional reg variable array is called a memory (see previous section).

An array cannot be assigned to another array using a single assignment statement. A slice or a range of an array cannot be assigned a value in a single assignment. Only an element of an array can be assigned. A bit-select or part-select of an element of an array can also be accessed and assigned.

```
smc_fifo[5] = 26; // Ok to assign to 5th element of array.
smc_fifo = req_stack; // Not allowed: cannot assign
  // a complete array.

biq_addr[0][1] = 32'b0;
biq_addr[1][0] = 32'b1;

push_bus[0:2] = 1; // Not allowed to write to a range
  // or slice of an array.

biq_addr[0][0][0:5] = 6'100011; // Ok to assign to a
  // slice of an element.
```

3.7.6 Difference between Reg and Wire

A reg is one of the variable types. A wire is one of the net types. Examples of other variable types are integer and time. Examples of other net types are wand and tri.

A reg variable can only be assigned a value in an always or an initial statement. A wire can only be assigned using a continuous assignment or via the output (and inout) port of a module instance.

Moreover, upon initialization, a reg variable has the value x, while a wire has the value z.

A wire can be assigned a strength whereas a reg variable cannot.

3.8 Parameters

A *parameter* is a constant. It is often used to specify delays and widths of variables. A parameter can be assigned a value only once, using a parameter declaration. A parameter declaration is of the form:

Guideline: Use all uppercase characters in a parameter name.

```
parameter [ signed ] [ [msb : lsb ]] param1 = const_expr1 ,
  param2 = const_exp2 , . . . ,paramN = const_exprN ;
```

Here are some examples.

```
parameter LINELENGTH = 132, ALL_X_S = 16'bx; // Implied
  // range of LINELENGTH is [31:0] and that
  // for ALL_X_S is [15:0].
parameter BIT = 1, WBYTE = 8, PI = 3.14; // Implied range
  // for BIT and WBYTE is [31:0] while PI is a real.
parameter STROBE_DELAY = (WBYTE + BIT) / 2;
parameter TQ_FILE = "/home/bhasker/TEST/add.tq";

parameter signed [3:0] MEM_DR = -5, CPU_SPI = 6;
  // MEM_DR and CPU_SPI are signed 4-bit values.
 `define WIDTH 16
parameter [`WIDTH-1:0] RED = 0, BLUE = 1, YELLOW = 2;

parameter LINEAR_SIZE = 2 * MEM_DR + CPU_SPI;
```

A parameter value can also be changed at compile time. This is done by using a defparam statement or by specifying the parameter value in the module instantiation statement (these two mechanisms are described in Chapter 9).

A parameter declaration can optionally specify a type (**integer**, **real**, **realtime**, or **time**), in which case, no range specification or keyword **signed** is allowed.

```
parameter time TRIG_TIME = 10, APPLY_TIME = 25;
parameter integer COUNT_LIMIT = 25;
```

Guideline: Use parameters to define constants and use macros to define ASCII text.

What is the difference between a parameter and a **`define**? A parameter is local to the module that it is declared in, while a **`define**'s definition stays through multiple files as they are compiled. So even though a **`define** can be defined within a module, the definition does not die until it is redefined, and the definition stays persistent through the many files in the compilation process. So the bottom line is, to be safe, reserve **`define** usage for strictly global variables and text substitution and use parameters for constants that are required to be scoped within a module.

3.8.1 Local Parameters

A local parameter is a parameter that is local to a module and which cannot be modified by a module instantiation statement or by a defparam assignment. Syntactically, a local parameter is declared exactly like a parameter declaration except for the keyword **localparam**.

```
localparam TC_IDLE = 2'b00;
localparam [3:0] INCR_BY = 12;
localparam signed [7:0] TSM_MAX = 56;
localparam real TWO_PI = 2 * 3.14;
```

If a local parameter is defined in terms of other non-local parameters, then the local parameter gets indirectly modified when the parameter value changes due to an external assignment.

```
parameter BYTE = 8;
localparam NIBBLE = 2 * BYTE;
```

If parameter BYTE gets modified during compile time, so does the local parameter NIBBLE.

3.9 Exercises

1. Identify the legal and illegal identifiers:
   COunT, 1_2Many, **1 , Real?, \wait , Initial

2. What first character identifies a system task or a system function?

3. Explain the text substitution compiler directive using an example.

4. Is there a Boolean type in Verilog HDL?

5. What are the bit patterns for the following:
7'o44, 'Bx0, 5'bx110, 'hA0, 10'd2, 'hzF

6. What is the bit pattern stored in `qpr` after the assignment?

```
reg [1:8*2] qpr;
. . .
qpr = "ME";
```

7. If a net `gnt` is declared but no assignment is made to it, what is its default value?

8. Verilog HDL allows a net not to be explicitly declared. If so, how is the net kind determined?

9. What is wrong with the following?

```
integer [0:3] ripple;
```

10. Write a system task to load a 32 by 64 word memory from a data file `memA.data`.

11. State two ways by which you can override a parameter value at compile time.

□

4

Expressions

This chapter describes the basics of how expressions are formed in Verilog HDL.

An expression is formed using operands and operators. An expression can be used wherever a value is expected.

4.1 Operands

An operand can be one of the following.

i. Constant
ii. Parameter
iii. Net
iv. Variable
v. Bit-select
vi. Part-select
vii. Memory and array element
viii. Function call

4.1.1 Constant

Constants were described in the previous chapter. Here are some examples.

```
256, 7              // Unsized decimal numbers
4'b10_11, 8'h0A // Sized integer constants
'b1, 'hFBA          // Unsized integer constants
90.00006            // Real constant
"BOND"              /* String constant; each character is
                       stored as a 8-bit ASCII value */
```

An integer value in an expression is interpreted as either a signed or an unsigned number. If it is a decimal integer, for example, 12, then it is interpreted as a signed number. If the integer is a based integer (unsized or sized), then it is treated as an unsigned number if no signed qualifier (no s) is used, else it is a signed number. Here are some examples.

```
12         is 01100 in 5-bit vector form (signed)
-12        is 10100 in 5-bit vector form (signed)
5'b01100 is decimal 12 (unsigned)
5'b10100 is decimal 20 (unsigned)
4'd12      is decimal 12 (unsigned)
8'shCF     is 11011111 in 8-bit vector form (signed)
```

More important is the fact that a negative value of an integer is treated differently for an integer with or without a base. The negative value of an integer with no base specifier is treated as a signed value, while the negative value of an integer with a base specifier is treated as an unsigned value. Thus, –44 is treated different from –6'o54 (decimal 44 is octal 54) as shown in the next example.

```
integer event_reg;
. . .
event_reg = - 44 / 4;
event_reg = - 6'o54 / 4;
```

Note that both –44 and –6'o54 are evaluated to the same bit pattern; however –44 is treated as a signed number, while –6'o54 is treated as an unsigned number. Thus `event_reg` in the first assignment has value –11, while `event_reg` has the value 1073741813 in the second assignment.

4.1.2 Parameter

Parameters were described in the previous chapter. A parameter is like a constant and is declared using a parameter declaration. Here are examples of parameter declarations.

```
parameter LOAD = 4'd12, STORE = 4'd10;
localparam [7:0] LIMIT = 112;
localparam [31:0] HIGH_BYTE_MASK = 32'hF000;
```

LOAD and STORE are examples of parameters that are declared to have the values 12 and 10 respectively. LIMIT and HIGH_BYTE_MASK are local parameters.

4.1.3 Net

Both scalar nets (1-bit) and vector nets (multi-bit) can be used in an expression. Here are examples of net declarations.

```
wire [0:3] gpio_port; // gpio_port is a 4-bit vector net.
wire intr;            // intr is a scalar net.
wire signed [3:0] jch; // 4-bit signed net.
```

A value in a net is interpreted as an unsigned value unless the keyword **signed** is specified in the net declaration. In the continuous assignment,

```
assign gpio_port = - 3;
```

gpio_port has the bit-vector 1101 assigned which is in effect the decimal value 13. In the following continuous assignment,

```
assign gpio_port = 4'HA;
```

gpio_port has the bit-vector 1010 assigned to it which is the decimal value 10.

4.1.4 Variable

Scalar and vector variables can be used in an expression. A variable is declared using a variable declaration. Here are some examples.

```
integer periph_id, test_input1;
reg [1:5] mis_state;
reg signed [3:0] raw_count;
time t_que [1:5];
```

A value in an integer variable is interpreted as a signed two's complement number while a value in a time variable is interpreted as an unsigned number. A value in a reg variable is interpreted as a signed number if the declaration for the reg variable contained the keyword **signed**, else the reg variable holds an unsigned number. Values in real and realtime variables are interpreted as signed floating point values.

```
periph_id = - 10; // periph_id has the bit-vector 10110,
                  // which is the two's complement of 10.
periph_id = 'b1011;  // periph_id has the decimal
                     // value 11.

mis_state = - 10; // mis_state has the bit-vector 10110,
                  // which is decimal 22.
mis_state = 'b1011; // mis_state has the bit-vector
                    // 01011, which is the decimal value 11.
```

4.1.5 Bit-select

A bit-select extracts a particular bit from a vector. It is of the form:

```
net_or_reg_vector [ bit_select_expr]
```

Here are examples of bit-selects used in expressions.

```
mis_state[1] && mis_state[4] // Variable bit-select
gpio_port[0] | intr          // Net bit-select
LIMIT[5]                     // Parameter bit-select
```

If the select expression evaluates to an x or a z or if it is out of bounds, the value of the bit-select is an x, for example, `mis_state[x]` is an x.

4.1.6 Part-select

In a part-select, a contiguous sequence of bits of a vector is selected. There are two forms of part-select: a constant part-select and an indexed part-select. A constant part-select is of the form:

```
net_or_reg_vector [ msb_const_expr :lsb_const_expr]
```

where the range expressions must be constant expressions. Here are some examples.

```
mis_state[1:4]        // Reg variable part-select
gpio_port[1:3]        // Net part-select
HIGH_BYTE_MASK[31:16] // Parameter part-select
```

An indexed part-select is of the form:

```
net_or_reg_vector [ base_expr +: const_width_expr ]
net_or_reg_vector [ base_expr -: const_width_expr ]
```

The base expression need not be a constant. The range of bits selected is the index specified by the base expression plus or minus the number of bits specified by the width. "+:" indicates that the part-select increases from the base (start) index. "–:" indicates that the part-select decreases from the start index. Here are some examples of indexed part-selects.

```
integer mark;
reg [0:15] inst_code;
wire [31:0] gpio_data;

inst_code[mark +: 2]    // Selects bits mark, mark + 1.
gpio_data[mark -: 4]    // Selects bits mark, mark - 1,
                        // mark - 2, mark - 3.
inst_code[0 +: 8]       // Same as inst_code[0:7].
gpio_data[31 -: 16]     // Same as gpio_data[31:16].

inst_code[mark -: 2]    // Selects bits mark - 1, mark.
gpio_data[mark +: 4]    // Selects bits mark + 3,
                        // mark + 2, mark + 1, mark.
inst_code[15 -: 4]      // Same as inst_code[12:15].
gpio_data[0 +: 8]       // Same as gpio_data[7:0].
```

The base expression (start index) can be a variable. However the width of the part-select must be a constant.

If either the range index is out of bounds or evaluates to an x or a z, the part-select value is an x.

4.1.7 Memory and Array Element

A memory element selects one word of a memory. It is of the form:

```
memory[ word_address]
```

Here is an example.

```
reg [1:8] hdlc_ram [0:63], intr_ack;
. . .
intr_ack = hdlc_ram[60]; // 60th element of memory.
```

An array element selects one word of an array. It is of the form:

```
array [ word_address]{[ word_address]}
```

Part-select or bit-select of a memory element or an array element is allowed. For example,

```
hdlc_ram[60][2] // Value at index 2 of the 60th element.
hdlc_ram[15][2:4]    // Value at index range [2:4] of
                     // the 15th element.
hdlc_ram[0:2]        // Is not allowed.
```

Here is another memory declaration.

```
reg [15:0] fill_pattern [0:63];
  // Memory of 64 words, each word of 16 bits.
```

To access the lower order byte of the word at address 10, use:

```
reg [7:0] test_pattern;
test_pattern = fill_pattern [10][7:0];
```

Here are some examples of arrays.

Part-select and bit-select of an element of a memory or an array is allowed.

```
reg [7:0] sense_data [15:0][15:0];
integer three_d [255:0][255:0][255:0];
wire xbar [3:0][3:0];

sense_data[2][3]       // Accesses the entire element.
sense_data[1][1][0]    // Accesses the 0th index of the
                       // element at index [1][1].

three_d[5][5][2]       // Ok.
three_d[2][1:2][8]     // Not ok; part-select of only an
                       // element is allowed.
xbar[0][2:0]           // Not ok.
```

4.1.8 Function Call

A function call can be used in an expression. It can either be a system function call (starts with the $ character) or an user-defined function call.

```
$time + sum_of_events (a, b)
  /* $time is a system function and sum_of_events is an
     user-defined function (defined elsewhere) */
```

Functions are described in greater detail in Chapter 10.

4.1.9 Signedness

An operand is either signed or unsigned. If all operands in an expression are signed, then the result is signed, else the result is unsigned. More on this later.

```
8'd2 + 8'sb0101    // Result is unsigned since 8'd2 is
                   // an unsigned number.
4'sb0110 - 4'sd1   // Result is signed since all
                   // operands are signed.
```

4.2 Operators

Operators in Verilog HDL are classified into the following categories.

i. Arithmetic operators
ii. Relational operators
iii. Equality operators
iv. Logical operators
v. Bitwise operators
vi. Reduction operators
vii. Shift operators
viii. Conditional operators
ix. Concatenation and replication operators

The following table shows the precedence and names of all the operators. The operators are listed from highest precedence (top row) to the lowest precedence (bottom row). Operators in the same row have identical precedence.

Operator	Name
+	Unary plus
–	Unary minus
!	Unary logical negation
~	Unary bit-wise negation
&	Reduction and
~&	Reduction nand
^	Reduction xor
^~ or ~^	Reduction xnor
|	Reduction or
~|	Reduction nor
**	Power (exponentiation)
*	Multiply
/	Divide
%	Modulus
+	Binary plus
–	Binary minus

<table>
<tr><td><<<
>>>
<<
>></td><td>Arithmetic left shift
Arithmetic right shift
Logical left shift
Logical right shift</td></tr>
<tr><td><
<=
>
>=</td><td>Less than
Less than or equal to
Greater than
Greater than or equal to</td></tr>
<tr><td>==
!=
===
!==</td><td>Logical equality
Logical inequality
Case equality
Case inequality</td></tr>
<tr><td>&</td><td>Bit-wise and</td></tr>
<tr><td>^
^~ or ~^</td><td>Bit-wise xor
Bit-wise xnor</td></tr>
<tr><td>|</td><td>Bit-wise or</td></tr>
<tr><td>&&</td><td>Logical and</td></tr>
<tr><td>||</td><td>Logical or</td></tr>
<tr><td>?:</td><td>Conditional operator</td></tr>
<tr><td>{}
{{}}</td><td>Concatenation
Replication</td></tr>
</table>

All operators associate left to right except for the conditional operator that associates right to left. The expression:

```
a + b - c
```

is evaluated as:

```
(a + b) - c          // Left to right
```

while the expression:

```
a ? b : c ? d : f
```

is evaluated as:

```
a ? b : (c ? d : f )      // Right to left.
```

Parentheses can be used to change the order of precedence, such as in the expression:

```
(a ? b : c) ? d : f
```

4.2.1 Arithmetic Operators

The arithmetic operators are:

- + (unary and binary plus)
- – (unary and binary minus)
- * (multiply)
- / (divide)
- % (modulus)
- ** (power)

Integer division truncates any fractional part. For example,

```
7 / 4             is 1
```

The % (modulus) operator gives the remainder with the sign of the first operand.

```
7 % 4             is 3
```

while:

```
-7 % 4            is -3
```

Here is an example usage of the power operator.

```
parameter ADDR_SIZE = 16;
localparam RAM_SIZE = 2 ** ADDR_SIZE - 1;
```

If any bit of an operand in an arithmetic operation is an x or a z, the entire result is an x. For example,

```
'b10x1 + 'b01111    is  'bxxxxx
```

Result Size

The size of the result of an arithmetic expression is determined by the size of the largest operand. In case of an assignment, it is determined by the size of the left-hand side target as well. Consider the following example.

```
reg [0:3] mask_intr, test_ctrl, raw_intr;
reg [0:5] intr_req;
. . .
mask_intr = test_ctrl + raw_intr;
intr_req = test_ctrl + raw_intr;
```

The result size of the first addition is determined by the size of `test_ctrl`, `raw_intr` and `mask_intr` which is four bits. The size of the second addition operation is decided similarly by the size of `intr_req` (largest of sizes `intr_req`, `test_ctrl`, `raw_intr`), which is six bits. So in the first assignment, any overflow from the plus operation is discarded while in the second assignment, any overflow bit is saved in the result bit `intr_req[1]`.

In larger expressions, how are the sizes of the intermediate results determined? Verilog HDL defines a rule which states that all intermediate results of an expression shall take the size of the largest operand (in case of an assignment, this also includes the left-hand side target). Consider another example.

```
wire [4:1] intr_ena, test_reg;
wire [1:5] next_iev;
wire [1:6] peg_intr;
wire [1:8] adt_sense;
. . .
assign adt_sense = (intr_ena + next_iev) +
                   (test_reg + peg_intr);
```

The size of the largest operand in the right-hand side expression is 6, but including the size of the left-hand side, the largest size is 8. So all additions are performed using 8 bits. For example, adding `intr_ena` and `next_iev` yields a result of size 8.

Unsigned and Signed

When performing arithmetic operations and assignments, it is important to note which operands are being treated as unsigned values and which are being treated as signed values. An unsigned value is stored in:

- a net
- a reg variable
- an integer in base format notation without signed qualifier (the s)

A signed value is stored in:

- an integer variable
- an integer in base format notation with signed qualifier (the s)
- an integer in decimal form
- a signed reg variable
- a signed net

Here are some examples of assignments.

```
reg [0:5] burst_data;
integer mtx_addr;
. . .
burst_data = - 4'd12;// Reg burst_data has the decimal
                     // value 52, which is the vector 110100.
mtx_addr = - 4'd12; // Integer mtx_addr has the value -12
                    // (bits 110100)

- 4'd12 / 4          // Result is 1073741821.
- 12 / 4             // Result is -3.
```

Since `burst_data` is a reg variable, it stores only unsigned values. The value of the right-hand side expression is 'b110100 (the two's complement of 12). Thus burst_data holds the decimal value 52 after the assignment. In the second assignment, the right-hand side expression is the same, whose value is 'b110100, but this time it is being assigned to an integer variable which holds signed quantities. Thus mtx_addr holds the decimal value –12 (the bit-vector 110100). Note that in both cases, the same bit-vector is stored; however, in the first case, the vector is interpreted as an unsigned number and in the second case, it is interpreted as a signed number.

Here are some more examples.

```
burst_data = - 4'd12 / 4;
mtx_addr = - 4'd12 / 4;

burst_data = - 12 / 4;
mtx_addr = - 12 / 4;
```

In the first assignment, burst_data gets the decimal value 61 (bit-vector 111101), while in the second assignment, mtx_addr gets the decimal value 1073741821 (bit-vector 0011...11101). burst_data gets the same value in the third assignment as in the first assignment. This is because burst_data holds only a 6-bit value. In the fourth assignment, mtx_addr gets the decimal value –3.

Here are some more examples.

```
burst_data = 4 - 6;
mtx_addr = 4 - 6;
```

burst_data gets the decimal value 62 (two's complement of –2), while mtx_addr gets the decimal value –2 (bit-vector 111110).

Here is another example.

```
burst_data = -2 + (-4);
mtx_addr = -2 + (-4);
```

burst_data gets the decimal value 58 (bit-vector 111010), while mtx_addr gets the decimal value –6 (bit-vector 111010).

The two system functions **$signed** and **$unsigned** can be used to convert values to signed or unsigned forms respectively.

```
$signed (4'b1101)     is a signed number, value of -3.
$unsigned (4'shA)     is an unsigned number, value of 10.
```

Be careful when mixing signed and unsigned operands in a single expression. If any one operand is unsigned, all operands are converted to unsigned before any operation takes place.

If any one operand is unsigned, all operands are converted to unsigned before any operation takes place.

```
'd2 + 4'sb1001     has unsigned decimal value 11.
```

To perform only a signed operation, convert the unsigned operand to a signed operand using the **$signed** system function. When signed and unsigned operators are mixed in an single expression, you can control the signed behavior by using the **$signed** and **$unsigned** system functions.

```
$signed ('d2) + 4'sb1001                      is -5.
$unsigned (5'sb11010 + 5'sh1C) - 5'b01001     is 13.
```

In the last example, the addition operation is signed which yields (–6) + (–4) = –10. Convert to unsigned yields +22. Unsigned subtraction with rightmost operand yields 13. In this particular case, if the **$signed** system function were used instead of the **$unsigned**, the exact same behavior would be produced. This is because of the previously stated rule that if any operand is unsigned, then all signed operands are implicitly converted to unsigned before any operation takes place.

To perform signed operation, use all signed operands in an expression.

```
2 + 8'shCA - $signed(8'o32)      // Signed.

reg signed [15:0] num_events;

num_events / 2                   // Signed.
num_events * $signed(4'd3)       // Signed.
```

4.2.2 Relational Operators

The relational operators are:

- > (greater than)
- < (less than)
- >= (greater than or equal to)
- <= (less than or equal to)

The result of a relational operator is true (the value 1) or false (the value 0). Result is an x if any bit in either of the operands is an x or a z. For example,

```
23 > 45
```

is false (value 0), while:

```
52 < 16'hxFF
```

is x. If operands are not of the same size and if any operand is unsigned, the smaller operand is zero-filled on the most significant bit side (the left). For example,

```
'b1000 >= 'b01110
```

is equivalent to:

```
'b01000 >= 'b01110
```

which is false (value 0). Consequently, if both operands are signed, then sign extension is performed on the smaller operand. For example,

```
4'sb1011 <= 8'sh1A
```

is equivalent to:

```
8'sb11111011 <= 8'sb00011010
```

which is true.

If one of the operands in the expression is unsigned, the rest of the expression is treated as unsigned as well.

```
(4'sd9 * 4'd2) < 4          is false (18 < 4).
(4'sd9 * 2) < 4             is true (-14 < 4).
```

4.2.3 Equality Operators

The equality operators are:

- == (logical equality)
- != (logical inequality)
- === (case equality)
- !== (case inequality)

The result is 0 if the comparison is false, else the result is a 1. In case comparisons, values x and z are compared strictly as values, that is, with no interpretations, and the result can never be an unknown, while in logical comparisons, values x and z have their usual meaning and the result may be unknown; that is, for logical comparisons if either operand contains an x or a z, and the comparison is ambiguous, the result is the unknown value (x).

Here is an example. Given:

```
sw_data = 'b11x0;
sw_addr = 'b11x0;
```

then:

```
sw_data == sw_addr
```

is unknown, that is, the value x, and:

```
sw_data === sw_addr
```

is true, that is, the value 1.

```
'b010x != 'b11x0
```

is true. Even though an x is present in both the operands, the result is not ambiguous - due to the difference in the first bit.

If the operands are of unequal lengths and if either operand is unsigned, the smaller operand is zero-filled on the most significant side, that is, on the left. For example,

```
2'b10 == 4'b0010
```

is same as:

```
4'b0010 == 4'b0010
```

which is true (the value 1). If the operands are of unequal lengths and if both operands are signed, the smaller operand is sign-extended.

Here is another example that multiplexes four bytes onto a bus.

```
`define WIDTH 8
wire [`WIDTH-1:0] mux_bus, byte_a, byte_b,
                  byte_c, byte_d;
wire [1:0] select;

assign mux_bus =  (select === 0) ? byte_a :
                  (select === 1) ? byte_b :
                  (select === 2) ? byte_c :
                  (select === 3) ? byte_d :
                  8'bz;
```

4.2.4 Logical Operators

The logical operators are:

- && (logical and)
- || (logical or)
- ! (unary logical negation)

These operators operate on logical values 0 or 1. The result of a logical operation is a 0, 1 or x. For example, given:

```
mlock = 'b0;      // 0 is false.
mprot = 'b1;      // 1 is true.
```

then:

```
mlock && mprot  is 0 (false)
mlock || mprot  is 1 (true)
! mprot         is 0 (false)
```

For vector operands, a non-zero vector is treated as a 1. For example, given:

```
rdy_bus = 'b0110;
intr_bus = 'b0100;
```

then:

```
rdy_bus || intr_bus  is 1
rdy_bus && intr_bus  is also 1
```

and:

```
! rdy_bus  is same as  ! intr_bus
```

which is 0.

If a bit in any of the operands is an x or a z, and if the result is ambiguous, the resultant value is an x.

```
'b1 || 'bx     is 1
'b0 && 'bz     is 0
!x             is x
```

4.2.5 Bit-wise Operators

The bit-wise operators are:

- ~ (unary negation)
- & (binary and)
- | (binary or)

- ^ (binary exclusive-or)
- ~^, ^~ (binary exclusive-nor)

These operators operate bit-by-bit, on corresponding bits of the input operands and produce a vector result. The following tables show the result of the bit-by-bit operation for the various operators.

& (and)	0	1	x	z
0	0	0	0	0
1	0	1	x	x
x	0	x	x	x
z	0	x	x	x

| (or)	0	1	x	z
0	0	1	x	x
1	1	1	1	1
x	x	1	x	x
z	x	1	x	x

^ (xor)	0	1	x	z
0	0	1	x	x
1	1	0	x	x
x	x	x	x	x
z	x	x	x	x

^~ (xnor)	0	1	x	z
0	1	0	x	x
1	0	1	x	x
x	x	x	x	x
z	x	x	x	x

~ (negation)	0	1	x	z
	1	0	x	x

Here is an example. Given,

```
a = 'b0110;
b = 'b0100;
```

then:

```
a | b        is 0110
a & b        is 0100
```

If the operands are unequal in length and either operand is an unsigned operand, the smaller operand is zero-filled on the most significant side. If both operands are signed, then the smaller operand is sign-extended to the width of the largest operand before the operation takes place. For example,

```
'b0110 ^ 'b10000
```

is same as:

```
'b00110 ^ 'b10000
```

which is 'b10110. Here is an example with signed operands.

```
4'sb1010 & 8'sb01100010
```

is expanded to:

```
8'sb11111010 & 8'sb01100010
```

to yield the result 8's01100010.

4.2.6 Reduction Operators

The reduction operators operate on all bits of a single operand and produce a 1-bit result. The operators are:

- & (reduction and):
  If any bit is 0, the result is 0, else if any bit is an x or a z, the result is an x, else the result is a 1.
- ~& (reduction nand):
  Invert of & reduction operator.
- | (reduction or):
  If any bit is a 1, the result is 1, else if any bit is an x or a z, the result is an x, else the result is 0.

- ~| (reduction nor):
  Invert of | reduction operator.
- ^ (reduction xor):
  If any bit is an x or a z, the result is an x, else if there are even number of 1's in the operand, the result is 0, else the result is 1.
- ~^ (reduction xnor):
  Invert of ^ reduction operator.

Here are some examples. Given,

```
a = 'b0110;
b = 'b0100;
```

then:

```
| b          is 1
& b          is 0
~^ a         is 1
```

The reduction xor operator can be used to determine if any bit of a vector is an x. Given,

```
addr_port = 4'b01x0;
```

then:

```
^addr_port is an x
```

This can be checked using an if statement such as:

```
if (^addr_port === 1'bx)
  $display ("There is an unknown in the ",
           "vector addr_port!");
```

Note that the logical equality (==) operator cannot be used for comparison; the logical equality operator comparison will only yield the result x. The case equality operator yields the value 1 which is the desired result.

4.2.7 Shift Operators

The shift operators are:

- << (logical left-shift)
- >> (logical right-shift)
- <<< (arithmetic left-shift)
- >>> (arithmetic right-shift)

The shift operation shifts the left operand by the right operand number of times. The right operand is always considered as an unsigned number. If the right operand evaluates to an x or a z, the result of the shift operation is an x. With the logical shift operators, the vacated bits are filled with 0's. With the arithmetic shift operators, left shift fills the vacated bits with 0's. In the case of right shift, if the left operand is unsigned, the vacated bits are filled with 0's, else it is filled with the sign bit (most significant bit).

Given:

```
reg [0:7] qreg;
reg signed [3:0] pmaster;
. . .
qreg = 8'h17;
pmaster = 4'sb1011;
```

then:

```
qreg >> 2          is 8'b00000101
qreg << 2          is 8'b01011100
qreg <<< 4         is 8'b01110000

qreg << -2         // Right operand is unsigned number,
                   // and hence shifted 2**31-2 times left.

qreg >> 4          is 8'b00000001
qreg >>> 2         is 8'b00000101
pmaster >>> 2      is 4'sb1110; sign bit used.
```

The shift operator can be used to perform exponentiation. For example, if you are interested in computing 2^{num_bits}, this can be achieved by using the shift operator, such as:

```
32'b1 << num_bits          // num_bits must be less than 32.

// The power operator can also be used to achieve this:
2 ** num_bits
```

In a similar vein, a 2-to-4 decoder can be modeled using a shift operator.

```
wire [0:3] decode_out = 4'd1 << address[0:1];
```

`address[0:1]` can have values 0, 1, 2, and 3. Correspondingly, `decode_out` has the values 4'b0001, 4'b0010, 4'b0100, and 4'b1000, thereby modeling a decoder.

An arithmetic right shift is a signed division by 2 with the fraction rounded downward to the next lowest integer.

```
qreg >>> 2              is 5 (23/4)
pmaster >>> 2           is -2 (-5/4)
```

In the case of arıunmetic shift operators, there is a special case under which a 0 is shifted in even if the operand is signed. This is the case described in Section 4.1.9 when in an expression, if any one operand is unsigned, then the entire expression is treated as unsigned. So if you need:

```
reg signed [3:0] xfer_port;
3'd4 + xfer_port >>> 1
```

then 0's will be shifted in as `xfer_port` is treated as an unsigned value.

4.2.8 Conditional Operator

The conditional operator selects an expression based on the value of the condition expression and it is of the form:

```
cond_expr ? expr1 : expr2
```

If *cond_expr* is true (that is, has value 1), *expr1* is selected, if *cond_expr* is false (value 0), *expr2* is selected. If *cond_expr* is an x or a z, the result is a bit-wise operation on *expr1* and *expr2* with the following logic: 0 with 0 gives 0, 1 with 1 gives 1, rest are x.

Here is an example.

```
wire [0:2] student = marks > 18 ? grade_a : grade_c;
```

The expression `marks > 18` is computed; if true, `grade_a` is assigned to `student`, if `marks` is <= 18, `grade_c` is assigned to `student`.

Here is another example.

```
always @(posedge clk)
  #5 dlc_ctr = (dlc_ctr != 25) ? (dlc_ctr + 1) : 5;
```

The expression in the procedural assignment says that if `dlc_ctr` is not equal to 25, increment `dlc_ctr`, else if `dlc_ctr` becomes 25, reset it to 5.

4.2.9 Concatenation and Replication

Concatenation is the operation of joining bits from smaller expressions to form larger expressions. It is of the form:

```
{ expr1 , expr2 , . . . , exprN }
```

Here are some examples.

```
wire [7:0] dbus;
wire [11:0] abus;

assign dbus[7:4] = {dbus[0], dbus[1], dbus[2], dbus[3]};
      // Assign lower four bits in reverse order to upper
      // four bits.
assign dbus = {dbus[3:0], dbus[7:4]};
      // Swap lower and upper four bits.
```

Concatenation of unsized constant numbers is not allowed as the size of these numbers are not known. For example,

```
{dbus, 5}    // Unsized constant in concatenation is not
             // allowed.
```

is not legal.

Replication is performed by specifying a repetition number. It is of the form:

{ *repetition_number* { *expr1* , *expr2* ,. . . , *exprN* }}

Here are some examples.

```
abus = {3{4'b1011}}; // The bit-vector 12'b101110111011
abus = {{4 {dbus[7]}}, dbus}; /* Sign extension */

{3{1'b1}}    is 111
{3{ack}}     is same as {ack, ack, ack}
```

The replication operation can be parameterized as shown next.

```
parameter LENGTH = 8;

{LENGTH {1'b0}}                is a string of eight 0's.
```

Here is another example that shows how parameterized concatenation can be used to compute a power of 2, a sign-extension and a zero-extension.

```
parameter POWER_OF = 4, PAD_BY = 5;
wire [7:0] cgr_reg;

wire [31:0] power_of_two = {1'b1, {POWER_OF{1'b0}}};
wire [12:0] sign_extension = {{PAD_BY{cgr_reg[7]}},
                               cgr_reg};
wire [11:0] zero_extension = {{4{1'b0}}, cgr_reg};
```

4.3 *Kinds of Expressions*

A *constant expression* is an expression that evaluates to a constant value at compile time. More specifically, a constant expression can be made up of:

i. constant literals, such as 'b10 and 326

ii. parameter names, such as `SIZE` from the parameter declaration:

```
parameter SIZE = 4'b1110;
```

iii. Bit-select and part-select of a parameter

iv. Constant function calls (see Chapter 10)

A *scalar expression* is an expression that evaluates to a 1-bit result. If a scalar result is expected but the expression produces a vector result, a non-zero vector is treated as 1.

The steps in evaluating an expression are:

i. Determine expression size - it is the size of the largest operand typically.

ii. Determine its signedness. If any operand in the expression is unsigned, then the expression is unsigned. If all the operands in the expression are signed, then the expression is signed. The type of left hand side (target) does not determine its signedness.

iii. All operands are coerced to the signedness.

iv. Size of each operand is extended to the size of the expression, sign extension for signed operands and zero extension for unsigned operands.

v. Evaluate the expression.

4.4 Exercises

1. Declare a parameter GATE_DELAY with a value of 5.

2. Given a memory of size 64 words, with 8 bits per word, write Verilog code to swap the contents of memory in reverse order, that is, transfer word at 0 to word at 63, word 1 to word 62, and so on.

3. Given a 32-bit bus, address_bus, write an expression that computes the reduction nand of bits 11 through 20.

4. Given one bus, control_bus[15:0], write an assignment statement that will split the bus into two buses, abus[0:9] and bbus[6:1].

5. Write an expression that performs the arithmetic shift of a 8-bit signed number contained in qparity.

6. Using a conditional operator, write an assignment statement that selects the value of next_state. If current_state is RESET, then next_state is GO, if current_state is GO, next_state is BUSY, if current_state is BUSY, next_state is RESET.

7. Model the behavior of the 2-to-4 decoder circuit shown in Figure 2-2 using a single continuous assignment statement. [Hint: Use shift operator, conditional operator and the concatenation operator].

8. How would you generate a bus, bus_q[0:3], from four scalar variables, a, b, c, and d?
   How would you form a new bus, bus_r[10:1], from two buses, bus_a[0:3] and bus_y[20:15]?

❑

5

Gate-level Modeling

This chapter describes the gate-level modeling capability of Verilog HDL. It describes the available built-in primitive gates and how these can be used to describe hardware.

5.1 The Built-in Primitive Gates

The following built-in primitive gates are available in Verilog HDL.

i. Multiple-input gates:
and, nand, or, nor, xor, xnor

ii. Multiple-output gates:
buf, not

iii. Tristate gates:
bufif0, bufif1, notif0, notif1

iv. Pull gates:
pullup, pulldown

v. MOS switches:
cmos, nmos, pmos, rcmos, rnmos, rpmos

vi. Bidirectional switches:
tran, tranif0, tranif1, rtran, rtranif0, rtranif1

A gate can be used in a design using a gate instantiation. Here is a simple format of a gate instantiation.

```
gate_type [instance_name ] ( term1 , term2 , . . . , termN );
```

Guideline: Use instance name of form *u<integer>* *<gate_type>*.

Note that the *instance_name* is optional; *gate_type* is one the gates listed earlier. The *terms* specify the nets and variables connected to the terminals of the gate.

Multiple instances of the same gate type can be specified in one construct. The syntax for this is the following.

```
gate_type
      [ instance_name1 ] ( term11 , term12 , . . . , term1N ),
      [ instance_name2 ] ( term21 , term22 ,. . . , term2N ),
      . . .
      [ instance_nameM ] ( termM1 , termM2 , . . . , termMN );
```

5.2 Multiple-input Gates

The multiple-input built-in gates are:

```
and    nand    nor    or    xor    xnor
```

These logic gates have only one output and one or more inputs. Here is the syntax of a multiple-input gate instantiation.

```
multiple_input_gate_type [ instance_name ]
  ( OutputA , Input1 , Input2 ,. . ., InputN );
```

The first terminal is the output and all others are the inputs. See Figure 5-1.

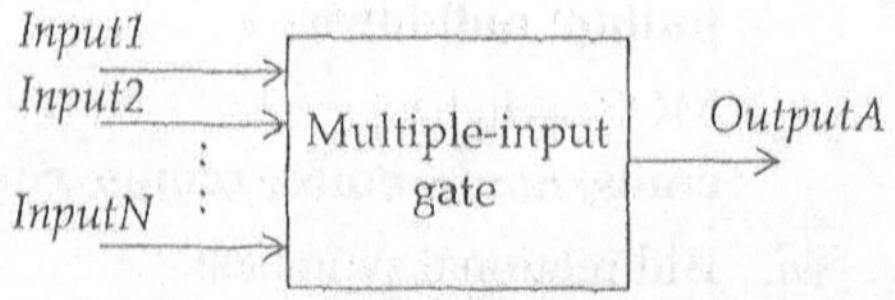

Figure 5-1 Multiple-input gate.

Here are some examples. The logic diagrams are shown in Figure 5-2.

```
and u1and (out1, in1, in2);

and u2and (
  req, sw_data[15], sw_data[14], ack[2], ack[1]
);
```

Instance name is optional.

```
xor
    (qpr, byte_a, byte_b, byte_c),
    (mlock, mprot[0], mprot[1]),
    (xparity, intr_vec[2], intr_vec[1],
     intr_vec[0], intr_vec[3]);
```

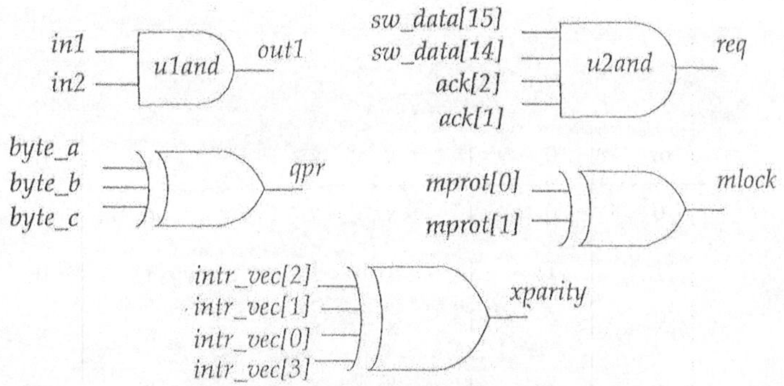

Figure 5-2 Multiple-input gate examples.

The first gate instantiation is a 2-input and gate with instance name u1and, output out1 and with two inputs, in1 and in2. The second gate instantiation is a 4-input and gate with instance name u2and, output req and four inputs, sw_data[15], sw_data[14], ack[2] and ack[1]. The third gate instantiation is an example of an xor gate with no instance name. Its output is qpr and it has three inputs, byte_a, byte_b and byte_c. Also, this instantiation has two additional instances of the same type.

The truth tables for these gates are shown next. Notice that a value z at an input is handled like an x; additionally, the output of a multiple-input gate can never be a z.

nand	0	1	x	z
0	1	1	1	1
1	1	0	x	x
x	1	x	x	x
z	1	x	x	x

and	0	1	x	z
0	0	0	0	0
1	0	1	x	x
x	0	x	x	x
z	0	x	x	x

or	0	1	x	z
0	0	1	x	x
1	1	1	1	1
x	x	1	x	x
z	x	1	x	x

nor	0	1	x	z
0	1	0	x	x
1	0	0	0	0
x	x	0	x	x
z	x	0	x	x

xor	0	1	x	z
0	0	1	x	x
1	1	0	x	x
x	x	x	x	x
z	x	x	x	x

xnor	0	1	x	z
0	1	0	x	x
1	0	1	x	x
x	x	x	x	x
z	x	x	x	x

5.3 Multiple-output Gates

The multiple-output gates are:

```
buf        not
```

These gates have only one input and one or more outputs. See Figure 5-3. The basic syntax for this gate instantiation is:

```
multiple_output_gate_type [ instance_name ]
  ( Out1 , Out2 , . . . , OutN , InputA );
```

The last terminal is the input, all remaining terminals are the outputs.

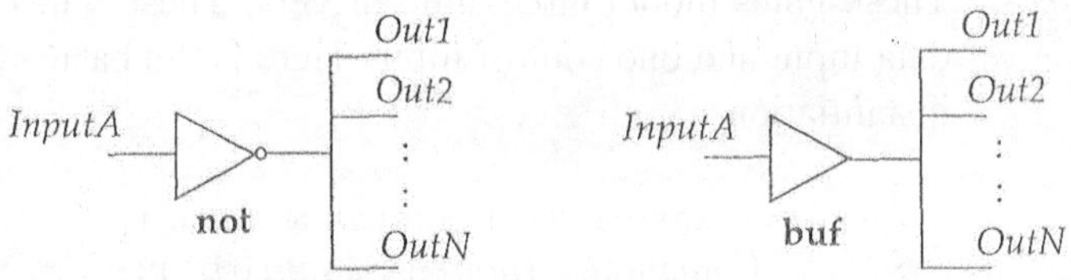

Figure 5-3 Multiple-output gates.

Here are some examples.

```
buf u5buf (
  clk_tx, clk_rx, clk_iol, clk_spi, clk_core
);
not u8not (
  phase_a_rdy, phase_b_rdy, ready
);
```

In the first gate instance, `clk_core` is the input to the buf gate; this gate instance has four outputs, `clk_tx`, `clk_rx`, `clk_iol` and `clk_spi`. In the second gate instance, `ready` is the only input to the not gate. This instance has two outputs, `phase_a_rdy` and `phase_b_rdy`.

The truth table for these gates are shown next.

buf	0	1	x	z
(output)	0	1	x	x

not	0	1	x	z
(output)	1	0	x	x

5.4 *Tristate Gates*

The tristate gates are:

```
bufif0   bufif1   notif0   notif1
```

These gates model three-state drivers. These gates have one output, one data input and one control input. Here is the basic syntax of a tristate gate instantiation.

```
tristate_gate [ instance_name ]
  ( OutputA , InputB , ControlC );
```

The first terminal *OutputA* is the output, the second terminal *InputB* is the data input, and the control input is *ControlC*. See Figure 5-4. Depending on the control input, the output can be driven to the high-impedance state, that is, to value z. For a bufif0 gate, the output is z if control is 1, else data is transferred to output. For a bufif1 gate, output is a z if control is 0. For a notif0 gate, output is at z if control is at 1 else output is the invert of the input data value. For notif1 gate, output is at z if control is at 0.

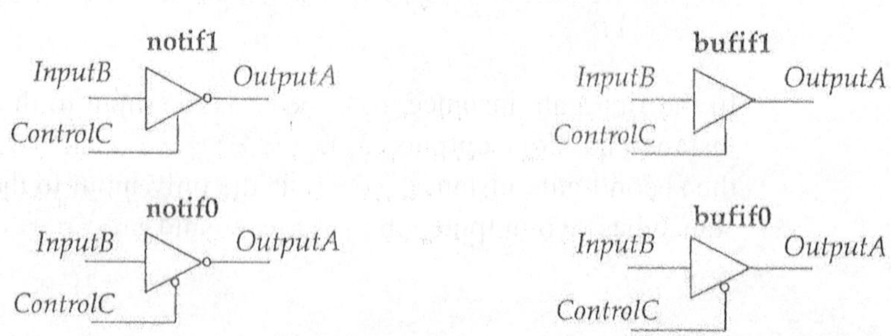

Figure 5-4 Tristate gates.

Here are some examples.

```
bufif1 u7bufif1 (dbus, mem_data, strobe);
notif0 u3notif0 (paddr, abus, probe);
```

The bufif1 gate `u7bufif1` drives the output `dbus` to high-impedance state when `strobe` is 0, else `mem_data` is transferred to `dbus`. In the second instantiation, when `probe` is 1, `paddr` is in high-impedance state, else `paddr` gets the inverted value of `abus`.

The truth table for these gates are shown next.

bufif0		Control			
		0	1	x	z
Data	0	0	z	x	x
	1	1	z	x	x
	x	x	z	x	x
	z	x	z	x	x

bufif1		Control			
		0	1	x	z
Data	0	z	0	x	x
	1	z	1	x	x
	x	z	x	x	x
	z	z	x	x	x

notif0		Control			
		0	1	x	z
Data	0	1	z	x	x
	1	0	z	x	x
	x	x	z	x	x
	z	x	z	x	x

notif1		Control			
		0	1	x	z
Data	0	z	1	x	x
	1	z	0	x	x
	x	z	x	x	x
	z	z	x	x	x

5.5 Pull Gates

The pull gates are:

```
pullup      pulldown
```

These gates have only one output with no inputs. A pullup gate places a 1 on its output. A pulldown gate places a 0 on its output. A gate instantiation is of the form:

```
pull_gate [ instance_name ] ( OutputA );
```

The terminal list of this gate instantiation contains only one output.

Here is an example.

```
pullup u0pullup (core_pwr);
```

This pullup gate has instance name `u0pullup` with output `core_pwr` tied to 1.

5.6 MOS Switches

The MOS switches are:

```
cmos   pmos   nmos   rcmos  rpmos   rnmos
```

These gates model unidirectional switches, that is, data flows from input to output and the data flow can be turned off by appropriately setting the control input(s).

The pmos (p-type MOS transistor), nmos (n-type MOS transistor), rnmos ('r' stands for resistive) and rpmos switches have one output, one input and one control input. The basic syntax for an instantiation is:

```
gate_type  [ instance_name ]
  ( OutputA , InputB , ControlC );
```

The first terminal is the output, the second terminal is the input and the last terminal is the control. If control is 0 for nmos and rnmos switches and 1 for pmos and rpmos switches, the switch is turned off, that is, output has value z; if control is 1 for nmos and rnmos switches and 0 for pmos and rpmos switches, data at input passes to output; see Figure 5-5. The resistive switches (rnmos and rpmos) have a higher impedance (resistance) between the input and output terminals as compared to the non-resistive switches (nmos and pmos). Thus when data passes from input to output, a reduction in strength occurs for resistive switches; strengths are described in Chapter 10.

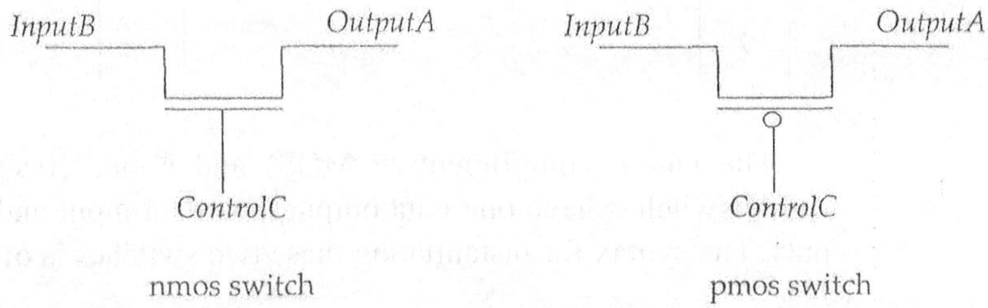

Figure 5-5 Nmos and pmos switches.

Here are some examples.

```
pmos u9pmos (iol_bus, read_data, gate_ctrl);
rnmos u2rnmos (control_bit, ready_bit, hold);
```

The first instance instantiates a pmos switch with instance name `u9pmos`. The input to the switch is `read_data` and the output is `iol_bus` and the control signal is `gate_ctrl`.

The truth tables for these switches are shown next.

pmos rpmos		Control			
		0	1	x	z
Data	0	0	z	x	x
	1	1	z	x	x
	x	x	z	x	x
	z	z	z	z	z

nmos rnmos		Control			
		0	1	x	z
Data	0	z	0	x	x
	1	z	1	x	x
	x	z	x	x	x
	z	z	z	z	z

The cmos (complimentary MOS) and rcmos (resistive version of cmos) switches have one data output, one data input and two control inputs. The syntax for instantiating these two switches is of the form:

```
(r)cmos  [ instance_name ]
  ( OutputA , InputB , NControl , PControl );
```

The first terminal is the output, the second is the input, the third is the n-channel control input and the fourth terminal is the p-channel control input. A cmos (rcmos) switch behaves exactly like a combination of a pmos (rpmos) and a nmos (rnmos) switch with common outputs and common inputs; see Figure 5-6.

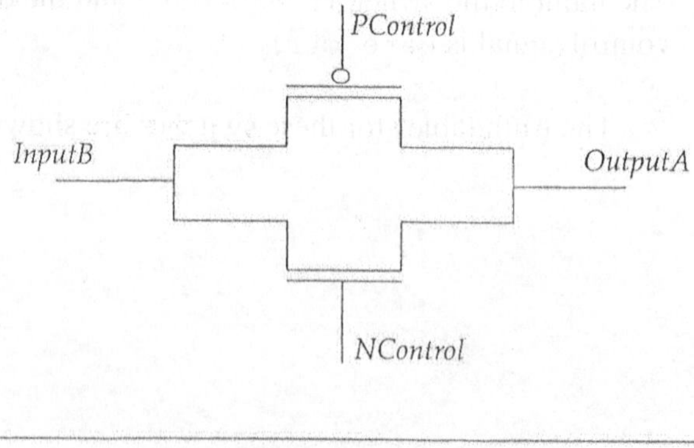

Figure 5-6 (r)cmos switch.

5.7 *Bidirectional Switches*

The bidirectional switches are:

```
tran  rtran tranif0 rtranif0 tranif1 rtranif1
```

These switches are bidirectional, that is, data flows both ways and there is no delay when data propagates through the switches. The last four switches can be turned off by setting a control signal appropriately. The tran and rtran switches cannot be turned off.

The syntax for instantiating a tran or a rtran (resistive version of tran) switch is:

```
(r)tran  [ instance_name ] ( SignalA , SignalB );
```

The terminal list has only two terminals and data flows unconditionally both ways, that is, from *SignalA* to *SignalB* and vice versa.

The syntax for instantiating the other bidirectional switches is:

```
gate_type  [ instance_name ]
  ( SignalA , SignalB , ControlC );
```

The first two terminals are the bidirectional terminals, that is, data flows from *SignalA* to *SignalB* and vice versa. The third terminal is the control signal. If *ControlC* is 1 for tranif0 and rtranif0, and 0 for tranif1 and rtranif1, the bidirectional data flow is disabled. For the resistive switches (rtran, rtranif0 and rtranif1), the strength of the signal reduces when it passes through the switch; strengths are discussed in Chapter 10.

5.8 *Gate Delays*

The signal propagation delay from any gate input to the gate output can be specified using a *gate delay.* The gate delay can be specified in the gate instantiation itself. Here is the syntax of a gate instantiation with the delay specification.

```
gate_type  [ delay ] [ instance_name ] ( terminal_list );
```

The delay specifies the gate delay, that is, the propagation delay from any gate input to the output. When no gate delay is specified, the default delay is zero.

A gate delay can be comprised of up to three values:

i. rise delay
ii. fall delay
iii. turn-off delay

A delay specification may contain zero, one, two, or all three values specified. The following table shows the values that are used for a delay based on the number of specified values.

	No delay	1 value (d)	2 values (d1, d2)	3 values (dA, dB, dC)
Rise	0	d	d1	dA
Fall	0	d	d2	dB
To_x	0	d	min[1] (d1, d2)	min (dA, dB, dC)
Turn-off	0	d	min (d1, d2)	dC

1. min: minimum

Notice that the transition to x delay (to_x) cannot be explicitly specified but is determined from the other specified values.

Here are some examples. Note that all delays in a Verilog HDL model are expressed in terms of time units. The association of time units with actual time is done using the **`timescale** compiler directive. In the following instantiation,

```
not u10not (qbar, q);
```

the gate delay is 0 since no delay has been specified. In the gate instantiation,

```
nand #6 (hmark, in1, in2);
```

all delays are 6, that is, the rise delay and fall delay are both 6. Turn-off delay does not apply to a nand gate since the output never goes into high-impedance. The transition to x delay is also 6.

```
and #(3, 5) (yout, a, b, c);
```

In this gate instantiation, the rise delay has been specified to be 3, the fall delay is 5 and the transition to x delay is the minimum of 3 and 5, which is 3. In the following gate instance,

```
notif1 #(2, 8, 6) (dout, din1, din2);
```

the rise delay is 2, the fall delay is 8, the turn-off delay is 6 and the transition to x delay is the minimum of 2, 8 and 6, which is 2.

Multiple-input gates, such as **and** and **or**, and multiple-output gates (**buf** and **not**) can have only up to two delays specified (since output never goes to z). Tristate gates can have up to three delays and the pull gates cannot have any delays.

5.8.1 Min:typ:max Delay Form

A delay for a gate (including all other delays such as in continuous assignments) can also be specified in a *min:typ:max* form. The form is:

```
minimum : typical : maximum
```

The minimum, typical and maximum values must be constant expressions. Here is an example of a delay in this form used in a gate instantiation.

```
nand #(2:3:4, 5:6:7) (pout, pin1, pin2);
```

The selection of which delay to use is usually made as an option during a simulation run. For example, if maximum delay simulation is performed, a rise delay of 4 and a fall delay of 7 is used for the nand gate instance.

A specify block can also be used to specify gate delays. Specify blocks are discussed in Chapter 10.

5.9 Array of Instances

When repetitive instances are required, a range specification can optionally be specified in a gate instantiation (a range specification can also be used in a module instantiation). The syntax of a gate instantiation in this case is:

```
gate_type [ delay ] instance_name
  [ leftbound : rightbound ]( list_of_ terminal_names );
```

The *leftbound* and *rightbound* values are any two constant expressions. It is not necessary for the left bound to be greater than the right bound and neither of the bounds is restricted to be a 0. Here is an example.

```
wire [3:0] irq, ctrl, sense;
. . .
nand u8nand [3:0] (irq, ctrl, sense);
```

Index range in an array of instances may also be negative, such as [-7:0].

This instantiation with the range specification is same as:

```
nand
    u8nand3 (irq[3], ctrl[3], sense[3]),
    u8nand2 (irq[2], ctrl[2], sense[2]),
    u8nand1 (irq[1], ctrl[1], sense[1]),
    u8nand0 (irq[0], ctrl[0], sense[0]);
```

Note that the instance name is not optional when specifying an array of instances.

Here is another example.

```
parameter NUM_BITS = 4;
wire [NUM_BITS-1:0] gated_d, din;
wire bypass;


and #(1, 2) u0and [NUM_BITS-1:0] (gated_d, din, bypass);
```

Notice that bypass is a scalar quantity. In such a case, the scalar signal is fanned out to all instances. The equivalent set of instances are:

```
and #(1, 2) u0and3 (gated_d[3], din[3], bypass);
and #(1, 2) u0and2 (gated_d[2], din[2], bypass);
and #(1, 2) u0and1 (gated_d[1], din[1], bypass);
and #(1, 2) u0and0 (gated_d[0], din[0], bypass);
```

Array of module instances are also supported; see Chapter 9 for an example.

5.10 Implicit Nets

If a net is not declared in a Verilog HDL model, by default, it is implicitly declared as a 1-bit wire. However the **`default_nettype** compiler directive can be used to override the default net type. This compiler directive is of the form:

```
default_nettype net_type
```

Here is an example.

```
`default_nettype wand
```

With this directive, all subsequent undeclared nets are of type **wand**.

The **`default_nettype** compiler directive occurs outside of a module definition and stays in effect until the next same directive is reached or a **`resetall** directive is found.

The implicit net inference can be disabled by using a value of **none** for the **`default_nettype** compiler directive. In such a case, any undeclared net is an error.

5.11 A Simple Example

Here is a gate-level description of a 4-to-1 multiplexer circuit shown in Figure 5-7. Note that no instance names are specified in the gate instantiations as these are optional (except when used in an array of instances).

```
module mux4x1 (y, d0, d1, d2, d3, s0, s1);
  output y;
  input d0, d1, d2, d3, s0, s1;

  and
      (t0, d0, s0bar, s1bar),
      (t1, d1, s0bar, s1),
      (t2, d2, s0, s1bar),
      (t3, d3, s0, s1);

  not
      (s0bar, s0),
      (s1bar, s1);

  or (y, t0, t1, t2, t3);
endmodule
```

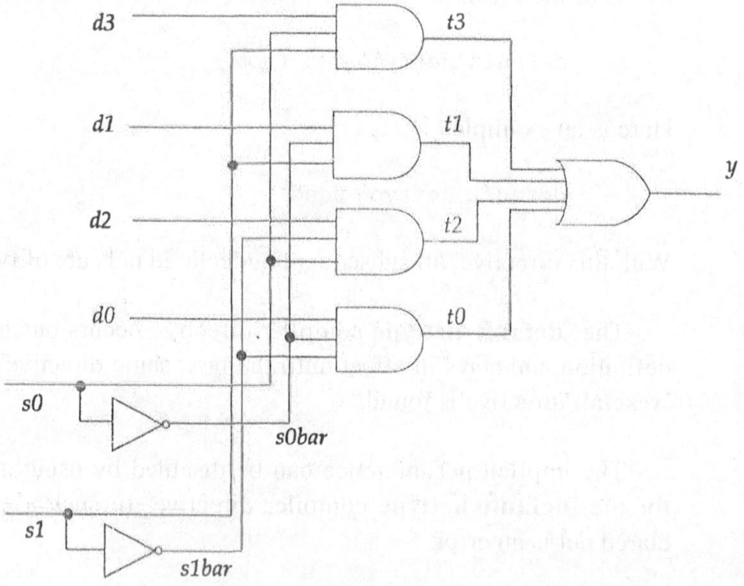

Figure 5-7 A 4-to-1 multiplexer.

What if the instantiation for the **or** gate was replaced by the following instantiation?

```
or y (y, t0, t1, t2, t3);        // Not legal Verilog HDL.
```

Notice that the instance name is also y and the net connected to the output of the gate is also y. This is not allowed in Verilog HDL. An instance name cannot be the same as a net name within one module.

5.12 A 2-to-4 Decoder Example

Here is a gate-level description of a 2-to-4 decoder circuit shown in Figure 5-8.

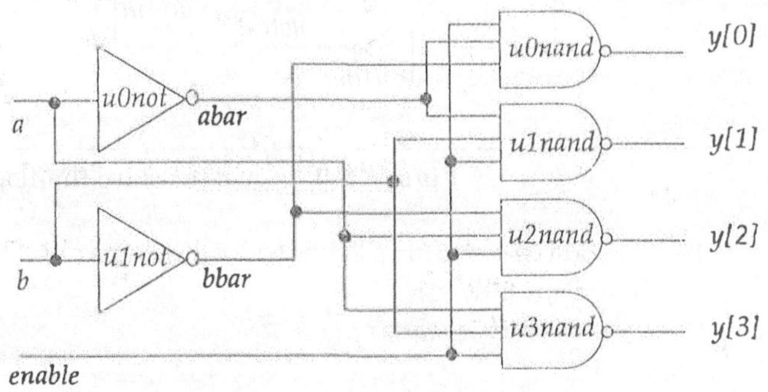

Figure 5-8 A 2-to-4 decoder circuit.

```
module dec2x4 (a, b, enable, y);
  input a, b, enable;
  output [0:3] y;
  wire abar, bbar;

  not #(1, 2)
    u0not (abar, a),
    u1not (bbar, b);

  nand #(4, 3)
    u0nand (y[0], enable, abar, bbar),
    u1nand (y[1], enable, abar, b),
    u2nand (y[2], enable, a, bbar),
    u3nand (y[3], enable, a, b);
endmodule
```

5.13 A Master-slave Flip-flop Example

Here is a gate-level description of a master-slave D-type flip-flop shown in Figure 5-9.

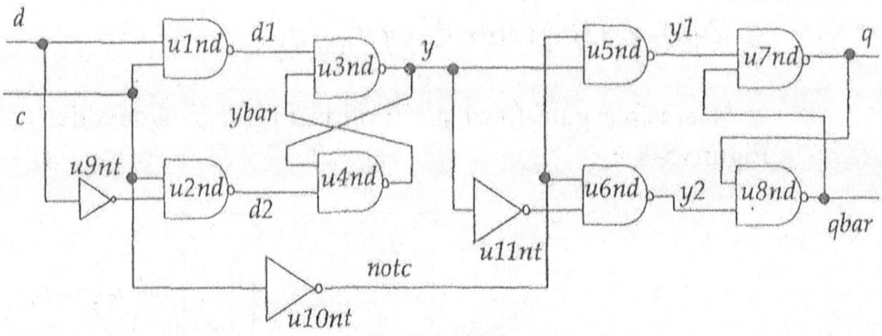

Figure 5-9 A master-slave flip-flop.

```
module ms_dflipflop (d, c, q, qbar);
  input d, c;
  output q, qbar;

  not
    u9nt (notd, d),
    u10nt (notc, c),
    u11nt (noty, y);

  nand
    u1nd (d1, d, c),
    u2nd (d2, c, notd),
    u3nd (y, d1, ybar),
    u4nd (ybar, y, d2),
    u5nd (y1, y, notc),
    u6nd (y2, noty, notc),
    u7nd (q, qbar, y1),
    u8nd (qbar, y2, q);
endmodule
```

5.14 A Parity Circuit

A gate-level model for a 9-bit parity generator, shown in Figure 5-10, is described next.

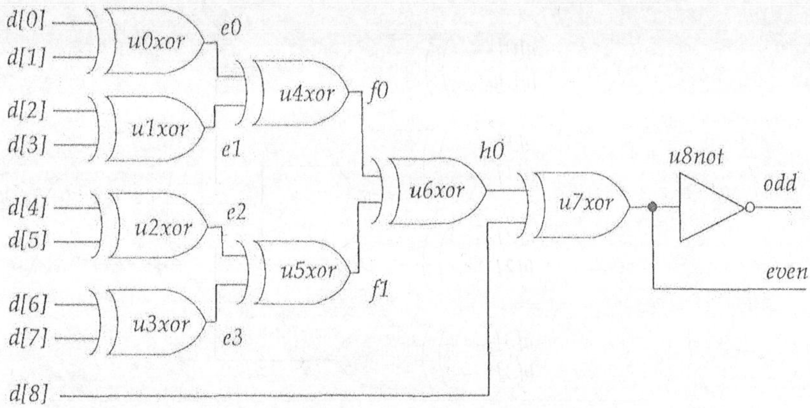

Figure 5-10 A parity generator.

```
module parity_9_bit (d, even, odd);
  input [0:8] d;
  output even, odd;

  xor #(5, 4)
    u0xor (e0, d[0], d[1]),
    u1xor (e1, d[2], d[3]),
    u2xor (e2, d[4], d[5]),
    u3xor (e3, d[6], d[7]),
    u4xor (f0, e0, e1),
    u5xor (f1, e2, e3),
    u6xor (h0, f0, f1),
    u7xor (even, d[8], h0);

  not #2
    u8not (odd, even);
endmodule
```

5.15 Exercises

1. Model the circuit shown in Figure 5-11 using primitive gates. Write a test bench to test out the circuit. Exercise the circuit with all possible values of inputs.

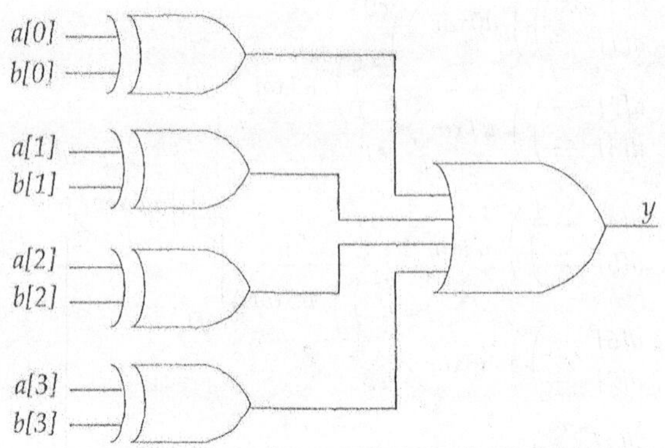

Figure 5-11 Logic for "*a* not equals *b*".

2. Model the circuit of a priority encoder shown in Figure 5-12 using primitive gates. Output `valid` is 0 when all inputs are 0, otherwise it is a 1. Write a test bench and verify that the model behaves as a priority encoder.

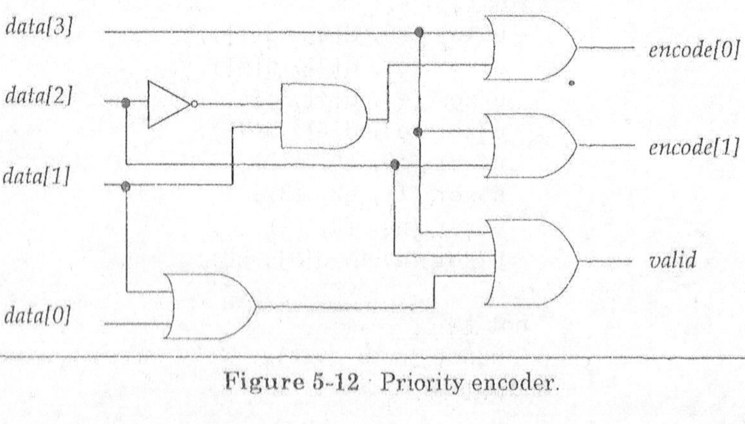

Figure 5-12 Priority encoder.

❑

6

User-Defined Primitives

In the previous chapter, we looked at the built-in primitive gates provided by Verilog HDL. This chapter describes the Verilog HDL capability of specifying user-defined primitives (UDP).

A UDP is instantiated exactly the same way as a primitive gate, that is, the syntax for a UDP instantiation is identical to that of a gate instantiation.

6.1 *Defining a UDP*

A UDP is defined using a UDP declaration which has the following syntax.

```
primitive UDP_name ( OutputName , List_of_inputs );
  Output_declaration
  List_of_input_declarations
  [ Reg_declaration ]
  [ Initial_statement ]

  table
    List_of_table_entries
  endtable
endprimitive
```

```
OR:

primitive UDP_name (
    Output_declaration, List_of_input_declarations );
  [ Reg_declaration ]
  [ Initial_statement ]

  table
    List_of_table_entries
  endtable
endprimitive
```

A UDP definition does not depend on a module definition and thus appears outside of a module definition. A UDP definition can also be in a separate text file. In the two syntax forms shown above, in the first form, only the port names are declared in the port list and their declarations appear later. In the second form, the declarations appear within the port list itself.

A UDP can have only one output and may have one or more inputs. The first port must be the output port. In addition, the output can have the value 0, 1 or x (z is not allowed). If a value z appears on the input, it is treated as an x. The behavior of a UDP is described in the form of a table.

The following two kinds of behavior can be described in a UDP.

i. Combinational.

ii. Sequential (edge-triggered and level-sensitive).

6.2 *Combinational UDP*

In a combinational UDP, the table specifies the various input combinations and their corresponding output values. Any combination that is not specified is an x for the output. Here is an example of a 2-to-1 multiplexer.

```
primitive mux_2by1 (y, a, b, select);
  output y;
  input a, b, select;

  table
    // Note: Next line is only a comment.
    //a    b    select : y
      0    ?    1      : 0 ;
      1    ?    1      : 1 ;
      ?    0    0      : 0 ;
      ?    1    0      : 1 ;
      0    0    x      : 0 ;
      1    1    x      : 1 ;
  endtable
endprimitive
```

The ? character represents a don't-care value, that is, it could either be a 0, 1 or x. The order of the input ports must match the order of entries in the table, that is, the first column in the table corresponds to the first input in the module port list (which is a), second column is b and the third column is select. In the table for the multiplexer, there is no table entry for one input combination **01x** (there are others as well); in this case, the output defaults to an **x** (as also for other unspecified entries).

Here is an example of a 4-to-1 multiplexer, shown in Figure 6-1, formed using 2-to-1 multiplexer primitives.

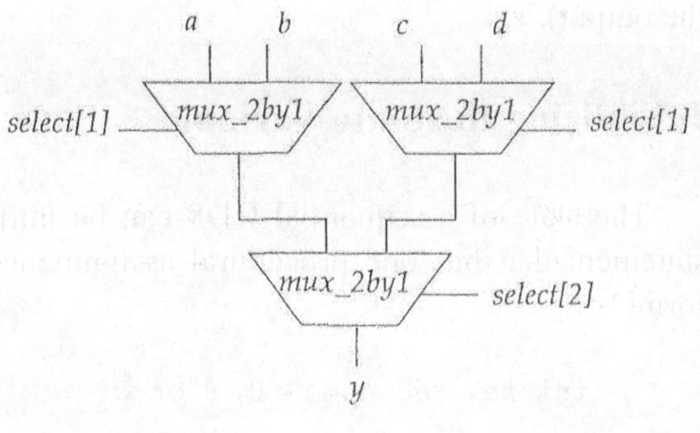

Figure 6-1 A 4-to-1 multiplexer built using UDPs.

```
module mux_4by1 (y, a, b, c, d, select);
  input a, b, c, d;
  input [2:1] select;
  output y;
  parameter tRISE = 2, tFALL = 3;

  mux_2by1 #(tRISE, tFALL)
     (temp1, a, b, select[1]),
     (temp2, c, d, select[1]),
     (y, temp1, temp2, select[2]);
endmodule
```

Instance name is optional.

In case of a UDP instantiation, up to two delays can be specified as shown in the above example. This is because the output of an UDP can either get a value 0 or a value 1, or the value x (there is no turn-off delay).

6.3 *Sequential UDP*

In a sequential UDP, the internal state is described using a 1-bit reg variable. The value of this reg variable is the output of the sequential UDP.

There are two different kinds of sequential UDP, one that models level-sensitive behavior and another that models edge-sensitive behavior.

A sequential UDP uses the current value of the reg variable and the input values to determine the next value of the variable (and consequently the output).

6.3.1 Initializing the State Variable

The state of a sequential UDP can be initialized by using an initial statement that has one procedural assignment statement. This is of the form:

```
initial reg_name = 0, 1 or x;
```

This initial statement appears within the UDP definition.

6.3.2 Level-sensitive Sequential UDP

Here is an example of a level-sensitive sequential UDP that models a D-type latch. As long as the clock is 0, data passes from the input to the output, else the value remains latched.

```
primitive latch (q, clk, d);
  output q;
  input clk, d;
  reg q;

  table
    // clk  d   q(state)  q(next)
       0    1   : ?    :   1 ;
       0    0   : ?    :   0 ;
       1    ?   : ?    :   - ;
  endtable
endprimitive
```

The – character implies a "no change". Note that the state of the UDP is stored in variable q.

6.3.3 Edge-triggered Sequential UDP

Here is an example of a D-type edge-triggered flip-flop modeled as a edge-triggered sequential UDP. An initial statement is used to initialize the state of the flip-flop.

```
primitive d_edge_flip_flop (q, clk, data);
  output q;
  input clk, data;
  reg q;

  initial q = 0;

  table
    // clk  data     q (state)  q(next)
       (01)   0   :     ?     :   0 ;
       (01)   1   :     ?     :   1 ;
       (0x)   1   :     1     :   1 ;
       (0x)   0   :     0     :   0 ;
```

```
        // Ignore negative edge of clock:
        (?0)    ?   :    ?    :   - ;
        // Ignore data changes on steady clock:
        ?       (??):    ?    :   - ;
    endtable
endprimitive
```

The table entry (01) indicates a transition from 0 to 1, the entry (0x) indicates a transition from 0 to x, the entry (?0) indicates a transition from any value (0, 1, or x) to 0, and the entry (??) indicates any transition. For any unspecified transition, the output defaults to an x.

Given the UDP definition of the `d_edge_flip_flop`, it can now be instantiated in a module just like a primitive gate as shown in the following example of a 4-bit register.

```
module register4 (clk, data_in, data_out);
  input clk;
  input [0:3] data_in;
  output [0:3] data_out;

  d_edge_flip_flop
    u0_d_edge_flip_flop (data_out[0], clk, data_in[0]),
    u1_d_edge_flip_flop (data_out[1], clk, data_in[1]),
    u2_d_edge_flip_flop (data_out[2], clk, data_in[2]),
    u3_d_edge_flip_flop (data_out[3], clk, data_in[3]);
endmodule
```

6.3.4 Mixing Edge-triggered and Level-sensitive Behavior

It is possible to mix level-sensitive entries and edge-triggered entries in one table. In such a case, the edge transitions are processed before the level-sensitive ones are processed, that is, the level-sensitive entries override the edge-triggered entries.

Here is an example of a D-type flip-flop with an asynchronous clear.

```
primitive d_async_ff (q, clock, clear, data);
  output q;
  input clock, clear, data;
  reg q;

  table
    // clock  clear  data    q(state)  q(next)
       (01)    0      0    :    ?    :   0 ;
       (01)    0      1    :    ?    :   1 ;
       (0x)    0      1    :    1    :   1 ;
       (0x)    0      0    :    0    :   0 ;
       // Ignore negative edge of clock:
       (?0)    0      ?    :    ?    :   - ;
       (??)    1      ?    :    ?    :   0;
       ?       1      ?    :    ?    :   0;
  endtable
endprimitive
```

6.4 Another Example

Here is a UDP description of a 3-bit majority circuit. The output is 1 if the input vector has two or more 1's. Notice that the alternate style of declaring ports, that is, the module port declaration style is used.

```
primitive majority_of_3 (
    output y,
    input a, b, c
  );
  // Ports are declared in the port list itself.

  table
    //a  b  c  :  y
      0  0  ?  :  0;
      0  ?  0  :  0;
      ?  0  0  :  0;
      1  1  ?  :  1;
      1  ?  1  :  1;
      ?  1  1  :  1;
  endtable
endprimitive
```

6.5 Summary of Table Entries

For sake of completion, listed in the table below are all the possible values that could be used in a table entry.

Symbol	Meaning
0	logic 0
1	logic 1
x	unknown
?	any of 0, 1, or x
b	any of 0 or 1
-	no change
(AB)	value change from A to B
*	same as (??)
r	same as (01)
f	same as (10)
p	any of (01), (0x), (x1)
n	any of (10), (1x), (x0)

6.6 Exercises

1. How is a combinational UDP different from a sequential UDP?
2. A UDP can have one or more outputs. True or False?
3. Can an initial statement be used to initialize a combinational UDP?
4. Write a UDP description for the priority encoder circuit shown in Figure 5-12. Verify the model using a test bench.
5. Write a UDP description for a toggle-type flip-flop. In a toggle flip-flop, if data input is 0, output does not change. If data input is a 1, then on every clock edge, the output toggles. Assume that the triggering clock edge is a negative clock edge. Verify the model using a test bench.

6. Model a rising-edge triggered JK flip-flop as a UDP. If both inputs, `J` and `K`, are 0, output does not change. If `J` is 0 and `K` is a 1, then output is 0. If `J` is 1 and `K` is 0, then output is 1. If `J` and `K` are both 1, output toggles. Verify the model using a test bench.

❑

7

Dataflow Modeling

This chapter describes the continuous assignment feature of Verilog HDL. Continuous assignments model dataflow behavior; in contrast, procedural assignments (the topic of next chapter) model sequential behavior. Combinational logic behavior can be best modeled using continuous assignments.

7.1 *Continuous Assignment*

A continuous assignment assigns a value to a net (it cannot be used to assign a value to a variable). It has the following form (a simple form):

```
assign LHS_target = RHS_expression ;
```

For example,

```
// Net declaration:
wire [3:0] frm_rdy, coh_rdy, hrd_tag;

// Continuous assignment:
assign hrd_tag = coh_rdy & frm_rdy;
```

The target of the continuous assignment is `hrd_tag` and the right-hand side expression is "`coh_rdy & frm_rdy`". Note the presence of the keyword **assign** in the continuous assignment.

When does a continuous assignment execute? Whenever an event (an event is a change of value) occurs on an operand used in the right-hand side expression, the expression is evaluated and if the result value is different, it is then assigned to the left-hand side target.

In the above example, if either `coh_rdy` or `frm_rdy` change, the entire right-hand side expression is evaluated. If this results in a change of value, then the resultant value is assigned to the net `hrd_tag`.

The target in a continuous assignment can be one of the following.

i. Scalar net

ii. Vector net

iii. Constant element-select of an array (which is a scalar net or a vector net)

iv. Constant bit-select of a vector

v. Constant part-select of a vector

vi. Concatenation of any of the above

Here are more examples of continuous assignments.

```
assign bus_error = dma_parity | (lock_data & OP_MASK);

assign y = ~ (a | b) & (c | d) & (e | f);
```

The last continuous assignment executes whenever there is a change of value in `a`, `b`, `c`, `d`, `e` or `f`, in which case, the entire right-hand side expression is evaluated and the result is then assigned to the target `y`.

In the next example, the target is a concatenation of a scalar net and a vector net.

```
wire carry_out, carry_in;
wire [3:0] sum, a, b;
```

```
. . .
assign {carry_out, sum} = a + b + carry_in;
```

Since a and b are 4-bits wide, the result of addition can produce a maximum of a 5-bit result. The left-hand side is specified to be five bits (one bit for carry_out and 4 bits of sum). The assignment therefore causes the rightmost four bits of the right-hand side expression result to be assigned to sum and the fifth bit (the carry bit) to carry_out.

The next example shows how multiple assignments can be written in one continuous statement.

```
assign mux_out = (select == 0) ? input_a : 'bz,
       mux_out = (select == 1) ? input_b : 'bz,
       mux_out = (select == 2) ? input_c : 'bz,
       mux_out = (select == 3) ? input_d : 'bz;
```

This is a short form of writing the following four separate continuous assignments.

```
assign mux_out = (select == 0) ? input_a : 'bz;
assign mux_out = (select == 1) ? input_b : 'bz;
assign mux_out = (select == 2) ? input_c : 'bz;
assign mux_out = (select == 3) ? input_d : 'bz;
```

Here is another example.

```
wire dtag;
parameter SIZE = 7;
wire [SIZE:0] padded_dtag;

assign padded_dtag = {{SIZE {1'b0}}, dtag};
```

If the target of a continuous assignment is not declared, an implicit scalar net of the default net type is assumed.

```
// No declaration for mc_noburst.
assign mc_noburst = dma_lock;
// mc_noburst is an implicit 1-bit net.
```

7.2 An Example

Here is an example of a 1-bit full-adder described using the dataflow style.

```
module full_adder_dataflow (
    a, b, carry_in, sum, carry_out
  );
  input a, b, carry_in;
  output sum, carry_out;

  assign sum = a ^ b ^ carry_in;
  assign carry_out = (a & carry_in) | (b & carry_in) |
                     (a & b);
endmodule
```

In this example, there are two continuous assignments. These assignments are concurrent in the sense that they are order independent. These continuous assignments execute based on events that occur on operands used in the right-hand side expression. If a changes, both the continuous assignments are evaluated, that is, the right-hand side expressions are evaluated and the results are assigned to the left-hand side targets concurrently.

7.3 Net Declaration Assignment

A continuous assignment can appear as part of a net declaration itself. Such an assignment is called a *net declaration assignment*. Here are some examples.

```
wire [3:0] qmv_wr = 4'b0;
wire frm_wait = 'b1;

wire ictr_gt_qctr = ictr > qctr,
     qctr_gt_ictr = qctr > ictr;
wire [(8*12-1):0] dbg_dump_rpt = "dbg_dump.rpt";
```

A net declaration assignment declares the net along with a continuous assignment. It is a convenient form of declaring a net and then writing a continuous assignment. See the example below.

```
wire wr_cycle;
assign wr_cycle = 'b1;
```

is equivalent to the net declaration assignment:

```
wire wr_cycle = 'b1;
```

Multiple net declaration assignments on the same net are not allowed. If multiple assignments are necessary, continuous assignments must be used.

7.4 Delays

If no delay is specified in a continuous assignment, as in the previous examples, the assignment of the right-hand side expression to the left-hand side target occurs with zero delay. A delay can be explicitly specified in a continuous assignment as shown in the following example.

```
assign #6 dbg_data = int_data || peg_cntxt;
```

The delay specified, #6, is the delay between the right-hand side and the left-hand side. For example, if a change of value occurs on `int_data` at time 5, then the expression on the right-hand side of the assignment is evaluated at time 5 and `dbg_data` will be assigned a new value at time 11 (= 5 + 6). The delay concept is illustrated in Figure 7-1.

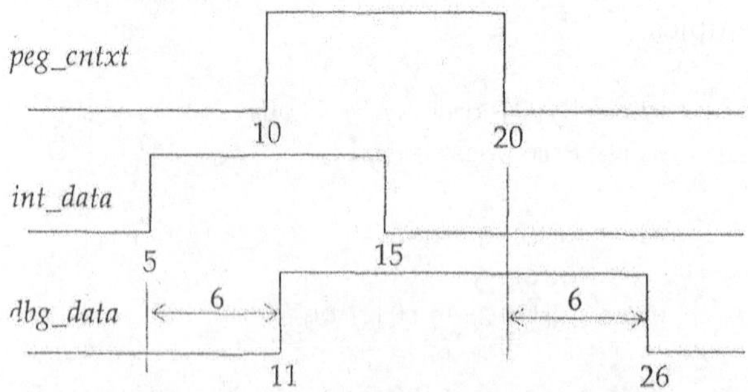

Figure 7-1 Delay in a continuous assignment.

What happens if the right-hand side changes before it had a chance to propagate to the left-hand side? In such a case, the latest value change is applied. Here is an example that shows this behavior.

```
assign #4 peg_free = xbid_par;
```

Figure 7-2 shows the effect. The changes on the right-hand side that occur within the delay interval are filtered out. For example, the rising edge on `xbid_par` at 5 gets scheduled to appear on `peg_free` at 9, however since `xbid_par` goes back to 0 at 8, the scheduled value on `peg_free` is deleted. Similarly, the pulse on `xbid_par` occurring between 18 and 20 gets filtered out. This corresponds to the inertial delay behavior; that is, a value change on the right-hand side must hold steady for at least the delay period before it can propagate to the left-hand side; if the value on the right-hand side changes within the delay period, the former value does not propagate to the output.

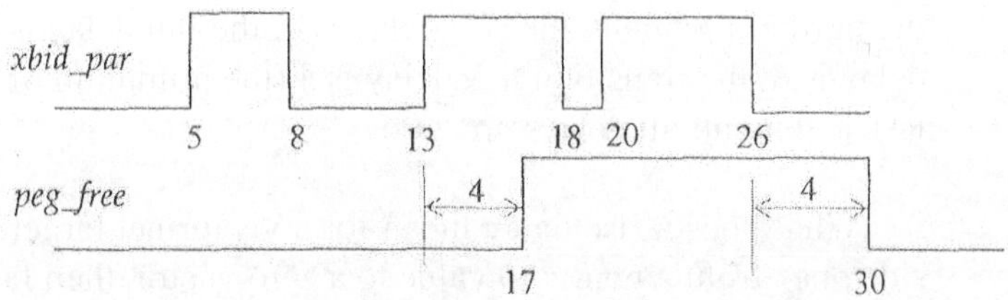

Figure 7-2 Values changing faster than delay interval.

For each delay specification, up to three delay values can be specified.

i. Rise delay
ii. Fall delay
iii. Turn-off delay

Here is the syntax for specifying the three delays.

```
assign #( rise , fall , turn-off )
    LHS_target = RHS_expression ;
```

Here are some examples that show how delays are interpreted when zero to three delay values are specified.

```
// One delay value:
assign #4 biu_par = fe_par || vsp_par;

// Two delay values:
assign #(4, 8) biu_par = rd_trg;

// Three delay values:
assign #(4, 8, 6) fe_arb = & fe_dbus;

// No delay value:
assign fe_dbus = rd_address[7:4];
```

In the first assignment statement, the rise delay, the fall delay and the turn-off delay and the transition to x delay are the same, which is 4. In the second statement, the rise delay is 4, the fall delay is 8 and the transition to x and z delay are the same, which is the minimum of 4 and 8, which is 4. In the third assignment, the rise delay is 4, the fall delay is 8 and the turn-off delay is 6; the transition to x delay is 4 (the minimum of 4, 8 and 6). In the last statement, all delays are zero.

What does a rise delay mean for a vector net target? If the right-hand side goes from a non-zero value to a zero vector, then fall delay is used. If right-hand side value goes to z, then turn-off delay is used; else rise delay is used.

7.5 *Net Delays*

A delay can also be specified in a net declaration, such as in the following declaration.

```
wire #5 mem_write;
```

This delay indicates the delay between a change of value of a driver for `mem_write` and the net `mem_write` itself. Consider the following continuous assignment to the net `mem_write`.

```
assign #2 mem_write = chunk_valid & flop_valid;
```

An event on `flop_valid`, say at time 10, causes the right-hand side expression to be evaluated. If the result is different, it is assigned to `mem_write` after 2 time units, that is, at time 12. However since `mem_write` has a net delay specified, the actual assignment to the net `mem_write` occurs at time 17 (= 10 + 2 + 5). The waveforms in Figure 7-3 illustrates the different delays.

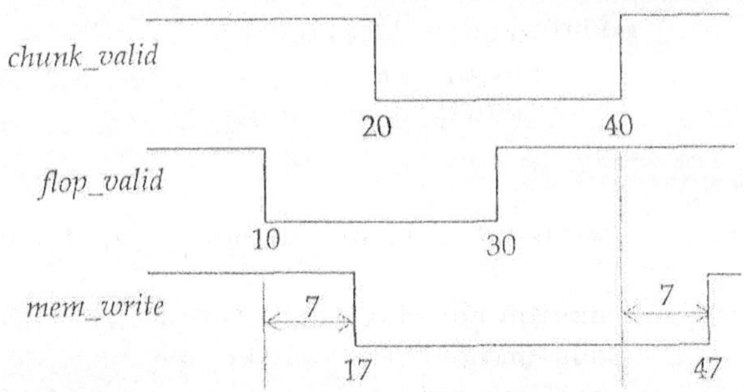

Figure 7-3 Net delay with assignment delay.

The effect of a net delay is best described as shown in Figure 7-4. First the assignment delay is used and then any net delay is added on.

If a delay is present in a net declaration assignment, then the delay is not a net delay but an assignment delay. In the following net declaration assignment for `nc_data`, 2 time units is the assignment delay, not the net delay.

```
// Assignment delay:
wire [3:0] #2 nc_data = si_data - mem_wdata;
```

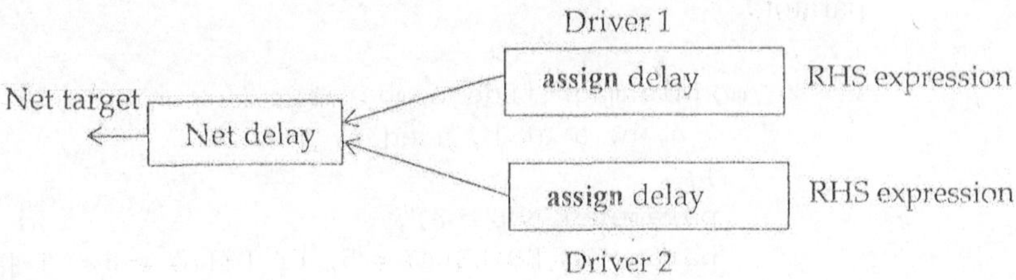

Figure 7-4 Effect of net delay.

7.6 *Examples*

7.6.1 Master-slave Flip-flop

Here is a Verilog HDL model for the master-slave flip-flop shown in Figure 5-9. Ports are declared using the module port declaration style.

```
module msdff_dataflow (
  input d, clk,
  output q, q_bar
 );

 wire not_clk, not_d, not_y, y, d1, d2, y_bar, y1, y2;

 assign not_d = ~ d;
 assign not_clk = ~ clk;
 assign not_y = ~ y;

 assign d1 = ~ (d & clk);
 assign d2 = ~ (clk & not_d);
 assign y = ~ (d1 & y_bar);
 assign y_bar = ~ (y & d2);
 assign y1 = ~ (y & not_clk);
 assign y2 = ~ (not_y & not_clk);
 assign q = ~ (q_bar & y1);
 assign q_bar = ~ (y2 & q);
endmodule
```

7.6.2 Magnitude Comparator

Here is a dataflow model for a 8-bit (parameterized) magnitude comparator.

```
module magnitude_comparator (
  a, b, a_gt_b, a_eq_b, a_lt_b
 );
 parameter BUS = 8;
 parameter EQ_DELAY = 5, LT_DELAY = 8, GT_DELAY = 8;
 input [BUS-1:0] a, b;
 output a_gt_b, a_eq_b, a_lt_b;
```

```
   assign #EQ_DELAY   a_eq_b = a == b;
   assign #GT_DELAY   a_gt_b = a > b;
   assign #LT_DELAY   a_lt_b = a < b;
endmodule
```

7.7 Exercises

1. Give an example of how turn-off delay is used in a continuous assignment.
2. When there are two or more assignments to the same target, how is the effective value for the target determined?
3. Write a dataflow model for the parity generator circuit shown in Figure 5-10. Use only two assignment statements. Specify rise and fall delays as well.
4. Using continuous assignment statements, describe the behavior of the priority encoder circuit shown in Figure 5-12.
5. Given:

```
tri0 [4:0] cell_data;
assign cell_data = vq_data;
assign cell_data = tim_ctr;
```

   What is the value on `cell_data` if both `vq_data` and `tim_ctr` are all z's.

❑

8

Behavioral Modeling

In previous chapters, we have examined gate-level modeling using gate and UDP instantiations, and dataflow modeling using continuous assignments. This chapter describes the third style of modeling in Verilog HDL, which is, behavioral modeling. To use the full power of Verilog HDL, a model may contain a mix of all the three styles of modeling.

8.1 *Procedural Constructs*

The primary mechanisms for modeling the behavior of a design are the following two statements.

i. Initial statement

ii. Always statement

A module may contain an arbitrary number of initial or always statements. These statements execute concurrently with respect to each other, that is, the order of these statements in a module is not important. An execution of an initial or an always statement starts a separate control flow. All initial and always statements execute concurrently starting at time 0.

8.1.1 Initial Statement

An initial statement executes only once. It begins its execution at start of simulation which is at time 0. The syntax for the initial statement is:

```
initial
    [ timing_control ] procedural_statement
```

where a *procedural_statement* is one of:

```
procedural_assignment (blocking or nonblocking)
procedural_continuous_assignment
conditional_statement
case_statement
loop_statement
wait_statement
disable_statement
event_trigger
sequential_block
parallel_block
task_enable (user or system)
```

The sequential block (**begin...end**) is the most commonly used procedural statement. Here *timing_control* can be a delay control, that is, wait for a certain time, or an event control, that is, wait for an event to occur or a condition to become true. The execution of an initial statement causes the procedural statement to execute once. Note that an initial statement starts execution at time 0. It may complete execution at a later time depending on any timing controls present in the procedural statement.

Here is an example of an initial statement.

```
reg intf_read;
. . .
initial
  intf_read = 2;
```

The initial statement contains a procedural assignment with no timing control. The initial statement executes at time 0, which causes `intf_read` to be assigned the value 2 at time 0. Here is another example of an initial statement, this time with a timing control.

```
reg fc_addr;
. . .
initial
  #2 fc_addr = 1;
```

Reg variable `fc_addr` gets assigned the value 1 at time 2. The initial statement starts execution at time 0 but completes execution at time 2.

If a variable needs to be assigned only once in an initial statement, then the assignment can be made in the declaration of the variable itself, using what is called a *variable declaration assignment*.

The equivalent initial statement has a blocking assignment.

```
reg intf_read = 2;
// Same as the declaration for intf_read followed by an
// initial statement that assigns to intf_read.

integer fe_count = 0;
// Same as:
// integer fe_count;
// initial fe_count = 0;
```

Here is an example of an initial statement with a sequential block.

```
parameter SIZE = 1024;
reg [7:0] vld_ram [0:SIZE-1];
reg speed_reg;

initial
  begin: seq_blk_a
    integer index;

    speed_reg = 0;

    for (index = 0; index < SIZE; index = index + 1)
      vld_ram[index] = 0;
  end
```

The sequential block, demarcated by the keywords **begin...end**, contains procedural statements that execute sequentially, as in a high-level programming language such as C. `seq_blk_a` is the label for the sequential block; this label is not required if no local declarations are present in the block, for example, if the declaration for `index` were outside the initial statement, no label would be required. An integer `index` has been locally declared within this block. Furthermore, the sequential block contains one procedural assignment followed by a for-loop statement. This initial statement, upon execution, initializes all memory locations with value 0.

Here is another example of an initial statement with a sequential block. In this example, the sequential block contains procedural assignments with timing controls.

```
// Waveform generation:
parameter APPLY_DELAY = 5;
reg [0:7] port_cmb;
. . .
initial
  begin
    port_cmb = 'h20;
     #APPLY_DELAY port_cmb = 'hF2;
     #APPLY_DELAY port_cmb = 'h41;
     #APPLY_DELAY port_cmb = 'h0A;
  end
```

Upon execution, `port_cmb` will get values as shown in Figure 8-1.

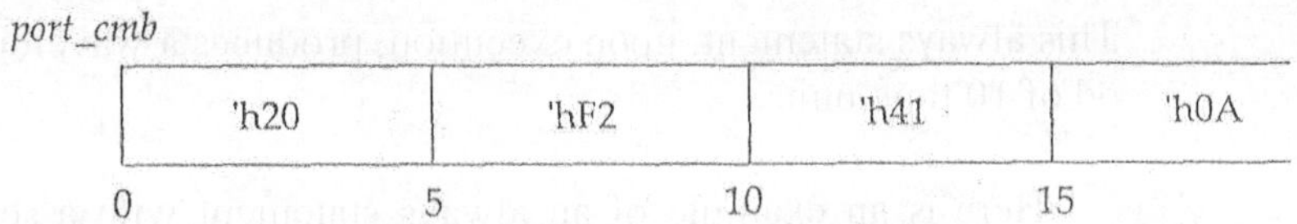

Figure 8-1 **A waveform produced using an initial statement.**

An initial statement is mainly used for initialization and waveform generation as shown in the examples above.

8.1.2 Always Statement

In contrast to the initial statement, an always statement executes repeatedly. Just like the initial statement, an always statement also begins execution at time 0. The syntax for an always statement is:

```
always
  [ timing_control ] procedural_statement
```

where *procedural_statement* and *timing_control* are as described in the previous section.

Here is an example of an always statement.

```
always
  clk_siob = ~ clk_siob;
// Will loop indefinitely.
```

This always statement has one procedural assignment. Since the always statement executes repeatedly and there is no timing control specified, the procedural assignment statement will loop indefinitely in zero time. Therefore, an always statement must always have some sort of timing control.

Here is the same always statement, this time with a delay control.

```
always
  #5 clk_siob = ~ clk_siob;
// Waveform on clk_siob of period 10.
```

This always statement, upon execution, produces a waveform with a period of 10 time units.

Here is an example of an always statement with a sequential block that is controlled by an event control.

```
reg [0:5] instr_reg;
reg [3:0] cpu_accum;
wire execute_cycle;

always
  @(execute_cycle)
   begin
     case (instr_reg[0:1])
       2'b00 : store_data (cpu_accum, instr_reg[2:5]);
       2'b11 : load_data (cpu_accum, instr_reg[2:5]);
       2'b01 : jump_to (instr_reg[2:5]);
       2'b10 : ;
```

```
        endcase
      end
  // store_data, load_data and jump_to are user-defined
  // tasks defined elsewhere.
```

Statements within a sequential block (**begin...end**) execute sequentially with respect to each other. This always statement implies that whenever an event occurs on `execute_cycle`, that is, whenever it changes, execute the sequential block; execution of the sequential block implies executing all statements within the block sequentially.

Here is another example. The model is that of a negative edge-triggered D-type flip-flop with an asynchronous preset.

```
module d_flipflop (clk, d, set, q, qbar);
  input clk, d, set;
  output reg q, qbar;

  always
    wait (set == 1)
      begin
        #3 q <= 1;
        #2 qbar <= 0;
        wait (set == 0);
      end

  always
    @(negedge clk)
      begin
        if (set != 1)
          begin
            #5 q <= d;
            #1 qbar <= ~q;
          end
      end
endmodule
```

This module has two always statements. The first always statement has a level-sensitive event control with a sequential block. The second always statement has an edge-triggered timing control with a sequential block.

8.1.3 In One Module

A module may contain multiple always statements and multiple initial statements. Each statement starts a separate control flow. Each statement starts execution at time 0.

Here is an example of a module with one initial statement and two always statements.

```
module test_xor_behavior;
  reg wave_a, wave_b, z_mon;

  initial
    begin
      wave_a = 0;
      wave_b = 0;
      #5 wave_b = 1;
      #5 wave_a = 1;
      #5 wave_b = 0;
    end

  always
    @(wave_a or wave_b) z_mon = wave_a ^ wave_b;
    // The event list can also be written as:
    // @(wave_a, wave_b), or simply @*

  always
    @(z_mon)
      $display (
        "At time %t, wave_a = %d, wave_b = %d, z_mon = %b",
        $time, wave_a, wave_b, z_mon);
endmodule
```

The order of the three statements in the module is not important since they all execute concurrently. The initial statement when executed causes the first statement in the sequential block to execute, that is, `wave_a` gets assigned 0; the next statement executes immediately after zero delay. The #5 in the third line of the initial statement indicates a "wait for 5 time units". Thus `wave_b` gets a 1 after 5 time units, `wave_a` gets a 1 after another 5 time units and finally `wave_b` gets a 0 after another 5 time units.

After the last statement in the sequential block is executed, the initial statement suspends forever.

The first always statement waits for an event to occur on `wave_a` or `wave_b`. Whenever such an event occurs, the statement within the always statement is executed and then the always statement again waits for an event to occur on `wave_a` or `wave_b`. Notice that based on the values assigned to `wave_a` and `wave_b` in the initial statement, the always statement will be executed at times 0, 5, 10 and 15 time units.

Similarly the second always statement executes whenever an event occurs on `z_mon`. In such a case, the **$display** system task is executed and then the always statement again waits for an event to occur on `z_mon`. Figure 8-2 shows the waveforms produced on `wave_a`, `wave_b` and `z_mon`. Here is the output produced when the module is simulated.

```
At time     5, wave_a = 0, wave_b = 1, z_mon = 1
At time     10, wave_a = 1, wave_b = 1, z_mon = 0
At time     15, wave_a = 1, wave_b = 0, z_mon = 1
```

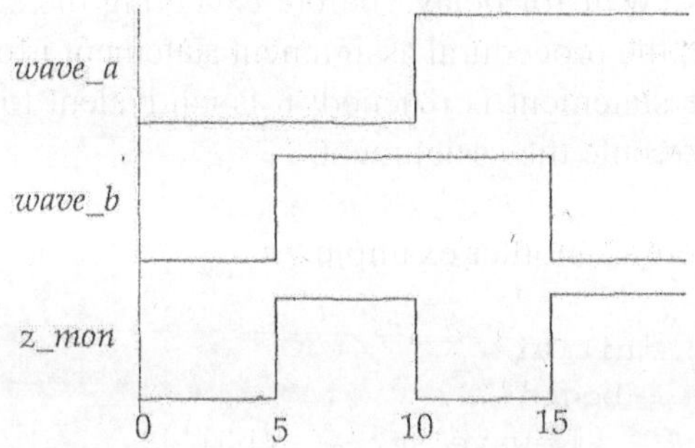

Figure 8-2 Waveforms produced on `wave_a`, `wave_b` and `z_mon`.

8.2 Timing Controls

A timing control may be associated with a procedural statement. Timing control is of two forms:

i. Delay control.
ii. Event control.

8.2.1 Delay Control

A delay control is of the form:

```
#delay procedural_statement
```

as in the example:

```
#2   tx_addr = rx_addr - 5;
```

A delay control specifies the time duration from the time the statement is initially encountered to the time the statement executes. Basically it means "wait for delay" before executing the statement. In the above example, the procedural assignment statement is executed two time units after the statement is reached; it is equivalent to wait for 2 time units and then execute the assignment.

Here is another example.

```
initial
  begin
    #3 wave_set_a = 'b0111;
    #6 wave_set_a = 'b1100;
    #7 wave_set_a = 'b0000;
  end
```

The initial statement executes at time 0. First, wait for 3 time units, execute the first assignment, wait for another 6 time units, execute the second statement, wait for 7 more time units, execute the third statement and then suspend indefinitely.

A delay control can also be specified in the form:

```
#delay ;
```

This statement causes a wait for the specified delay before the next statement is executed. Here is an example of such an usage.

```
parameter ON_DELAY = 3, OFF_DELAY = 5;
always
  begin
    #ON_DELAY;            // Wait for ON_DELAY.
    clk_ref = 0;
    #OFF_DELAY;           // Wait for OFF_DELAY.
    clk_ref = 1;
  end
```

The delay in a delay control can be an arbitrary expression, that is, it need not be restricted to a constant. See the following examples.

```
#strobe_delay
  start_ptr = tx_addr ^ MASK;

#(PERIOD / 2)
  clk_crd = ~ clk_crd;
```

If the value of the delay expression is 0, then it is called an *explicit zero delay*.

```
#0;           // Explicit zero delay.
```

An explicit zero delay causes a wait until all other events that are waiting to be executed at the current simulation time are completed, before it resumes; the simulation time does not advance.

If the value of a delay expression is an x or a z, it is the same as zero delay. If the delay expression evaluates to a negative value, the two's complement signed integer value is used as the delay.

If a delay value includes a space character, use parentheses to enclose the value.

```
next_frame <= #(5 'b11011) curr_frame;
coh_hdr = #(i + j) pkt_load;
```

Use parentheses when using expressions for delays as well. The same rule applies to delays in continuous assignments as well.

```
assign #(soh_dly * 2) crd_update = feq_data;
```

8.2.2 Event Control

With an event control, a statement executes based on events. There are two kinds of event control.

i. Edge-triggered event control
ii. Level-sensitive event control

Edge-triggered Event Control

An edge-triggered event control is of the form:

```
@event   procedural_statement
```

as in the example:

```
@(posedge clock)
  curr_state = next_state;
```

An event control with a procedural statement delays the execution of the statement until the occurrence of the specified event. In the above example, if a positive edge occurs on `clock` the assignment statement executes, otherwise execution is suspended until a positive edge occurs on `clock`.

Here are some more examples.

```
@(negedge reset) intf_count = 0;

@cell_byte
  per_frame = cell_data;
```

In the first statement, the assignment statement executes only when a negative edge occurs on `reset`. In the second statement, `cell_data` is assigned to `per_frame` when an event occurs on `cell_byte`, that is, wait for an event to occur on `cell_byte`, and when it does occur, assign `cell_data` to `per_frame`.

Event control can also be of the form:

```
@event ;
```

Guideline: Write clock names using `clk` as a prefix or as a suffix.

This statement causes a wait until the specified event occurs. Here is an example of such an usage in an initial statement that determines the on-period of a clock.

```
time rise_edge, on_delay;

initial
  begin
    // Wait until positive edge on clock occurs:
    @(posedge clk_cell);
    rise_edge = $time;
    // Wait until negative edge on clock occurs:
    @(negedge clk_cell);
    on_delay = $time - rise_edge;
    $display ("The on-period of clock is %t.", on_delay);
  end
```

Events can also be or'ed to indicate "if any of the events occur". This is shown in the following examples.

```
@(posedge clear or negedge reset)
  q = 0;

@(ctrl_a or ctrl_b)
  token_bus = 'bz;
```

Note that the keyword **or** does not imply a logical-or such as in an expression.

posedge and **negedge** are keywords in Verilog HDL that indicate a positive edge and a negative edge respectively. A negative edge is one of the following transitions:

```
1 -> x
1 -> z
1 -> 0
x -> 0
z -> 0
```

A positive edge is one of the following transitions:

```
0 -> x
0 -> z
0 -> 1
x -> 1
z -> 1
```

A simple event control is of the form:

```
@(negedge clk_core)
```

When more than one expression is in an event control, the **or** keyword or a comma can be used. For example:

```
// Comma-separated event list:
@(negedge clk_core, posedge reset_core)

// Or-separated event list:
@(request or grant)
```

It is possible to have an implicit event control that contains all (wildcard) the variables and nets read within the associated procedural statement as part of the event list. The `@*` indicates that the associated procedural statement is sensitive to any change of value used in the procedural statement. For example, in:

```
always
  @* procedural_statement
```

the @* includes all variables read within the procedural statement as part of the event list.

```
always
  @* cpu_req = master_req + control_reg;
```

would implicitly include `master_reg` and `control_reg` in the event list. This is a shortcut form of writing:

A comma-separated event list is same as an or-separated event list.

```
always
  @(master_reg, control_reg)
    cpu_reg = master_reg + control_reg;
```

The `@*` represents all variables or nets whose values are used in any statement within the associated block. This includes index variables used in a left-hand side assignment as well.

```
always
  @*
    valid_ptr[k] = ram_wrn & chip_sel;
```

In this example, `@*` is equivalent to:

```
@(ram_wrn, chip_sel, k)
```

Here is another example.

```
always
  @*
    case (select)
      2'b00: y = a;
      2'b01: y = b;
      2'b10: y = c;
      2'b11: y = d;
    endcase
```

In this case the `@*` represents `@(a, b, c, d, select)`.

I shall continue to use the or-separated event list form throughout the rest of the book, though both forms are identical in semantics.

Level-sensitive Event Control

In a level-sensitive event control, the procedural statement is delayed until a condition becomes true. This event control is written in the form:

```
wait (condition)
  procedural_statement
```

The procedural statement executes only if the condition is true, else it waits until the condition becomes true. If the condition is already true when the statement is reached, then the procedural statement is executed immediately. The procedural statement is optional.

Here are some examples.

```
wait (token_sum > 22)
  token_sum = 0;

wait (data_ready)
  spi_data = intf_bus;

wait (preset);
```

In the first statement, only when `token_sum` becomes greater than 22 will the assignment of 0 to `token_sum` occur. In the second example, `intf_bus` is assigned to `spi_data` only if `data_ready` is true, that is, `data_ready` has the value 1. In the last example, the execution is simply delayed until `preset` becomes true.

8.3 Block Statement

A block statement provides a mechanism to group two or more statements to act syntactically like a single statement. There are two kinds of blocks in Verilog HDL. These are:

i. Sequential block (**begin...end**): Statements are executed sequentially in the given order.

ii. Parallel block (**fork...join**): Statements in this block execute concurrently.

A block can be labeled optionally. If so labeled, variables can be declared locally within the block. Blocks can also be referenced; for example, a block can be disabled using a disable statement. A block label, in addition, provides a way to uniquely identify variables. However, there is one word of caution. All local variables are static, that is, their values remain valid throughout the entire simulation run.

8.3.1 Sequential Block

Statements in a sequential block execute in sequence. A delay value in each statement is relative to the simulation time of the execution of the previous statement. Once a sequential block completes execution, execution continues with the next statement following the sequential block. Here is the syntax of a sequential block.

```
begin
  [ : block_id { declarations } ]
  procedural_statement(s)
end
```

Here is an example of a sequential block.

```
// Waveform generation:
begin
  #2 ve_stream = 1;
  #5 ve_stream = 0;
  #3 ve_stream = 1;
  #4 ve_stream = 0;
  #2 ve_stream = 1;
  #5 ve_stream = 0;
end
```

Assume that the sequential block gets executed at 10 time units. The first statement executes after 2 time units, that is at 12 time units. After this execution has completed, the next statement is executed at 17 time units (because of the delay). Then the next statement is executed at 20 time units and so on. Figure 8-3 shows the waveform produced due to the sequential execution behavior of this example.

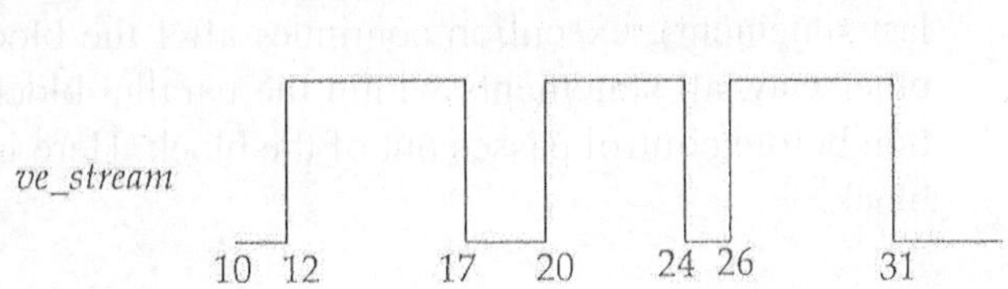

Figure 8-3 Delays are cumulative in a sequential block.

Here is another example of a sequential block.

```
begin
  mem_rdata = sms_result | mem_status;

  @(negedge clk_sms)
    update_rw = & mem_rdata;
end
```

In this example, the first statement executes first and then the second statement executes. Of course, the assignment in the second statement occurs only when a negative edge appears on `clk_sms`. Here is another example of a sequential block.

```
begin: lbl_seq_blk
  reg [3:0] dmac_channel;

  dmac_channel = dmac_breq & dmac_clear;
  dmac_parity = ^ dmac_channel;
end
```

In this example, the sequential block has a label `lbl_seq_blk` and it has a local reg variable declared. Upon execution, the first statement is executed, then the second statement is executed.

8.3.2 Parallel Block

A parallel block has the delimiters **fork** and **join** (a sequential block has the delimiters **begin** and **end**). Statements in a parallel block execute concurrently. Delay values specified in each statement within a parallel block are relative to the time the block starts its execution. When the last activity in the parallel block has completed execution (this need not be the last statement), execution continues after the block statement. Stated another way, all statements within the parallel block must complete execution before control passes out of the block. Here is the syntax of a parallel block.

```
fork
  [ :block_id { declarations } ]
  procedural_statement(s)
join
```

Here is an example.

```
// Waveform generation:
fork
  #2 req_stream = 1;
  #7 req_stream = 0;
  #10 req_stream = 1;
  #14 req_stream = 0;
  #16 req_stream = 1;
  #21 req_stream = 0;
join
```

If the parallel block gets executed at 10 time units, all statements execute concurrently and all delay values are relative to 10. For example, the third assignment executes at 20 time units, the fifth assignment executes at 26 time units, and so on. Figure 8-4 shows the waveform produced.

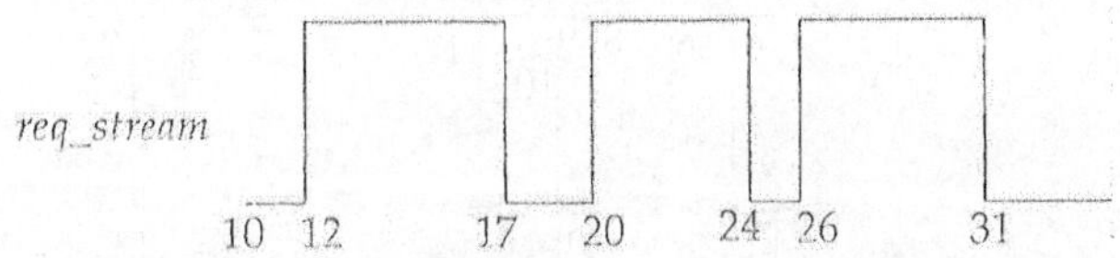

Figure 8-4 Delays are relative in a parallel block.

Here is an example that uses a mix of sequential and parallel blocks to emphasize their differences.

```
always
  begin: blk_seq_a
    #4 pm_write = 5;                    // S1

    fork: blk_par_a                     // S2
      #6 pm_select = 7;                 // P1

      begin: blk_seq_b                  // P2
        wdog_rst = pm_enable;           // S6
        #5 wdog_intr = wdog_rst;        // S7
      end
```

```
        #2 frc_sel = 3;                        // P3
        #4 pm_itcr = 2;                        // P4
        #8 itop = 4;                           // P5
      join

      #8 pm_lock = 1;                          // S3
      #2 pcell_id = 52;                        // S4
      #6 $stop;                                // S5
    end
```

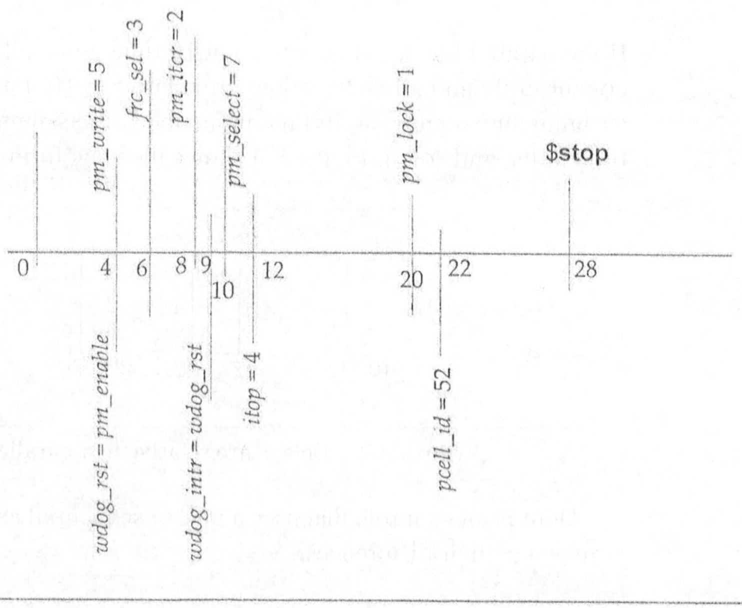

Figure 8-5 Delays due to a mix of sequential and parallel blocks.

The always statement contains a sequential block `blk_seq_a` and all statements within the sequential block (`S1`, `S2`, `S3`, `S4`, `S5`) execute sequentially. Since the always statement executes at time 0, `pm_write` gets assigned 5 at 4 time units, and the parallel block `blk_par_a` begins its execution at 4 time units. All statements within the parallel block (`P1`, `P2`, `P3`, `P4`, `P5`) execute concurrently, that is, at 4 time units. Thus `pm_select` gets assigned a value at 10 time units, `frc_sel` gets assigned at 6, `pm_itcr` gets assigned at 8, and `itop` gets assigned at 12. The sequential block `blk_seq_b` starts execution at 4 time units, causing statements `S6` and then `S7` to execute. `wdog_intr` gets its new value at 9.

Since all statements within the parallel block `blk_par_a` complete execution at time 12, statement `S3` is executed at 12 time units, assignment to `pm_lock` occurs at 20, then statement `S4` executes, assignment to `pcell_id` occurs at 22, then the next statement executes. Finally the system task **$stop** executes at time 28. Figure 8-5 shows the events that occur upon the execution of the always statement.

8.4 *Procedural Assignments*

A procedural assignment is an assignment within an initial statement or an always statement. It is used to assign to only a variable data type. The right-hand side of the assignment can be any expression. Here is an example.

```
reg [3:0] prn_data, lock_write, data_reg;
. . .
#5 prn_data = ~lock_write & ~data_reg;
```

`prn_data` is a reg variable. Due to the delay control, the assignment statement executes 5 time units after the statement is initially encountered. The right-hand side expression is then evaluated and its value is assigned to `prn_data`.

A procedural assignment executes sequentially with respect to other statements that appear around it. Here is an example of an always statement.

```
always
  @(a, b, c, d)                // Same as @(a or b or c or d)
    begin: blk_aoi
      reg temp1, temp2;

      temp1 = a & b;
      temp2 = c & d;
      temp1 = temp1 | temp2;
      y = ~ temp1;
    end

  /* It is possible to replace the above four statements
     with one statement, such as:
       y = ~ ((a & b) | (c & d));
```

```
However, it has been used here as such to illustrate
the sequential nature of the statements in a
sequential block */
```

The sequential block within the always statement starts execution when an event occurs on a, b, c or d. The assignment to temp1 takes place first. Then the second assignment occurs. The values of temp1 and temp2 computed in the previous assignment are used in the third assignment statement. The last assignment uses the value of temp1 computed in the third statement.

There are two kinds of procedural assignments.

i. Blocking.

ii. Nonblocking.

But before we discuss these, let us first briefly discuss the notion of intra-statement delays.

8.4.1 Intra-statement Delay

A delay appearing on the left of an expression in an assignment statement is an intra-statement delay. It is the delay by which the right-hand side value is delayed before it is applied to the left-hand side target. Here is an example.

```
frc_done = #5 'b1;
```

The important thing to note about this delay is that the right-hand side expression is evaluated before the delay, then the wait occurs and then the value is assigned to the left-hand side target. To understand the difference between inter-statement delays and intra-statement delays, here are some examples that illustrate this.

```
frc_done = #5 'b1;    // Intra-statement delay control.

// is the same as:
begin
  temp = 'b1;
```

```
  #5 frc_done = temp; // Inter-statement delay control.
end

q = @(posedge clk_iol) d;
  // Intra-statement event control.

// is the same as:
begin
  temp = d;

  @(posedge clk_iol)  // Inter-statement event control.
    q = temp;
end
```

In addition to the two forms of timing controls (delay control and event control) that can be specified for intra-statement delay, there is yet another form called the repeat event control that can be used to specify intra-statement delay. It is of the form:

```
repeat ( expression ) @ ( event_expression )
```

This form of control is used to specify a delay that is based on the number of occurrences of one or more events. Here is an example.

```
hresult = repeat (2) @(negedge tclk) hw_data + hr_data;
```

This statement when executed evaluates the value of the right-hand side, that is, `hw_data + hr_data`, waits for two negative edges on clock `tclk` and then assigns the value of the right-hand side to `hresult`. The equivalent form of this repeat event control example is shown next.

```
begin
  temp = hw_data + hr_data;
  @(negedge tclk);
  @(negedge tclk);
  hresult = temp;
end
```

This form of delay is useful in synchronizing assignments to certain edges or with a count of edges.

8.4.2 Blocking Procedural Assignment

A procedural assignment in which the assignment operator is an "=" is a blocking procedural assignment. For example,

```
p_address = 52;
```

is a blocking procedural assignment. A blocking procedural assignment is executed before any of the statements that follow it are executed, that is, the assignment statement is executed completely before the next statement is executed. Here is another example.

```
always
  @(a or b or cin)
    begin: blk_carry_out
      reg t1, t2, t3;

      t1 = a & b;
      t2 = b & cin;
      t3 = a & cin;
      cout = t1 | t2 | t3;
    end
```

The `t1` assignment occurs first, `t1` is computed, then the second statement executes, `t2` is assigned and then the third statement is executed and `t3` is assigned, and so on.

Here is another example of a blocking procedural assignment using intra-statement delays.

```
initial
  begin
    scan_clear = #5 0;
    scan_clear = #4 1;
    scan_clear = #10 0;
  end
```

The first statement executes at time 0 and `scan_clear` gets assigned 0 after 5 time units, then the second statement executes causing `scan_clear` to get assigned a 1 after 4 time units (9 time units from time 0), and then the third statement executes causing `scan_clear` to get a 0 after 10 time units (19 time units from time 0). The waveform produced on `scan_clear` is shown in Figure 8-6.

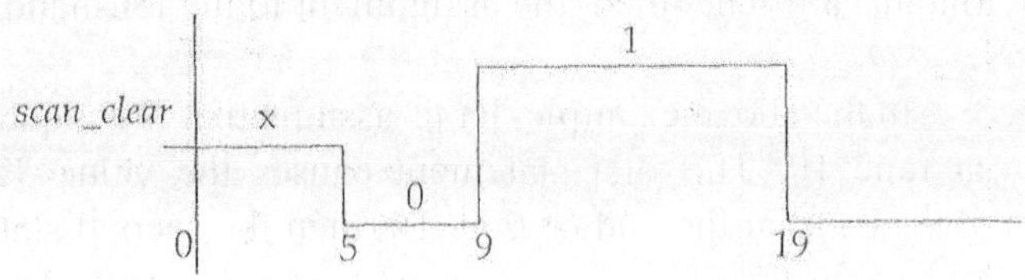

Figure 8-6 Blocking procedural assignments with intra-statement delays.

Here is another example.

```
begin
  itc_reset = 0;
  itc_reset = 1;
end
```

In this case, `itc_reset` gets assigned the value 1. This is because, first `itc_reset` gets assigned 0, then the next statement executes that causes `itc_reset` to get 1 after zero delay.

8.4.3 Nonblocking Procedural Assignment

In a nonblocking procedural assignment, the assignment symbol "<=" is used. Here are some examples of nonblocking procedural assignments.

```
begin
  rms_load <= 32;
  wr_enable <= rms_load;
  rd_strobe <= rms_store;
end
```

In a nonblocking procedural assignment, the assignment to the target is not blocked (due to delays) but are scheduled to occur in the future (based on the delays; if zero delay, then at the end of the current time step). When a nonblocking procedural assignment is executed, the right-hand side expression is evaluated and its value is scheduled to be assigned to the left-hand side target, and execution continues with the next statement. The earliest an output would be scheduled is at the end of the current time step; this case would occur if there were no delay in the assignment statement. At the end of the current time step or whenever the outputs are scheduled, the assignment to the left-hand side target occurs.

In the above example, let us assume that the sequential block executes at time 10. The first statement causes the value 32 to be assigned to `rms_load` at the end of time 10, then the second statement executes, the old value of `rms_load` is used (note that time has not advanced and `rms_load` in the first assignment has not yet been assigned a new value); the assignment to `wr_enable` is scheduled at the end of time step 10, the next statement executes and `rd_strobe` is scheduled to be assigned a value at the end of time 10. After all events at time 10 have occurred, all scheduled assignments to the left-hand side target are made.

Here is another example that explains this further.

```
initial
  begin
    timer_clr <= #5 1;
    timer_clr <= #4 0;
    timer_clr <= #10 0;
  end
```

The execution of the first statement causes a 1 to be scheduled to appear on `timer_clr` at 5 time units, the execution of the second statement causes `timer_clr` to get a value 0 at 4 time units (4 time units from time 0), and finally the execution of the third statement causes a 0 to be scheduled on `timer_clr` at 10 time units (10 time units from 0). Note that all the three statements execute at time 0. In addition, notice that the order of execution of nonblocking assignments become irrelevant in this case. Figure 8-7 shows the waveform produced on `timer_clr`.

Here is another example, but this time with zero delays.

```
initial
  begin
    wdog_intr <= 0;
    wdog_intr <= 1;
  end
```

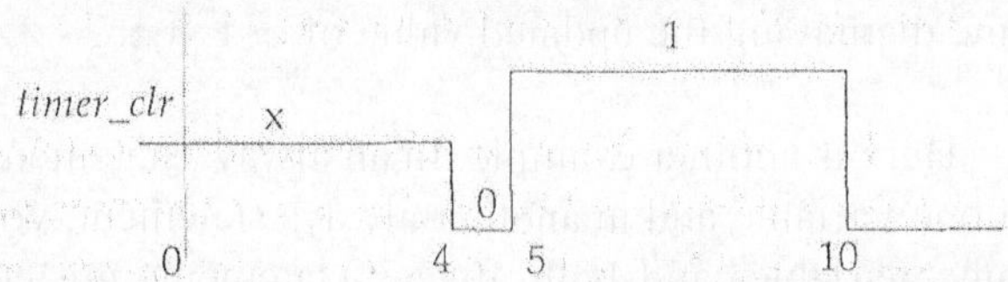

Figure 8-7 Nonblocking assignments with intra-statement delays.

The value of `wdog_intr` after the initial statement executes is 1 since the Verilog HDL standard specifies that all nonblocking assignments to a variable shall occur in the order the assignment statements are executed. Thus, `wdog_intr` gets the value 0 first and then 1.

Here is an example that uses both blocking and nonblocking assignments and highlights their differences.

```
reg [0:2] qstate;

initial
  begin
    qstate = 3'b011;
    qstate <= 3'b100;
    $display ("Current value of qstate is %b", qstate);
    #5;          // Wait for some time.
    $display ("The delayed value of qstate is %b",
              qstate);
  end
```

The execution of the initial statement produces the result:

```
Current value of qstate is 011
The delayed value of qstate is 100
```

The first blocking assignment causes `qstate` to get the value of 3'b011. The execution of the second assignment statement, which is a nonblocking one, causes the value 3'b100 to be scheduled for `qstate` at the end of the current time step (which is 0). Therefore when the first **$display** task is executed, `qstate` still has the value from the first assignment, which is 3'b011. When the #5 delay is executed, this causes the scheduled assignment of `qstate` to occur, `qstate` gets updated with its new value, a delay of 5 time units occurs and then the next **$display** task is executed, this time displaying the updated value of `qstate`.

Here is another example. In an always statement, if you read the value of one variable and in another always statement, you assign a value to the same variable, and both always statements are controlled by the same clock edge, then how do you ensure that the read occurs before the write? The answer is to use nonblocking assignments.

```
always
  @(negedge clock)
    reg_a <= data;              // reg_a assigned here.

always
  @(negedge clock)              // Same clock edge.
    reg_b <= reg_a;             // reg_a read here.
```

When the falling edge of the clock occurs, `reg_a` value is read first in the second always statement. The update to the `reg_a` in the first always statement occurs after the read (that is, at the end of the simulation time step). If blocking assignments were used, then depending on which always statement executed first, you may end up with different results.

So which procedural assignment do you use when? Here is a recommendation: Use nonblocking assignment ("<=") when assigning to a variable that is used outside the enclosing always statement. Use blocking assignment ("=") for computing intermediate results. Here is an example.

```
always
  @(posedge clk_piol) begin
    bdir_data = ^ spi_rdata; // Use blocking assignment
      // to compute intermediate result.
    spi_wdata <= bdir_data + rst_cnt; // Use nonblocking
      // assignment as value of spi_wdata is used in
      // another always block.
  end

always
  @(spi_wdata)
    spi_parity <= ^ spi_wdata;
```

We shall follow this guideline in the rest of the examples in this book.

8.4.4 Continuous Assignment vs Procedural Assignment

What are the differences between continuous assignments and procedural assignments? Table 8-1 illustrates this.

Table 8-1 Difference between procedural and continuous assignment.

Procedural assignment	Continuous assignment
Occurs inside an always statement or an initial statement.	Occurs within a module.
Execution is with respect to other statements surrounding it.	Executes concurrently with other statements; executes whenever there is a change of value in an operand on its right-hand side.
Drives variables.	Drives nets.
Uses "=" or "<=" assignment symbol.	Uses "=" assignment symbol.
No **assign** keyword (except in a procedural continuous assignment; see Sec. 8.8).	Uses **assign** keyword.

Here is an example explaining this difference further.

```
module m_procedural;
  reg t_select, t_enable, wr_reset;

  always
    @(t_enable) begin
      wr_reset <= t_select;
      t_select <= t_enable;
    end
endmodule

module m_continuous;
  wire t_select, t_enable, wr_reset;

  assign wr_reset = t_select;
  assign t_select = t_enable;
endmodule
```

Say that `t_enable` has an event at time 10ns. In module `m_procedural`, the two procedural statements are executed sequentially and `t_select` gets the new value of `t_enable` at 10ns. `wr_reset` does not get the value of `t_enable` since the assignment to `wr_reset` occurs before the assignment to `t_select`. In module `m_continuous`, the second continuous assignment is triggered since there is an event on `t_enable`. This in turn causes an event on `t_select`, which causes the first continuous assignment to be executed, which in turn causes `wr_reset` to get the value of `t_select` which is really `t_enable`. However, if an event occurred on `t_select`, the always statement in module `m_procedural` does not execute since `t_select` is not in the timing control event list for that always statement. However the first continuous assignment in the module `m_continuous` executes and `wr_reset` gets the new value of `t_select`.

8.5 Conditional Statement

The syntax of an `if` statement is:

```
if ( condition_1 )
  procedural_statement_1
{ else if ( condition_2 )
  procedural_statement_2 }
[ else
  procedural_statement_3 ]
```

1 is a non-zero known value.

If *condition_1* evaluates to a non-zero known value, then the *procedural_statement_1* is executed. If *condition_1* evaluates to a value 0, x or z, the *procedural_statement_1* is not executed, and an `else` branch, if it exists, is executed. Here is an example.

```
if (sum < 60)
  begin
    grade = C;
    total_c = total_c + 1;
  end
else if (sum < 75)
  begin
    grade = B;
    total_b = total_b + 1;
  end
```

```
else
  begin
    grade = A;
    total_a = total_a + 1;
  end
```

Note that the condition expression must always be within parentheses. Also there is a possibility for an ambiguity if an `if-if-else` form is used, as shown in this example.

```
if (fclk)
  if (reset)
    q = 0;
  else
    q = d;
```

The question is to which `if` does the last `else` belong? Does it belong to the first `if` condition (`fclk`) or to the second `if` condition (`reset`)? This is resolved in Verilog HDL by associating the `else` with the closest `if` that does not have an `else`. In this example, the `else` is associated with the inner `if` statement.

Here are some more examples of `if` statements.

```
if (sum < 100)
  sum = sum + 10;

if (nickel_in)
  deposit = 5;
else if (dime_in)
  deposit = 10;
else if (quarter_in)
  deposit = 25;
else
  deposit = ERROR;

if (p_ctrl)
  begin
    if (~w_ctrl)
      mux_out = 4'd2;
    else
      mux_out = 4'd1;
```

```
      end
    else
      begin
        if (~w_ctrl)
          mux_out = 4'd8;
        else
          mux_out = 4'd4;
      end
```

8.6 Case Statement

A case statement is a multi-way conditional branch. It has the following syntax:

```
case ( case_expr )
  case_item_expr { , case_item_expr } :
                  procedural_statement
  . . .
  . . .
  [ default: procedural_statement ]
endcase
```

The case expression is evaluated first. Next the case item expressions are evaluated and compared in the order given. The set of statements that match the first true condition is executed. Multiple case item expressions can be specified in one branch; these values need not be mutually-exclusive. The default case covers all values that are not covered by the case item expressions.

Neither the case expression nor the case item expressions need be constant expressions. In a case statement, the x and z values are compared as their literal values. Here is an example of a case statement.

```
localparam
    MON = 0, TUE = 1, WED = 2,
    THU = 3, FRI = 4,
    SAT = 5, SUN = 6;
reg [0:2] today;
integer pocket_money;
```

```
case (today)
  TUE      : pocket_money = 6;     // Branch 1
  MON,
  WED      : pocket_money = 2;     // Branch 2
  FRI,
  SAT,
  SUN      : pocket_money = 7;     // Branch 3
  default  : pocket_money = 0;     // Branch 4
endcase
```

Branch 2 is chosen if `today` has the value `MON` or `WED`. Branch 3 covers the values `FRI`, `SAT`, `SUN`, while branch 4 covers the remaining values, `THU` and the bit-vector 111. Here is another example of a case statement.

```
module alu (a, b, op_code, y);
  input [3:0] a, b;
  input [1:2] op_code;
  output reg [7:0] y;

  localparam
      ADD_INSTR = 2'b10,
      SUB_INSTR = 2'b11,
      MULT_INSTR = 2'b01,
      DIV_INSTR = 2'b00;

  always
    @(a or b or op_code)
      case (op_code)
        ADD_INSTR:  y <= a + b;
        SUB_INSTR:  y <= a - b;
        MULT_INSTR: y <= a * b;
        DIV_INSTR:  y <= a / b;
      endcase
endmodule
```

What happens if the case expression and the case item expressions are of different lengths? In such a situation, all case expressions are made equal to the largest size of any of these expressions before any comparisons are made. Here is an example that illustrates this.

```
case (3'b101 << 2)
  3'b100    : $display ("First branch taken!");
  4'b0100   : $display ("Second branch taken!");
  5'b10100 : $display ("Third branch taken!");
  default   : $display ("Default branch taken!");
endcase
```

produces:

```
Third branch taken!
```

Since the third case item expression is of size 5 bits, all case item expressions and the case expression are made equal to size 5. So when 3'b101 << 2 is computed, the result is 5'b10100, and the third branch is taken.

8.6.1 Don't-cares in Case

In the case statement described in the previous section, the values x and z are interpreted literally, that is, as x and z values. There are two other forms of case statements: casex and casez, that use a different interpretation for x and z values. The syntax is exactly identical to that of a case statement except for the keywords **casex** and **casez**.

In a casez statement, the value z that appears in the case expression and in any case item expression is considered as a don't-care, that is, that bit is ignored (not compared).

In a casex statement, both the values x and z are considered as don't-cares. Here is an example of a casez statement.

```
casez (intr_mask)
  4'b1??? :  rtc_wdata[4] = 0;
  4'b01?? :  rtc_wdata[3] = 0;
  4'b001? :  rtc_wdata[2] = 0;
  4'b0001 :  rtc_wdata[1] = 0;
endcase
```

The ? character can be used instead of the character z to imply a don't-care. The casez statement example implies that if the first bit of `intr_mask` is 1 (other bits of `intr_mask` are ignored), then 0 is assigned to `rtc_wdata[4]`, if first bit of `intr_mask` is 0 and the second bit is 1 (other bits are ignored), then `rtc_wdata[3]` gets assigned the value 0, and so on.

8.7 Loop Statement

There are four kinds of loop statements. These are:

i. Forever-loop
ii. Repeat-loop
iii. While-loop
iv. For-loop

8.7.1 Forever-loop Statement

The syntax for this form of loop statement is:

```
forever
  procedural_statement
```

This loop statement continuously executes the procedural statement. Thus to get out of such a loop, a disable statement may be used with the procedural statement. Also, some form of timing controls must be used in the procedural statement, otherwise the forever-loop will loop forever in zero delay.

Here is an example of this form of loop statement.

```
initial
  begin
    clk1hz = 0;

    #5 forever
      #10 clk1hz = ~ clk1hz;
  end
```

This example generates a clock waveform; `clk1hz` first gets initialized to 0 and stays at 0 until 5 time units. After that `clk1hz` toggles every 10 time units.

8.7.2 Repeat-loop Statement

This form of loop statement has the form:

```
repeat ( loop_count )
  procedural_statement
```

It executes the procedural statement the specified number of times. If loop count expression is an x or a z, then the loop count is treated as a 0. Here are some examples.

```
repeat (count)
  sum = sum + 10;

repeat (shift_by)
  wdog_reg = wdog_reg << 1;
```

The repeat-loop statement differs from repeat event control. Consider,

```
repeat (load_count)     // Repeat-loop statement.
  @(posedge clk_rtc) accum = accum + 1;
```

which means for `load_count` times, wait for positive edge of `clk_rtc` and when this occurs, increment `accum`. Whereas,

```
accum = repeat (load_count) @(posedge clk_rtc)
        accum + 1;                 // Repeat event control.
```

means to compute `accum+1` first, then wait for `load_count` positive edges on `clk_rtc`, then assign to left-hand side.

What does the following mean?

```
repeat (NUM_OF_TIMES) @(negedge zclk);
```

It means to wait for `NUM_OF_TIMES` negative clock edges before executing the statement following the repeat statement.

8.7.3 While-loop Statement

The syntax of this form of loop statement is:

```
while ( condition )
  procedural_statement
```

This loop executes the procedural statement until the specified condition becomes false. If the expression is false to begin with, then the procedural statement is never executed. If the condition is an **x** or a **z**, it is treated as a 0 (false). Here are some examples.

```
while (shift_by > 0)
  begin
    acc = acc << 1;
    shift_by = shift_by - 1;
  end
```

8.7.4 For-loop Statement

This loop statement is of the form:

```
for ( initial_assignment ; condition ; step_assignment )
  procedural_statement
```

A for-loop statement repeats the execution of the procedural statement a certain number of times. The *initial_assignment* specifies the initial value of the loop index. The *condition* specifies the condition when loop execution must stop. As long as the condition is true, the statements in the loop are executed. The *step_assignment* specifies the assignment to modify, typically to increment or decrement, the step count.

```
integer k;

for (k = 0; k < MAX_RANGE; k = k + 1)
  if (hold_data[k] == 0)
    hold_data[k] = 1;
  else if (hold_data[k] == 1)
    hold_data[k] = 0;
  else
    $display ("hold_data[k] is an x or a z");
```

8.8 Procedural Continuous Assignment

A procedural continuous assignment is a procedural assignment, that is, it can appear within an always statement or an initial statement. This assignment can override all other assignments to a net or a variable. It allows the expression in the assignment to be driven continuously into a variable or a net. Note, this is not a continuous assignment; a continuous assignment occurs outside of an initial or an always statement.

There are two kinds of procedural continuous assignments.

i. assign and deassign procedural statements: these assign to variables.

ii. force and release procedural statements: these assign primarily to nets, though they can also be used for variables.

The assign and force statements are "continuous" in the sense that any change of operand in the right-hand side expression causes the assignment to be redone while the assign or force is in effect.

The target of a procedural continuous assignment cannot be a part-select or a bit-select of a variable.

8.8.1 Assign - deassign

An assign procedural statement overrides all procedural assignments to a variable. The deassign procedural statement ends the continuous assignment to a variable. The value in the variable is retained until assigned again.

```
module d_flip_flop (d, clear, clock, q);
  input d, clear, clock;
  output reg q;

  always
    @(clear)
      if (! clear)
        assign q = 0;        // d has no effect on q.
      else
        deassign q;
```

```
   always
     @(negedge clock) q <= d;
endmodule
```

If `clear` is 0, the assign procedural statement causes `q` to be stuck at 0 irrespective of any clock edges, that is, `clock` and `d` have no effect on `q`. If `clear` becomes 1, the deassign statement is executed; this causes the override to be removed, so that in the future `clock` can effect `q`.

If an assign is applied to an already assigned variable, it is deassigned first before making the new procedural continuous assignment. Here is another example.

```
reg [3:0] load_ctr;
. . .
load_ctr = 0;
. . .
assign load_ctr = nibble ^ rtc_count;
. . .
assign load_ctr = 2; // Will deassign load_ctr and
                     // then assign.
. . .
deassign load_ctr;   // load_ctr continues to have 2.
. . .
assign load_ctr[2] = 1; /* Error: Bit-select of a reg
    variable cannot be a target of a procedural
    continuous assignment */
```

The second assign statement will cause the first assign to be deassigned before making the next assign. After the deassign is executed, `load_ctr` continues to keep the value 2 until another assignment to the variable occurs.

An assign statement is "continuous" in the sense that after the first assign is executed and before the second assign gets executed, any change on `nibble` or `rtc_count` will cause the first assign statement to be reevaluated.

8.8.2 Force - release

The force and release procedural statements are very similar to assign and deassign, except that force and release can be applied to nets as well as to variables.

The force statement, when applied to a variable, causes the current value of the variable to be overridden by the value of the force expression. When a release on the variable is executed, the current value is held in the variable unless a procedural continuous assignment was already in effect (at the time the force statement was executed) in which case, the continuous assignment establishes the new value of the variable.

A force procedural statement on a net overrides all the drivers for the net until a release procedural statement is executed on that net.

```
wire test_reset;
. . .
or #1 (test_reset, penable, rtc_intr);

initial
  begin
    force test_reset = penable & rtc_intr;
    #5;                          // Wait for 5 time units.
    release test_reset;
  end
```

The execution of the force statement causes the value of `test_reset` to override the value from the `or` gate primitive until the release statement is executed, upon which the driver of `test_reset` from the `or` gate primitive takes back its effect. While the force assignment is in effect (first 5 time units), any changes on `penable` and `rtc_intr` cause the assignment to be executed again.

Here is another example.

```
reg [2:0] pr_data;
. . .
pr_data = 2;
force pr_data = 1;
. . .
```

```
release pr_data;            // pr_data retains value 1.
. . .
assign pr_data = 5;
. . .
force pr_data = 3;
. . .
release pr_data;            // pr_data gets the value 5.
. . .
force pr_data[1:0] = 3; /* Error: target of a procedural
    continuous assignment cannot be a part-select of a
    reg variable */
```

The first release of `pr_data` causes the value of `pr_data` to be retained (as 1). This is because there was no procedural continuous assignment applied to the variable at the time force was applied. In the latter release statement, `pr_data` gets back the value 5 because the procedural continuous assignment on `pr_data` becomes active again.

8.9 A Handshake Example

Always statements can be used to capture the behavior of interacting processes, for example, that of interacting finite-state machines. These statements within a module communicate with each other using variables that are visible to all the always statements. It is not recommended to use variables declared within an always statement to pass information between always statements (though this is possible through the use of hierarchical path names, described in Chapter 10).

Consider the following example of two interacting processes: `rx`, a receiver, and `mp`, a microprocessor. The `rx` process reads the serial input data and sends a signal `ready` indicating that the data can be read into the `mp` process. The `mp` process, after it assigns the data to the output, sends an acknowledge signal, `ack`, back to the `rx` process to begin reading new input data. The block diagram for the two processes is shown in Figure 8-8.

The behavior for these two interacting processes is expressed in the following design description.

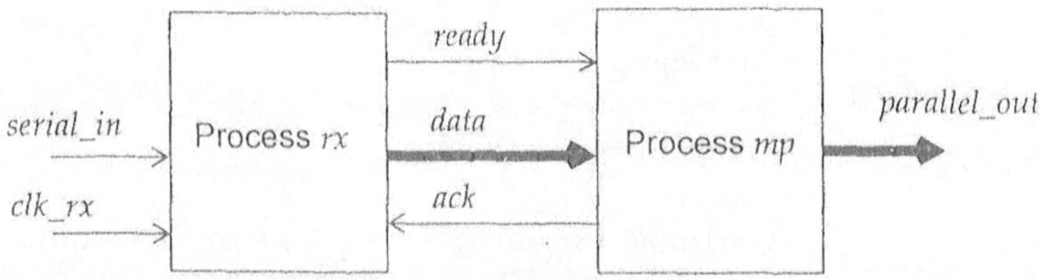

Figure 8-8 Two interacting processes.

```
`timescale 1ns/100ps
module interacting (serial_in, clk_rx, parallel_out);
  input serial_in, clk_rx;
  output reg [7:0] parallel_out;

  reg ready, ack;
  reg [0:7] data;

  `include "read_word.v" // Task read_word is defined in
                         // this file.
  always
    begin: RX
      read_word (serial_in, clk_rx, data);
      // The task read_word reads the serial data on every
      // clock cycle and converts to a parallel data in
      // signal data. It takes 10ns to do this.
      ready <= 1;
      wait (ack);
      ready <= 0;
      #40;
    end

  always
    begin: MP
      #25;
      parallel_out <= data;
      ack <= 1;
      #25 ack <= 0;
      wait (ready);
    end
endmodule
```

The interaction of these two processes via variables `ready` and `ack` is shown in the waveforms in Figure 8-9.

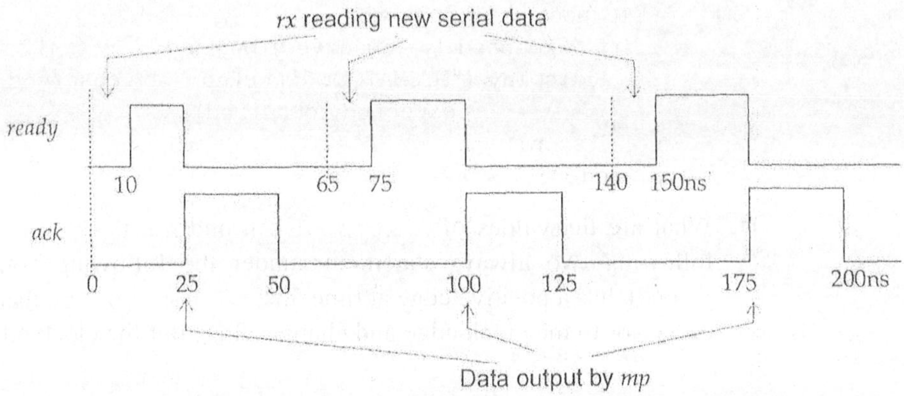

Figure 8-9 Handshaking protocol between the two processes.

8.10 *Exercises*

1. Which statement executes repeatedly, initial or always statement?
2. What is the difference between a sequential block and a parallel block? Explain using an example. Can a sequential block appear within a parallel block?
3. When is a label required for a block?
4. Is it necessary to specify a delay in an always statement?
5. What is the difference between an intra-statement delay and an inter-statement delay? Explain using an example.
6. How are blocking assignments different from nonblocking assignments?
7. How does the casex statement differ from the case statement?
8. Can a net type (for e.g. a wire) be assigned in an always statement?
9. Generate a clock waveform with an off-period of 5ns and an on-period of 10ns.

10. Express the following always statement using an initial statement and a forever loop statement.

```
always
  @(expected or observed)
    if (expected !== observed) begin
      $display ("MISMATCH: expected = %b, observed = %b",
                expected, observed);
      $stop;
    end
```

11. What are the values of `next_state_h` and `next_state_l` in the following two always statements under the following conditions: `pclock` has a positive edge at time 5ns; `current_state` has a value of 5 prior to the clock edge and changes 3ns after the clock edge to 7?

```
always
  @(posedge pclock)
    #7 next_state_h <= current_state;

always
  @(posedge pclock)
    next_state_l <= #7 current_state;
```

12. Write a model using the behavioral modeling style to describe the following finite state machine.

Input (tmr)	*PresentState*	*NextState*	*Output (tclr)*
0	NO_ONE	NO_ONE	0
1	NO_ONE	ONE_ONE	0
0	ONE_ONE	NO_ONE	0
1	ONE_ONE	TWO_ONE	0
0	TWO_ONE	NO_ONE	0
1	TWO_ONE	THREE_ONE	1
0	THREE_ONE	NO_ONE	0
1	THREE_ONE	THREE_ONE	1

13. Describe the behavior of a JK flip-flop using an always statement.

14. Describe the behavior of a circuit that sets the output `wr_asm` to 1 if a pattern 1011 is found on the input `usb_clr`. The data on the input is checked on every falling clock edge.

15. Describe the behavior of a majority circuit. The input is a 12-bit vector. If the number of 1's exceeds the number of 0's, the output is set to 1. The input data is checked only when `data_ready` is a 1.

16. Express the following behavior: `data_out` should assert when posedge of `strobe` occurs and get deasserted when posedge of `spi_select` occurs.

9

Structural Modeling

This chapter describes the structural modeling style of Verilog HDL. Structural modeling is described using:

- Gate instantiation
- UDP instantiation
- Module instantiation

Chapters 5 and 6 have discussed gate-level modeling and UDP modeling. This chapter describes module instantiations, generate statements and configurations.

9.1 *Module*

A module defines a basic unit in Verilog HDL. It is of the form:

```
module module_name ( port_list );
  Declarations_and_Statements
endmodule
```

The port list gives the list of ports through which the module communicates with the external modules.

9.2 Ports

A port can be declared as input, output or inout. A port by default is a net. However, it can be explicitly declared as a net. An output port can optionally be redeclared as a reg variable. In either the net declaration or the variable declaration, the net or variable must have the same size as the one specified in the port declaration. Here are some examples of port declarations.

```
module micro_proc (prog_ctr, instr_reg, next_addr);
  // Port declarations:
  input [3:1] prog_ctr;
  output [1:8] instr_reg;
  inout [16:1] next_addr;

  // Redeclarations:
  wire [16:1] next_addr; // Optional; but if specified
    // must have same range as in its port declaration.

  reg [1:8] instr_reg;
  /* instr_reg has been redeclared as a reg so that it can
    be assigned a value within an always statement or an
    initial statement. */
  . . .
endmodule
```

Port and data type declarations can be merged into one declaration, if need be. For example, for the module micro_proc, the port declarations can be rewritten as:

```
input wire [3:1] prog_ctr; // prog_ctr is a wire
                           // by default.
output reg [1:8] instr_reg;
inout wire [16:1] next_addr;
```

Port declarations can alternately appear in the port list directly rather than as declarations within the module - called the *module port declaration style* (the other style is the *module port list style*). Here is the above example rewritten using this style.

Guideline: Use the module port declaration style as the declaration of the port and its data type is in one place.

```
module micro_proc (
   // Port declarations:
   input wire [3:1] prog_ctr,   // Note comma-separated.
   output reg [1:8] instr_reg,
   inout wire [16:1] next_addr
  );

  // No port declarations within module.
  . . .
endmodule
```

Once a port is declared in the port list, you can not redeclare it within the module body. The ports can further be qualified as reg ports and/or as signed ports. Here is another example.

```
module remap_ctrl (
   input [31:0] rpc_addr,// Default is net and unsigned.
   input signed [31:0] rpc_rdata,    // Net and signed.
   output reg remap, ready,        // Reg and unsigned.
   output reg signed [31:0] rpc_wdata
     // rpc_wdata is a reg and signed.
  );
  . . .
endmodule
```

Note that all the port declarations are comma-separated, including multiple ports that share a common declaration such as `remap` and `ready`.

9.2.1 Parameter Ports

In addition to parameters being declared within a module, parameters can also be declared as a parameter port list. This is of the form:

```
module module_name
  # ( parameter param1 = value1, param2 = value2, . . .,
      parameter param3 = value3, . . .)
    ( port_list );
  . . .
endmodule
```

A range and signed specification can optionally be specified in the parameter declaration. Here is an example.

Guideline: Use the parameter port style for specifying parameters.

```
module sspm
  # ( parameter SIZE = 256, WIDTH = 8,
      parameter [WIDTH-1:0] HOLD_VALUE = 56,
      parameter DUMP_FILE = "dump.rpt")
    ( input chip_select, read_write,
      output [WIDTH-1:0] data
    );
  . . .
endmodule
```

If a parameter does not vary from one instance to another, that is, not instance-specific, then the parameter should be declared as a local parameter. Otherwise a parameter can either be declared within a module or as a parameter port.

9.3 Module Instantiation

A module can be instantiated in another module, thus creating hierarchy. A module instantiation statement is of the form:

```
module_name instance_name ( port_associations );
```

Guideline: Use u_<module_name> as instance name.

Port associations can be by position or by name; however, associations cannot be mixed. A port association is of the form:

```
port_expr                    // By position.
.PortName ( port_expr )      // By name.
```

Guideline: Use similar names for port name and port expression where possible.

where *port_expr* can be any of the following:

i. an identifier (a variable or a net)
ii. a bit-select
iii. a part-select
iv. a concatenation of the above
v. an expression (only for input ports)

In positional association, the port expressions connect to the ports of the module in the specified order. In association by name, the connection between the module port and the port expression is explicitly specified and thus the order of port associations is not important. Here is an example of a full-adder built using two half-adder modules; the logic diagram is shown in Figure 9-1.

Guideline: Always use named association when associating ports and parameters.

```
module half_adder (a, b, s, c);
  input a, b;
  output s, c;
  parameter AND_DELAY = 1, XOR_DELAY = 2;

  assign #XOR_DELAY s = a ^ b;
  assign #AND_DELAY c = a & b;
endmodule

module full_adder (p, q, cin, sum, cout);
  input p, q, cin;
  output sum, cout;
  parameter OR_DELAY = 1;
  wire s1, c1, c2;

  // Two module instantiations:
  // Associating by position.
  half_adder u1ha (p, q, s1, c1);

  // Associating by name.
  half_adder u2ha (.a(cin), .s(sum), .b(s1), .c(c2));

  // Gate instantiation:
  or #OR_DELAY u3or (cout, c1, c2);
endmodule
```

In the first module instantiation, `half_adder` is the name of the module, `u1ha` is the instance name and ports are associated by position, that is, `p` is connected to module (`half_adder`) port `a`, `q` is connected to module port `b`, `s1` to `s` and `c1` to module port `c`. In the second instantiation, the port association is by name, that is, the connections between the module (`half_adder`) ports and the port expressions are specified explicitly.

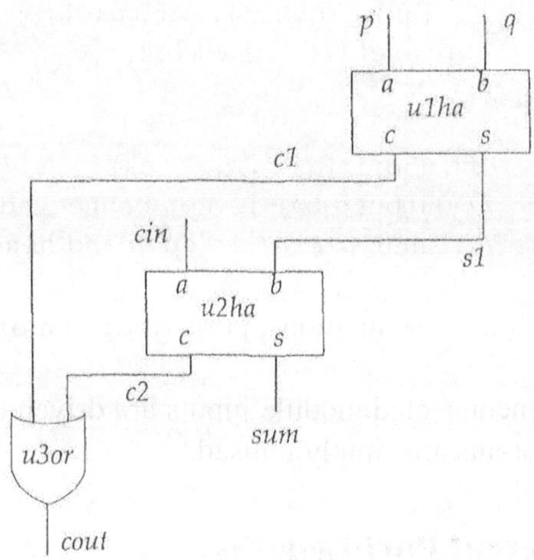

Figure 9-1 A full-adder using half-adder modules.

Here is another example of a module instantiation that uses different forms of port expression.

```
micro_proc u9micro_proc (
  urd_in[3:0], {wr_n, rd_n},
  status[0], status[1],
  & urd_out[0:7], tx_data
);
```

This instantiation shows that a port expression can be an identifier (`tx_data`), a bit-select (`status[0]`), a part-select (`urd_in[3:0]`), a concatenation (`{wr_n, rd_n}`), or an expression (`&urd_out[0:7]`); an expression can only be connected to an input port.

9.3.1 Unconnected Ports

Unconnected ports in an instantiation can be specified by leaving the port expression blank, such as in the following example.

```
dff u0dff (
  .q(qs), .qbar(), .data(d),
  .preset(), .clock(ck)
);                              // Associate by name.

dff u5dff (qs, , d, , ck);      // Associate by position.
// Output qbar is not connected.
// Input preset is open and hence set to value z.
```

In both the instantiations, ports `qbar` and `preset` are not connected.

Unconnected module inputs are driven to value z. Unconnected module outputs are simply unused.

9.3.2 Different Port Lengths

An implicit continuous assignment is assumed to exist between a port and a port expression. So when a port and the port expression are of different lengths, port matching is performed by using the same rules as that for a continuous assignment. Here is an example of port matching.

```
module child (psa, ppy);
  input [5:0] psa;
  output [2:0] ppy;
  . . .
endmodule

module top;
  wire [1:2] bdl;
  wire [2:6] mpr;

  child u6child (.psa(bdl), .ppy(mpr));
endmodule
```

In the module instantiation for `child`, there are two implicit continuous assignments.

```
// From port expression to port since psa
// is an input:
assign psa = bdl;
```

```
// From port to port expression since ppy is
// an output:
assign mpr = ppy;
```

bdl[2] is connected to psa[0] and bdl[1] is connected to psa[1]. Remaining input ports, psa[5],psa[4],psa[3],psa[2] are not connected and therefore have the value z. Similarly, mpr[6] is connected to ppy[0], mpr[5] is connected to ppy[1] and mpr[4] is connected to ppy[2]. See Figure 9-2.

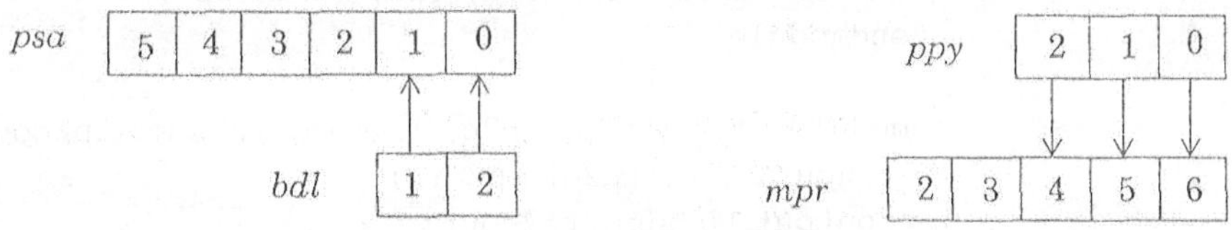

Figure 9-2 Port matching.

9.3.3 Module Parameter Values

When a module is instantiated in another module, the higher level module can change the value of the parameters in a lower level module. This can be done in two ways.

i. Defparam statement
ii. Module instance parameter value assignment

Defparam Statement

A defparam statement is of the form:

```
defparam hier_path_name1 = value1,
         hier_path_name2 = value2, . . . ;
```

The hierarchical path names of the parameters in a lower level module can be explicitly set by using such a statement (hierarchical path names are described in the next chapter). Here is an example. Modules full_adder and half_adder have been declared previously in this section.

```
module top (tpa, tpb, tps, tpc);
  input tpa, tpb;
  output tps, tpc;
  defparam u5ha.XOR_DELAY = 5,
                 // Parameter XOR_DELAY in instance u5ha.
           u5ha.AND_DELAY = 2;
                 // Parameter AND_DELAY in instance u5ha.

  half_adder u5ha (tpa, tpb, tps, tpc);
endmodule

module top2 (tp2p, tp2q, tp2cin, tp2sum, tp2cout);
  input tp2p, tp2q, tp2cin;
  output tp2sum, tp2cout;
  defparam
    u8fa.u1ha.XOR_DELAY = 2,     // Parameter XOR_DELAY
                    // in instance u1ha of instance u8fa.
    u8fa.u1ha.AND_DELAY = 3,     // Parameter AND_DELAY
                    // in instance u1ha of instance u8fa.
    u8fa.OR_DELAY = 3;           // Parameter OR_DELAY
                    // in instance u8fa.

  full_adder u8fa (tp2p, tp2q, tp2cin, tp2sum, tp2cout);
endmodule
```

Module Instance Parameter Value Assignment

In this method, the new parameter values are specified in the module instantiation itself. There are two forms in which parameter values can be specified:

i. Parameter value assignment by position (positional association): The first value corresponds to the first declared parameter, the second value corresponds to the second declared parameter, and so on.

ii. Parameter value assignment explicitly by name (named association): The values and the names of the parameters are explicitly specified. Therefore ordering of the parameter values is not important, and parameter values can be passed in any order. More importantly, not all parameter values have to be explicitly specified.

Here are the same examples as shown in the previous section, but this time, module instance parameter value assignment is used.

```
module top3 (tp3a, tp3b, tp3s, tp3c);
  input tp3a, tp3b;
  output tp3s, tp3c;

  half_adder #(5, 2) u4ha (tp3a, tp3b, tp3s, tp3c);
    // First value, 5, is that for parameter AND_DELAY,
    // the first parameter declared in module half_adder.
    // Second value, 2, is that for parameter XOR_DELAY,
    // the second parameter declared in module
    // half_adder. This is parameter value assignment by
    // position.

  // Following is parameter value assignment
  // explicitly by name.
  half_adder #(.XOR_DELAY(5), .AND_DELAY(2)) u12ha (
    tp3a, tp3b, tp3s, tp3c
  );
endmodule

module top4 (tp4p, tp4q, tp4cin, tp4sum, tp4cout);
  input tp4p, tp4q, tp4cin;
  output tp4sum, tp4cout;
  defparam
    u22fa.u1ha.XOR_DELAY = 2,      // Parameter XOR_DELAY
                                // in instance u1ha of instance u22fa.
    u22fa.u1ha.AND_DELAY = 3;      // Parameter AND_DELAY
                                // in instance u1ha of instance u22fa.

  full_adder #(3) u22fa (
    tp4p, tp4q, tp4cin, tp4sum, tp4cout
  ); // Value 3 is the new value for parameter OR_DELAY.
endmodule
```

In parameter value assignment by position, the order of parameter values in the instantiation must match the order of parameters declared in the lower-level module. In instance u4ha of the module top3, AND_DELAY has been set as 5 and XOR_DELAY has been set as 2.

The two modules, top3 and top4, illustrate the fact that module instance parameter value assignment can be used only to pass parameter values down one level of hierarchy (e.g. OR_DELAY), whereas the defparam statement can be used to override parameter values at any level of the hierarchy.

Note that the positional notation for specifying parameter values appears identical to that of a delay specified in a gate instantiation. This is no case for concern in a module instantiation since delays cannot be specified for a module in the same way as that for a gate instantiation.

Parameter values could also represent sizes. Here is an example that models a generic M-by-N multiplier.

```
module multiplier (opd_1, opd_2, result);
  parameter EM = 4, EN = 2; // Default values.
  input [EM : 1] opd_1;
  input [EN : 1] opd_2;
  output [EM + EN : 1] result;

  assign result = opd_1 * opd_2;
endmodule
```

This parameterized multiplier can now be instantiated in another design. Here is an instantiation of an 8-by-6 multiplier.

```
wire [1:8] pipe_reg;
wire [1:6] dbus;
wire [1:14] addr_counter;
. . .
multiplier #(.EN(6), .EM(8)) u0multiplier (
  pipe_reg, dbus, addr_counter
);
```

The first value 6 specifies a new value for parameter EN and the second value 8 specifies a new value for parameter EM.

When using named association, it is not necessary to specify values for all the parameters. Only those that need to be overriden need to be explicitly specified. Whereas when positional association is used to specify parameter values, if the last parameter was the only one that had to be changed, the entire list of parameter values have to be specified. The recommended practice is to specify parameter values using named association as it both provides the freedom of specifying only the ones you want and it is very clear and explicit as to which parameters are getting what values.

Guideline: Use named association when overriding parameter values.

Here is another example. This is a generic N-bit serial shift register.

```
module serial_shift
  # ( parameter SIZE = 8)
    ( input serial_in, sclk,
      output reg serial_out
    );
  reg [SIZE-1:0] save;

  always
    @(negedge sclk)
      {serial_out, save} <= {save, serial_in};
endmodule
```

This module can be instantiated in another module as:

```
// 5-bit shift register:
serial_shift #(.SIZE(5)) u0serial_shift (. . .);

// 8-bit shift register:
serial_shift u_serial_shift (. . .);
```

9.4 External Ports

In the module definition we have seen so far, the port list describes the list of ports visible outside the module. For example,

```
module scram_a (arb, ctrl, mem_blk, byte);
  input [0:3] arb;
  input ctrl;
  input [8:0] mem_blk;
```

```
  output [0:3] byte;
  . . .
endmodule
```

The module ports are arb, ctrl, mem_blk and byte. These are also the external ports, that is, in an instantiation, the external port names are used to specify the interconnections when associating ports by name. Here is an example of an instantiation of module scram_a.

```
scram_a u_scram_a (
  .byte(b1), .mem_blk(m1), .ctrl(c1), .arb(a1)
);
```

In module scram_a, the external port names are implicitly specified. Verilog HDL provides an explicit way to specify external port names. This is done by specifying a port of the form:

```
. external_port_name ( internal_port_name )
```

Here is the same example, but this time the external ports are explicitly specified.

```
module scram_b (
    .data(arb), .control(ctrl),
    .mem_word(mem_blk), .addr(byte)
  );
  input [0:3] arb;
  input ctrl;
  input [8:0] mem_blk;
  output [0:3] byte;
  . . .
endmodule
```

The module scram_b has external ports specified in this case which are data, control, mem_word and addr. The port list explicitly shows the connections between the external ports and the internal ports. Note that the external ports need not be declared whereas the internal ports of the module must be declared. The external ports are not visible within the module but are used in a module instantiation whereas internal ports must be declared within the module since they are visible within the module. In a module instantiation, the external ports are used as shown in the following example.

```
scram_b u_scram_b (
  .addr(a1), .data(d1), .control(c1),.mem_word(m1)
);
```

The two types of notation can be mixed in a port list for a module definition, that is, only some ports in a module definition may have external port names.

External port names are not used in module instantiations if module ports are being connected by position.

An internal port name can not only be an identifier, it can also be one of the following.

- a bit-select
- a part-select
- a concatenation of bit-select, part-select and identifier

Here is an example.

```
module scram_c (
    arb[0:2], ctrl,
    {mem_blk[0], mem_blk[1]}, byte[3]
  );
  input [0:3] arb;
  input ctrl;
  input [8:0] mem_blk;
  output [0:3] byte;
  . . .
endmodule
```

In the module definition for `scram_c`, the port list contains a part-select (`arb[0:2]`), an identifier (`ctrl`), a concatenation (`{mem_blk[0], mem_blk[1]}`) and a bit-select (`byte[3]`). In the case where the internal port is a bit-select, part-select or a concatenation, no external port name is implicitly specified. Consequently, in such a module instantiation, module ports must be connected through positional associations. Here is an example of such an instantiation.

```
scram_c u_scram_c (
  cab[4:6], ram_ctl, mmy[1:0], tcb
);
```

In this instantiation, ports are connected by positional associations; thus, cab[4:6] is connected to arb[0:2], ram_ctl is connected to ctrl, mmy[1] is connected to mem_blk[0], mmy[0] to mem_blk[1], and tcb is connected to byte[3]. arb[3] and mem_blk[8:2] are not connected to any signal and hence by default, these input signals would have the value z.

To use association by name in this situation (where an internal port is not an identifier), external port names must be explicitly specified for the ports in the module. This is shown in the following module definition for scram_d.

```
module scram_d (
    .data(arb[0:2]), .control(ctrl),
    .mem_word({mem_blk[0], mem_blk[1]}),
    .addr(byte[3])
  );
  input [0:3] arb;
  input ctrl;
  input [8:0] mem_blk;
  output [0:3] byte;
  . . .
endmodule
```

In the instantiation for module scram_d, ports can be connected by position or by name, but not mixed. Here is an example of an instantiation where ports are connected by name.

```
scram_d u_scram_d (
  .data(cab[4:6]), .control(ram_ctl),
  .mem_word(mmy[1:0]), .addr(tcb)
);
```

It is possible for a module to have an external port with no internal port. Here is an example of such a module.

```
module scram_e (
    .data( ), .control(ctrl),
    .mem_word({mem_blk[0], mem_blk[1]}),
    .addr( )
  );
  input ctrl;
  input [8:0] mem_blk;
  . . .
endmodule
```

Module scram_e has two external ports, data and addr, that are not connected to anything internal to the module.

Can an internal port be connected to more than one external port? Yes, Verilog HDL allows this. Here is an example.

```
module fan_out (
    .a(ctrl_in), .b(cond_out), .c(cond_out)
  );
  input ctrl_in;
  output cond_out;

  assign cond_out = ctrl_in;
endmodule
```

The internal port cond_out is connected to two external ports, b and c. So the value on cond_out appears on both b and c.

Consider the following example.

```
module ssp_ctrl (
    .wdata({write_bus[15:12], write_bus[3:0]})
  );
  input [15:0] write_bus;
endmodule
```

```
module top_ssp_ctrl;
  reg [7:0] ssp_select;

  ssp_ctrl u_ssp_ctrl (.wdata(ssp_select), . . .);
endmodule
```

What does this do? The external port name of module `ssp_ctrl` is `wdata` and the module `top_ssp_ctrl` selectively connects the eight bits of `ssp_select` to `write_bus[15:12]` and `write_bus[3:0]`.

9.5 Examples

Here is an example of a decade counter written in the structural style. The logic diagram is shown in Figure 9-3.

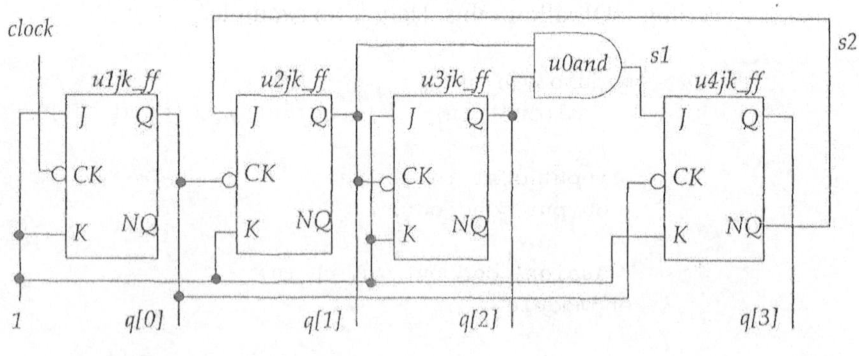

Figure 9-3 A decade counter.

```
module decade_ctr (clock, q);
  input clock;
  output [0:3] q;
  wire s1, s2;

  // Primitive gate instantiation:
  and u0and (s1, q[2], q[1]);
```

```
// Four module instantiations:
jk_ff
  u1jk_ff (
    .J(1'b1), .K(1'b1), .CK(clock), .Q(q[0]), .NQ()
  ),
  u2jk_ff (
    .J(s2), .K(1'b1), .CK(q[0]), .Q(q[1]), .NQ()
  ),
  u3jk_ff (
    .J(1'b1), .K(1'b1), .CK(q[1]), .Q(q[2]), .NQ()
  ),
  u4jk_ff (
    .J(s1), .K(1'b1), .CK(q[0]), .Q(q[3]), .NQ(s2)
  );
endmodule
```

Notice the usage of constants as values to input ports; also notice the unconnected ports.

Here is another example, this one is that of a three-bit up-down counter shown in Figure 9-4. The structural model follows.

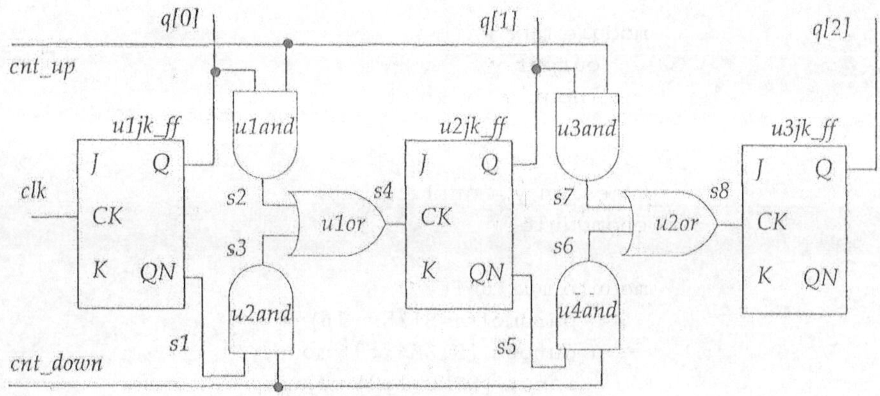

(J and K inputs of all flip-flops connected to 1)

Figure 9-4 A 3-bit up-down counter.

```
module up_down (clk, cnt_up, cnt_down, q);
  input clk, cnt_up, cnt_down;
  output [0:2] q;
  wire s1, s2, s3, s4, s5, s6, s7, s8;

  jk_ff
    u1jk_ff (1'b1, 1'b1, clk, q[0], s1),
    u2jk_ff (1'b1, 1'b1, s4, q[1], s5),
    u3jk_ff (1'b1, 1'b1, s8, q[2], );

  and
    u1and (s2, cnt_up, q[0]),
    u2and (s3, s1, cnt_down),
    u3and (s7, q[1], cnt_up),
    u4and (s6, s5, cnt_down);

  or
    u1or (s4, s2, s3),
    u2or (s8, s7, s6);
endmodule
```

Here is an example that shows how a replicated set of modules can be written as an array of instances.

```
module mux_unit (
    output y,
    input a, b, ctrl
  );

  assign y = ctrl ? a : b;
endmodule

module mux16bit
  # ( parameter SIZE = 16)
    ( output [SIZE-1:0] mout,
      input [SIZE-1:0] ma, mb,
      input select
    );

  mux_unit umux_unit [SIZE-1:0]
    (.y(mout), .a(ma), .b(mb), .ctrl(select));
endmodule
```

The instance `umux_unit` is an array of 16 instances. The scalar signal `select` fans out to all instances. The array of instances is equivalent to the following set of instantiations.

```
mux_unit umux_unit15 (.y(mout[15]), .a(ma[15]),
  .b(mb[15]), .ctrl(select));
mux_unit umux_unit14 (.y(mout[14]), .a(ma[14]),
  .b(mb[14]), .ctrl(select));
. . .
mux_unit umux_unit0 (.y(mout[0]), .a(ma[0]),
  .b(mb[0]), .ctrl(select));
```

9.6 Generate Statement

A generate statement allows for elaboration-time selection or replication of certain statements. Such statements include, amongst others, module instantiation, continuous assignment, always statement, initial statement and gate instantiation. Elaboration time is the phase before simulation starts when all design modules are linked together and hierarchical references are resolved. The generate statement is demarcated by the keywords **generate . . . endgenerate**. There are three kinds of statements that can appear within a generate statement.

i. Generate-loop
ii. Generate-case
iii. Generate-conditional

A generate statement is of the form:

```
generate
  // Generate-loop statements
  // Generate-case statements
  // Generate-conditional statements
  // Nested generate statements
endgenerate
```

9.6.1 Generate-loop

A generate-loop statement is used to replicate statements during elaboration, basically, it allows you to write a for loop on a structural element. Here is an example of a generic N-bit exclusive-or gate.

```
module nbit_xor
  # ( parameter SIZE = 16)
    ( input [SIZE-1:0] a, b,
      output [SIZE-1:0] y
    );
  genvar gv_i;

  generate
    for (gv_i = 0; gv_i < SIZE; gv_i = gv_i + 1)
      begin: sblka
        xor uxor (y[gv_i], a[gv_i], b[gv_i]);
      end
  endgenerate
endmodule
```

During elaboration time, the generate-loop is expanded. The body of the for-loop is replicated once for each value of the iteration. For the above example, after elaboration, you get:

```
xor sblka[0].uxor (y[0], a[0], b[0]);
xor sblka[1].uxor (y[1], a[1], b[1]);
xor sblka[2].uxor (y[2], a[2], b[2]);
. . .
```

In general, a generate-loop is of the form:

```
for ( initial_expression ; final_expression ;
      assignment )
  begin : label
    statements
  end
```

In the for-loop, a variable is needed that is initialized and modified on every iteration. Such a variable that is used is called a *genvar variable*. This variable must be declared using a *genvar declaration* and can only be used within a generate-loop statement. The genvar variable is used in forming the initial value and the genvar assignment. In the module nbit_xor, the genvar variable is gv_i. It is assigned to 0 initially and then incremented once through each iteration of the loop.

The generate block label is required and is used to reference any instance names that are local to the generate-loop. In the module nbit_xor, the block label is sblka. The hierarchical references to instance uxor are:

```
nbit_xor.sblka[0].uxor
nbit_xor.sblka[1].uxor
nbit_xor.sblka[2].uxor
. . .
```

It is possible to have local declarations within a generate statement as well. For example, if we were to include the following declaration in the block sblka:

```
wire phy2;
```

then there would be sixteen instances of wire phy2 with their hierarchical reference names as:

```
sblka[0].phy2
sblka[1].phy2
. . .
```

During elaboration, the for-loop is expanded, that is, the body of the for-loop is replicated once for each iteration. If there are multiple statements within the generate statement, all statements are replicated. Even though the example above showed only one gate instantiation, a generate statement can contain procedural statements as well. Here is another example, that of a ripple counter.

```
module ripple_counter
   # ( parameter BITS = 8)
     ( input count_clk, nreset,
       output [BITS-1:0] q
     );
  genvar gv_a;
```

```
jk_ff u0jk_ff (
  .J(1'b1), .K(1'b1), .NRESET (nreset),
  .CK(count_clk), .Q(q[0]), .NQ()
);

generate
  for (gv_a = 1; gv_a < BITS; gv_a = gv_a + 1)
    begin: gblk_a
      jk_ff  u1jk_ff (
        .J(1'b1), .K(1'b1), .NRESET (nreset),
        .CK(q[gv_a-1]), .Q(q[gv_a]), .NQ()
      );
    end
  endgenerate
endmodule
```

The genvar variable is `gv_a`. There is one module instance `u0jk_ff` instantiated outside of the generate statement. There are `BITS-1` number of other instances declared within the generate statement.

9.6.2 Generate-conditional

The generate-conditional statement allows for conditional selection of statements at elaboration time. The general form of this statement is:

```
if ( condition )
  statements
[ else
  statements ]
```

The *condition* must be a static condition, that is, computable at elaboration time (such a condition expression is dependent only on constants and parameters). The *statements* can be any set of statements that can appear in a module, for example, always statement, module instantiation and gate instantiation. During elaboration, based on the value of the condition, the appropriate set of statements are selected. Note that the condition may depend on a parameter whose value is passed in from a parent module and thus may not be fully computable until elaboration time.

Here is an example of a shift register that uses both a generate-loop statement and a generate-conditional statement.

```
module shift_register
  # ( parameter BITS = 8)
   ( input shift_in, clk, nreset,
     output shift_out
   );
  wire [BITS-1 : 0] tq;
  genvar gv_k;

  generate
    for (gv_k = 0; gv_k < BITS; gv_k = gv_k + 1)
      begin: gblk_x
        if (gv_k == BITS-1)
          dflip_flop u0dff (
            .d(serial_in), .nreset(nreset), .ck(clk),
            .q(tq[gv_k])
          );
        else
          if (gv_k == 0)
            dflip_flop u1dff (
              .d(tq[gv_k+1]), .nreset(nreset), .ck(clk),
              .q(serial_out)
            );
          else
            dflip_flop u2dff (
              .d(tq[gv_k+1]), .nreset(nreset), .ck(clk),
              .q(tq[gv_k])
            );
      end
  endgenerate
endmodule
```

During elaboration, the for-loop is expanded. If the value of the generate variable `gv_k` is `BITS-1`, then the first stage of the shift register is built (serial input goes into the `d` input of the flop). If the generate variable has the value 0, then the last stage of the shift register is instantiated (output of flop goes to `serial_out`). For all other values of the generate variable, the intermediate stages of the shift register are generated (`d` of the flop connects to the `q` of the previous flop). After elaboration (assuming value of `BITS` is 8), you get:

The value of BITS can be modified during the instantiation of the shift_register module or by using a defparam statement.

```
dflip_flop gblk_x[7].u0dff (
  .d(serial_in), .nreset(nreset), .ck(clk),
  .q(tq[7])
);
dflip_flop gblk_x[6].u2dff (
  .d(tq[7]), .nreset(nreset), .ck(clk), .q(tq[6])
);
dflip_flop gblk_x[5].u2dff (
  .d(tq[6]), .nreset(nreset), .ck(clk), .q(tq[5])
);
. . .
dflip_flop gblk_x[0].u1dff (
  .d(tq[1]), .nreset(nreset), .ck(clk),
  .q(serial_out)
);
```

Here is another example of a generate statement with the generate-conditional form.

```
module adder
  # ( parameter SIZE = 4 )
   ( input [SIZE-1:0] a, b,
     output [SIZE-1:0] sum,
     output carry_out
   );
  wire [SIZE-1:0] carry;
  genvar gv_k;

  generate
   for (gv_k = 0; gv_k < SIZE; gv_k = gv_k + 1)
     begin: gen_blk_adder
      if (gv_k == 0)
        half_adder u_ha (
          .a(a[gv_k]), .b(b[gv_k]), .sum(sum[gv_k]),
          .carry_out(carry[gv_k])
        );
      else
        full_adder u_fa (
          .a(a[gv_k]), .b(b[gv_k]),
          .carry_in(carry[gv_k-1]), .sum(sum[gv_k]),
          .carry_out(carry[gv_k])
        );
     end
```

```
    endgenerate
  endmodule
```

9.6.3 Generate-case

A generate-case is similar to a generate-conditional except that a case statement is used to model conditional selection. The general form of this statement is:

```
case ( case_expression )
  case_value1 , case_value2 , case_valueN :
    statements
  case_valueM :
    statements
  . . .
  default :
    statements
endcase
```

The value of the case expression must be computable at elaboration time. And based on its value, the set of statements that belong to the appropriate branch are selected for execution. Here is an example of a generate-case statement that selects an appropriate behavior for the add operation based upon a parameter IMPLEMENTATION_LEVEL.

```
module my_special_adder
  # ( parameter SIZE = 16,
      parameter IMPLEMENTATION_LEVEL = 0 )
    ( input [SIZE-1:0] arg1, arg2,
      output [SIZE-1:0] result
    );
  generate
    case (IMPLEMENTATION_LEVEL)
      0 : assign result = arg1 + arg2;
      1 : ripple_adder u_ra (
              .sum(result), .a(arg1), .b(arg2)
          );
      2 : cla u_cla (
              .sum(result), .a(arg1), .b(arg2)
          );
```

```
        3 : fast_cla u_fcla (
              .sum(result), .a(arg1), .b(arg2)
            );
      endcase
    endgenerate
  endmodule
```

The default branch is optional. If IMPLEMENTATION_LEVEL has a value greater than 3, then none of the statements specified are selected for execution.

9.7 *Configurations*

Before configurations are presented, let us first describe the notion of libraries. A library is a place where compiled configurations, UDPs and modules (also collectively called *cells*) are stored. The library is a logical or a symbolic library. It contains a number of compiled source descriptions.

A library with its contents is declared using a *library declaration.*

```
library library_name "file_name(s)" ;
```

The specified file names are compiled into the logical library.

A list of such library declarations is specified in a *library map file*. A library map file can be included in another library map file using the *include statement*.

```
include library_map_file ;
```

Here is an example of a library map file.

A cell is a UDP, configuration or a module.

```
// File: esoc_library.map
library lib_global "gbl/global_blocks.vg";
library lib_rtl    "./*.vg";
library lib_work   "/home/bond/IP/usb*.v";
include            "../../global_lib_definitions";
library lib_gate   "./syn/gate/*.vg";
```

The library map file esoc_library.map contains four library declarations and one include statement. The four libraries declared are lib_global, lib_rtl, lib_work, and lib_gate. File gbl/global_blocks.vg is compiled into library lib_global. All files in current directory with file extension ".vg" are compiled into library lib_rtl, and so on. Paths specified in the file names are relative to the location of the library map file.

The library map file is read by the Verilog HDL parser before parsing any of the source code. You can have multiple library map files. A tool that supports Verilog HDL must provide a mechanism to support specification of such multiple library map files.

As source files are compiled, the cells within each source file are saved in the corresponding library as specified in the library map file. For example, when the file usb_host.v is compiled, all cells within the file get stored in the library lib_work.

Getting back to configurations, a configuration is used to specify the bindings of instances to modules in a library, that is, it specifies which module source code is to be used for each instance of a module. An example of such a binding is: bind instance u1 in module timer to module fsm_rtl in library lib_fsm.

A configuration, along with a UDP and a module, is a top-level block in Verilog HDL. It is specified outside of a module. It can be in the same file as the library map file or it can be in a separate file.

Guideline: Put configurations in a separate file from the design.

So basically a configuration specifies a set of rules to be used in mapping instances to cells in a library. The basic syntax of a configuration is:

```
configuration config_name ;
  design rootModuleName ;
  default liblist list_of_libraries ;
  instance instance_name use library .cell ;
  instance instance_name liblist list_of_libraries ;
  cell cell_name use library.cell ;
  cell cell_name liblist list_of_libraries ;
endconfig
```

Here is a simple example of a configuration.

```
config config_usb;
  design lib_work.usb;
  default liblist lib_global lib_rtl;
  instance u6 use lib_work.usb_fsm;
endconfig
```

The name of configuration is config_usb. The next line specifies the design or the module that is being configured, module usb that resides in library lib_work. The default search rule for cells is specified by the default statement to be the libraries lib_global and lib_rtl, in the order specified. The instance statement provides an exception to the default binding rules. For instance u6, map to module usb_fsm in library lib_work.

When a configuration has an instance statement such as:

```
instance u2 liblist lib_a lib_b lib_c;
```

this implies that for instance u2, search library lib_a first, then lib_b, and then library lib_c.

Configurations can even be hierarchical. For example, an instance binding can specify a binding to a configuration such as:

```
instance u8 use lib_usb.my_config;
```

Here is an example scenario.

```
// File: f1.v; contains 2 cells.
module m1;
  m3 u0 . . .
  m3 u1 . . .
endmodule

module m2;
  m3 u2 . . .
  m3 u3 . . .
endmodule
```

```
// File: f2.v; contains 2 cells.
module m3;
  m4 u4 . . .
endmodule

primitive p1;
. . .
endprimitive

// File: f3.v; contains 2 cells.
module m3;
  . . .
endmodule

config c1;
  . . .
endconfig
```

The library map contains:

```
// File: f_lib.map
library lib_p f1.v;
library lib_q f2.v;
library lib_r f3.v;
```

After compilation, the following are the contents of the libraries.

```
Library lib_p   contains cells m1, m2
Library lib_q   contains cells m3, p1
Library lib_r   contains cells m3, c1
```

Notice that libraries `lib_q` and `lib_r` each contain a module called `m3` which are distinct. An example configuration for a top module `m1` may look like this.

```
config m1_config;
  design lib_p.m1;
  default liblist lib_q lib_r;
  instance m1.u0 use lib_r.m3;
  instance m1.u1 use lib_p.m2;
endconfig
```

Here is another example.

```
config uart_config;
  design lib_blocks.uart;
  default liblist lib_rtl;
  instance receive.urx use lib_gates.rxo;
endconfig
```

The name of the configuration is `uart_config`. The configuration is described for module `uart` that resides in library `lib_blocks`. The default search path for linking all instances is to look in library `lib_rtl`. Therefore link all instances in design `uart` to corresponding modules in `lib_rtl`, except link the instance `receive.urx` to the module `rxo` in library `lib_gates`.

9.8 *Exercises*

1. What is the difference between a gate instantiation and a module instantiation?
2. What are the values of ports when they are left open, that is, they are not connected?
3. Write a module that instantiates the module `full_adder` described in Section 9.3 with an `OR_DELAY` of 4, an `XOR_DELAY` of 7 and an `AND_DELAY` of 5.
4. Using the module `full_adder` described in this chapter, write a structural model for a 4-bit ALU that performs addition and subtraction.
5. Using the module `mux4x1` described in Section 5.11, write a structural model for a 16-to-1 multiplexer.
6. Describe a generic `N`-bit counter with asynchronous negative level reset. Instantiate this generic counter as a 5-bit counter. Verify this 5-bit counter using a test bench.

7. Using a generate statement, write a model for a priority multiplexer that selects a bit in an `N`-bit vector `qmv_addr` whose index matches the leftmost 1 in another `N`-bit vector `pr_select`.

❑

10

Other Topics

This chapter describes miscellaneous topics such as functions, tasks, hierarchy, value change dump file and compiler directives.

10.1 *Tasks*

A task is like a procedure, it provides the ability to execute common pieces of code from several different places in a description. This common piece of code is written as a task (using a task definition) so that it can be called (by a task call) from different places in a design description. A task can contain timing controls, that is, delays, and it can call other tasks and functions as well.

10.1.1 Task Definition

A task is defined using a task definition. It is of the form:

```
task [automatic] task_id ;
  [ declarations ]
  procedural_statement
endtask
```

A task can have zero, one, or more arguments. Values are passed to and from a task through arguments. In addition to input arguments (receive values for a task), a task can have output arguments (return values from a task) and inout arguments as well. A task definition is written within a module declaration. Here is an example of a task definition.

```
module esoc;
  parameter MAXBITS = 8;

  task reverse_bits;
    input [MAXBITS -1 : 0] data_in;
    output [MAXBITS -1 : 0] data_out;
    integer k;

    begin
      for (k = 0; k < MAXBITS; k = k + 1)
        data_out[MAXBITS - k - 1] = data_in[k];
    end
  endtask
  . . .
endmodule
```

The inputs and outputs of a task are declared at the beginning of the task. The order of these inputs and outputs specify the order to be used in a task call. Here is another example of a task.

```
task rotate_left;
  inout [1:16] input_array;
  input [0:3] start_bit, stop_bit, rotate_by;
  reg fill_value;
  integer mac1, mac3;

  begin
    for (mac3 = 1; mac3 <= rotate_by; mac3 = mac3 + 1)
      begin
        fill_value = input_array[stop_bit];

        for (mac1 = stop_bit; mac1 >= start_bit + 1;
              mac1 = mac1 - 1)
          input_array[mac1] = input_array[mac1 - 1];

        input_array[start_bit] = fill_value;
```

```
        end
      end
    endtask
```

fill_value is a local variable that is directly visible only within the task. The first argument in this task is the inout array, input_array, followed by the three inputs, start_bit, stop_bit and rotate_by.

In addition to the task arguments, a task can reference any variable defined in the module in which the task is declared. An example is shown in the next section.

A task can be declared as *automatic*. In such a task, all local variables that are declared within the task are allocated dynamically for each task call, that is, the local variables in a task call cannot influence two separate or concurrent task calls. In a static (non-automatic) task, each task call shares the same storage space for local variables. A task is specified as automatic by using the keyword **automatic** such as:

```
task automatic rotate_right;
  integer mac_addr;
  . . .
endtask
```

In this case, each task call gets its own storage space for variable mac_addr.

The arguments of a task can alternately be defined using the *inline argument declaration style.*

Guideline: Use the inline argument declaration style.

```
task [automatic] task_id ( [ argument_declarations ] );
  [ other_declarations ]
  procedural_statement
endtask
```

Here is an example of a task written using this style.

```
task automatic apply_address (
    input [SIZE-1:0] address,
    output success
  );
```

```
    reg check_flag;
    . . .
  endtask
```

10.1.2 Task Calling

A task is called (or enabled, as it is said in Verilog HDL) by a task enable statement that specifies the argument values passed to the task and the variables that receive the results. A task enable statement is a procedural statement and can thus appear within an always or an initial statement. It is of the form:

```
task_id [ ( expr1 , expr2 , . . . , exprN ) ] ;
```

The list of arguments must match the order of input, output and inout declarations in the task definition. In addition, arguments are passed by value, not by reference. An important distinction between a task and a procedure in other high-level programming languages such as Pascal is that a task can be called more than once concurrently with each call having its own control. The biggest point to be careful of is that a variable declared within a task is static, that is, it never disappears or gets re-initialized. Thus one task call might modify a local variable whose value may be read by another task call. However if it is an automatic task, then the local variables are not static but get redefined for every task call (and therefore behave as procedures in other high-level programming languages).

Here is an example of a task call for the task `reverse_bits` whose definition was given in the previous section.

```
// Reg variable declaration:
reg [MAXBITS - 1 : 0] hdlc_ctr, save_ctr;

reverse_bits (hdlc_ctr, save_ctr);   // Calling task.
```

The value of `hdlc_ctr` is passed as the input value, that is, to `data_in`. The output of the task `data_out` is returned back to `save_ctr`. Note that because a task can contain timing controls, a task may return a value later in time than when it was called.

The output and inout arguments in a task call must be variables because a task enable statement is a procedural statement. In the above example, `save_ctr` must be declared as a variable.

Here is an example of a task that references a variable that is not passed in through its argument list. Even though referencing global variables is considered bad programming style, it is sometimes useful as shown in the following example.

```
module global_var;
  reg [0:7] qram [0:63];
  integer index;
  reg check_bit;

  task get_parity;
    input [7:0] address;
    output parity_bit;

    parity_bit = ^ qram[address];
  endtask

  initial
    for (index = 0; index <= 63; index = index + 1)
      begin
        get_parity (index, check_bit);
        $display ("Parity bit of memory word %d is %b.",
                  index, check_bit);
      end
endmodule
```

The address of the memory `qram` is passed as an argument and the memory is referenced directly within the task.

A task can have delays and/or it can wait for certain events to occur. However, an assignment to an output argument is not passed to the calling argument until the task exits.

```
module task_wait;
  reg no_clock;

  task generate_waveform;
    output qclock;
    begin
      qclock = 1;
      #2 qclock = 0;
      #2 qclock = 1;
      #2 qclock = 0;
    end
  endtask

  initial
    generate_waveform (clk_ssp);
endmodule
```

The assignments to `qclock` do not appear on `clk_ssp`, that is, no waveform appears on `clk_ssp`; only the final assignment to `qclock`, which is 0, appears on `clk_ssp` after the task returns. One way to avoid this problem is to make `qclock` as a global variable, that is, declare it outside the task.

Here is an example that illustrates the differences between an automatic and a non-automatic task.

```
task automatic check_cnt;
  reg [3:0] count;
  begin
    $display ("At beginning of task, count = ", count);

    if (reset)
      count = 0;

    count = count + 1;

    $display ("At end of task, count = ", count);
  end
endtask
```

Since `check_cnt` is an automatic task, for each task call, a separate reg variable `count` is allocated.

```
reg reset;
. . .
reset = 1;
check_cnt ();
. . .
reset = 0;
check_cnt ();
. . .
```

causes the following to print:

```
. . .
At beginning of task, count = xxxx
At end of task, count = 1
. . .
At beginning of task, count = xxxx
At end of task, count = xxxx
```

If the task `check_cnt` were not an automatic task (by removing the keyword **automatic**), then the following would print:

```
. . .
At beginning of task, count = xxxx
At end of task, count = 1
. . .
At beginning of task, count = 1
At end of task, count = 2
```

Since the reg variable `count` is static, that is, not destroyed, the second call to task `check_cnt` used the value of `count` from the previous call to task `check_cnt` and therefore `count` has the value 1 when `check_cnt` is called the second time.

10.2 Functions

Functions, similar to tasks, also provide the capability to execute common code from different places in a module. The difference from a task is that a function can return only one value, it cannot contain any delays (must execute in zero time) and it cannot call any other task. In addition, a function must have at least one input. No output or inout declarations are allowed in a function. A function may call other functions.

10.2.1 Function Definition

A function definition can appear anywhere in a module declaration. It is of the form:

```
function [automatic] [signed]
   [range_or_type] function_id;
  input_declaration
  other_declarations
  procedural_statement
endfunction
```

An input to the function is declared using the input declaration. If no range or type is specified with the function definition, then a 1-bit return value is assumed. The return type can be one of **real**, **integer**, **time** or **realtime**. The return value of a function can be declared to be a signed value by using the keyword **signed**. Here is an example of a function.

```
module function_example;
  parameter MAXBITS = 8;

  function [MAXBITS-1:0] reverse_bits;
    input [MAXBITS-1:0] data_in;
    integer k;
    begin
      for (k = 0; k < MAXBITS; k = k + 1)
        reverse_bits[MAXBITS - k - 1] = data_in[k];
    end
  endfunction
  . . .
endmodule
```

The name of the function is `reverse_bits`. The function returns a vector of size `MAXBITS`. The function has one input, `data_in`. `k` is a local integer.

The function definition implicitly declares a reg variable internal to the function, with the same name and range as the function. A function returns a value by assigning a value to this variable explicitly in the function definition. An assignment to this variable must therefore be present within a function definition. Here is another example of a function.

```
function parity;
  input [0:31] par_vector;
  reg [0:3] result;
  integer j;
  begin
    result = 0;

    for (j = 0; j <= 31; j = j + 1)
      if (par_vector[j] == 1)
        result = result + 1;

    parity = result % 2;
  end
endfunction
```

In this function, `parity` is the name of the function. Since no size has been specified, the function returns a 1-bit value. `result` and `j` are local variables. Note that the last procedural assignment assigns a value to the variable which returns the value from the function (a variable with the same name as function is implicitly declared within the function).

Here is an example of a function that returns a signed value.

```
parameter SIZE = 32;
localparam ADD = 0, SUB = 1, AND = 2, OR = 3;
. . .
function signed [SIZE-1:0] alu;
  input signed [SIZE-1:0] opd1, opd2;
  input [1:0] operation;

  case (operation)
    ADD : alu = opd1 + opd2;
    SUB : alu = opd1 - opd2;
    AND : alu = opd1 & opd2;
    OR  : alu = opd1 | opd2;
```

```
    endcase
  endfunction
```

A function can be specified as an automatic function by using the keyword **automatic**. For example,

```
function automatic parity;
. . .
endfunction
```

In an automatic function, all local variables are allocated new for each function call. In a non-automatic function, the local variables are static, that is, there is only one copy of the local variables that are used by all calls to the function. Automatic functions support writing recursive functions (since each call allocates its own storage space). Here is an example of a recursive function that computes the factorial of a number.

```
function automatic [31:0] factorial;
  input [31:0] fac_of;

  factorial = (fac_of == 1) ? 1 :
                factorial(fac_of - 1) * fac_of;
endfunction
```

There is an alternate style for describing the arguments to a function, that of using inline argument declaration style.

Guideline: Use inline argument declaration style.

```
function [automatic] [signed]
     [range_or_type] function_id (
   input_declarations
  );
  [ other_declarations ]
  procedural_statement
endfunction
```

Here is the factorial example written using this style.

```
function automatic [31:0] factorial (
    input [31:0] fac_of
  );

  factorial = (fac_of == 1) ? 1 :
                 factorial(fac_of - 1) * fac_of;
endfunction
```

Here is another example of an automatic function that converts a 3-digit string to its equivalent string form, for example, an integer value of 329 is converted to the string "329".

```
parameter NUM_DIGITS = 3, BYTE = 8;

function automatic [NUM_DIGITS*BYTE:1] to_string (
    input integer number // The 3-digit number.
  );
  integer unit_digit, ten_digit, hun_digit;
  begin
    unit_digit = number % 10;
    ten_digit = (number / 'd10) % 10;
    hun_digit = (number / 'd100) % 10;

    to_string[3*BYTE:2*BYTE+1] = "0" + hun_digit;
    to_string[2*BYTE:BYTE+1] = "0" + ten_digit;
    to_string[BYTE:1] = "0" + unit_digit;
    /* to_string now contains the string equivalent
       of the three-digit integer */
  end
endfunction
```

10.2.2 Function Call

A function call is part of an expression. It is of the form:

func_id (expr1 , expr2 , . . . , exprN)

Here is an example of a function call.

```
// Reg declaration:
reg [MAXBITS-1:0] remap_reg, rmp_rev;
```

```
rmp_rev = reverse_bits(remap_reg);
  // Function call in right-hand side expression.
```

Similar to a task, all local variables declared within a function definition are static, that is, local variables within a function retain their values between multiple invocations of the function; this is true only for non-automatic functions. In an automatic function, all variables are allocated dynamically for each call.

A parameter value in a function can be overriden by using a defparam statement.

```
module test;
  time current_time;

  function watch (
      input time ctime
    );
    parameter RESOLUTION = 60;
    . . .
  endfunction

  defparam watch.RESOLUTION = 3600;

  assign print_time = watch(current_time);
endmodule
```

10.2.3 Constant Functions

A constant function is a function that can be evaluated to a constant value at elaboration time (that is before simulation starts). A constant function can be used wherever constant expressions are allowed, such as in vector width declarations.

The syntax and format of a constant function is exactly identical to that of a regular function except that certain modeling style has to be followed in describing the behavior of the function so that the function is computable at elaboration time. For example, no access to global variables are allowed, and no system functions can be called. System tasks are ignored and a constant function can call another constant function. Here is an example of an use of a constant function.

```
module pack_a;
  parameter VECTOR_LSB = 0, VECTOR_MSB = 7;
  reg [get_largest(VECTOR_LSB, VECTOR_MSB) : 0]
     mmc_address;

  function integer get_largest ( // Constant function.
    input integer first_bound, second_bound
   );

    get_largest = (first_bound > second_bound) ?
                          first_bound : second_bound;
  endfunction
endmodule
```

10.3 System Tasks and Functions

Verilog HDL provides built-in system tasks and system functions, that is, tasks and functions that are predefined in the language. These are grouped as follows:

i. Display tasks
ii. File I/O tasks
iii. Timescale tasks
iv. Simulation control tasks
v. PLA modeling tasks
vi. Stochastic modeling tasks
vii. Conversion functions
viii. Probabilistic distribution functions
ix. String formatting
x. Command line arguments

PLA modeling tasks and stochastic modeling tasks are outside the scope of this book.

10.3.1 Display Tasks

The display system tasks are used for displaying and printing information. These system tasks are further characterized into:

- Display and write tasks.
- Strobed monitoring.
- Continuous monitoring.

Display and Write Tasks

The syntax is of the form:

```
task_name ( format_specification1 , argument_list1 ,
            format_specification2 , argument_list2 ,
            . . . ,
            format_specificationN , argument_listN );
```

where a *task_name* is one of:

```
$display   $displayb $displayh $displayo
$write     $writeb   $writeh   $writeo
```

The display task prints the specified information to standard output with a end-of-line character, while the write task prints the specified information without an end-of-line character. The following escape sequences can be used for format specification.

```
%h or %H   : hexadecimal
%d or %D   : decimal
%o or %O   : octal
%b or %B   : binary
%c or %C   : ASCII character
%v or %V   : net signal strength
%m or %M   : hierarchical name
%s or %S   : string
%t or %T   : current time format
```

If no format specification exists for an argument, then the default is:

```
decimal     : for $display and $write
binary      : for $displayb and $writeb
octal       : for $displayo and $writeo
hexadecimal : for $displayh and $writeh
```

Special characters can be printed using the following escape sequences.

```
\n       newline
\t       tab
\\       the \ character
\"       the " character
\OOO     the character with octal value OOO
%%       the % character
```

Here are some examples.

```
$display ("Simulation time is %t", $time);

$display ($time, " : r=%b, s=%b, q=%b, qb=%b",
   r, s, q, qb); // Time is displayed in decimal since no
               // format specification has been specified.

//Can have multiple arguments and split
//over multiple lines:
$display ("At time %t,", $time,
              " the value is %d.", tube_rst);

$write ("Simulation time is");
$write (" %t\n", $time);
```

The following is what is displayed when above statements are executed for some values of **$time**, r, s, q, qb, and tube_rst.

```
Simulation time is          10
                            10 : r=1, s=0, q=0, qb=1
At time 10, the value is 6.
Simulation time is          10
```

Strobe Tasks

The strobe tasks are:

```
$strobe    $strobeb    $strobeh $strobeo
```

These system tasks display the simulation data at the specified time but at the end of the time step. "End of time step" implies that all events have been processed for the specified time step.

```
always
  @(posedge reset)
    $strobe ("The flip-flop value is %b at time %t",
             q, $time);
```

When `reset` has a positive edge, the **$strobe** task prints the values of `q` and the current simulation time. Here is the output generated for some values of `q` and **$time**. Values are printed every time `reset` has a positive edge.

```
The flip-flop value is 1 at time 17
The flip-flop value is 0 at time 24
The flip-flop value is 1 at time 26
```

Format specifications are same as that for display and write tasks.

The strobe task differs from the display task in that the display task is executed at the time the statement is encountered, while the execution of the strobe task is postponed to the end of the time step. The following example helps clarify this further.

```
integer wait_timer;

initial
  begin
    wait_timer = 1;
    $display ("After first assignment, ",
              "wait_timer has value %d", wait_timer);
    $strobe ("When strobe is executed, ",
            "wait_timer has value %d", wait_timer);
```

```
    wait_timer = 2;
    $display ("After second assignment, ",
              "wait_timer has value %d", wait_timer);
  end
```

The output produced is:

```
After first assignment, wait_timer has value 1
After second assignment, wait_timer has value 2
When strobe is executed, wait_timer has value 2
```

The first **$display** task prints the value of `wait_timer` as 1 (from the first assignment to `wait_timer`). The second **$display** task prints the value of `wait_timer` as 2 (from the second assignment to `wait_timer`). The **$strobe** task prints the value of `wait_timer` as 2, the value it holds at the end of the time step.

Monitor Tasks

The monitor tasks are:

```
$monitor   $monitorb   $monitorh   $monitoro
```

These tasks monitor the specified arguments continuously. Whenever there is a change of value in an argument in the argument list, the entire argument list is displayed at the end of the time step. Here is an example.

```
initial
  $monitor ("At %t, d = %d, clk = %d ", $time, d, clk,
            "and q is %b", q);
```

When the monitor task is executed, a continuous monitor is set on `d`, `clk` and `q`. If any of these change values, the entire argument list is displayed. Here is a sample output for some changes on `d`, `clk` and `q`.

```
At        24, d = x, clk = x and q is 0
At        25, d = x, clk = x and q is 1
At        30, d = 0, clk = x and q is 1
At        35, d = 0, clk = 1 and q is 1
At        37, d = 0, clk = 0 and q is 1
At        43, d = 1, clk = 0 and q is 1
```

The format specification is the same as that for a display task. Only one monitor can be active at any time.

A monitor cannot be set on time variables or functions returning time values; this includes the system function **$time**. Furthermore, **$monitor** values are displayed only if there is at least one change in value of the variables being monitored. The **$monitor** tracks only changes in the displayed variables. Consider the following example.

```
$monitor ("Net value, as a 4-state value, is %b",
                matrix_enable);
```

If the strength changes from `St0` to `Pull0`, nothing will be displayed. However if the task call were changed to:

```
$monitor ("Net in full-strength form is %v",
                matrix_enable);
```

then the **$monitor** is executed and the message displayed.

Monitoring can be turned on and off by using the following two system tasks.

```
$monitoroff;  // Disables active monitor.

$monitoron;   // Enables most recent monitor.
```

These provide a mechanism to control dumping of value changes. The **$monitoroff** task turns off monitoring so that no more messages are displayed. The **$monitoron** task is used to enable monitoring.

10.3.2 File I/O Tasks

Opening and Closing Files

A system function **$fopen** is available for opening a file.

```
integer file_pointer = $fopen (file_name, mode) ;
  // The $fopen system function returns an integer value
  // (a pointer) to the file after opening the file in
  // the specified mode.
```

while the following system task can be used to close a file.

```
$fclose (file_pointer);
```

The *mode* can be one of :

- "r", "rb": Open file for reading at beginning of file. Issue error if file does not exist.
- "w", "wb": Open file for writing at beginning of file or create file if it does not exist.
- "a", "ab": Open file for writing at end of file or create file if it does not exist.
- "r+", "r+b", "rb+": Open file for reading and writing at beginning of file. Issue error message if file does not exist.
- "w+", "w+b", "wb+": Open file for reading and writing at beginning of file or create file it it does not exist.
- "a+", "a+b", "ab+": Open file for reading and writing at end of file or create file if it does not exist.

The "b" refers to opening binary files. Here is an example of its usage.

```
integer tq_file;

initial
  begin
    tq_file = $fopen ("~/jb/div.tq", "r+");
    . . .
    $fclose (tq_file);
  end
```

Writing out to a File

The display, write, strobe and monitor system tasks have a corresponding counterpart that can be used to write information to a file. These are:

```
$fdisplay $fdisplayb $fdisplayh $fdisplayo
$fwrite   $fwriteb   $fwriteh   $fwriteo
$fstrobe  $fstrobeb  $fstrobeh  $fstrobeo
$fmonitor $fmonitorb $fmonitorh $fmonitoro
$fflush
```

The first argument for all these tasks is a file pointer. Remaining arguments for the task is a list of pairs of format specification followed by an argument list. Here is an example that illustrates this.

```
integer vec_file;

initial
  begin
    vec_file = $fopen ("div.vec", "w");
    . . .
    $fdisplay (vec_file, "The simulation time is %t",
                $time);
      // The first argument vec_file is the file pointer.
    $fclose (vec_file);
  end
```

Upon execution of the **$fdisplay** task, the following statement appears in the file `div.vec`.

```
The simulation time is              0
```

The **$fflush** task flushes the output buffer to the output.

The `%u` (`%U`) or `%z` (`%Z`) format can be used to write out data in binary unformatted two-value or four-value respectively. Any **x** or **z** values is treated as a 0 by the `%u` format specification. The `%z` format writes out a 4-value binary representation of the data. The values **x** and **z** are also supported.

```
$fwrite (fp, "%u", usb_phase1);
$fdisplay (fp, "%z", i2c_mem[index]);
```

Reading from a File

There are two system tasks available for reading memory data from a file. These tasks read data from a text file and load the data into memory. These system tasks are:

```
$readmemb    $readmemh
```

The text file can contain white spaces, comments and binary (for **$readmemb**) or hexadecimal (for **$readmemh**) numbers. Each number is separated by white space. When the system task is executed, each number read is assigned to an address in memory. The beginning address corresponds to the leftmost index of the memory.

```
reg [0:3] rx_mem [0:63];

initial
  $readmemb ("ones_and_zeros.vec", rx_mem);
    // Each number read in is assigned to memory
    // locations starting from 0 to 63.
```

Optionally an explicit address can also be specified in the system task call, such as:

```
$readmemb ("rx.vec", rx_mem, 15, 30);
  // The first number read from the file "rx.vec" is
  // stored in address 15, next one at 16, and so on until
  // address 30.
```

An address may explicitly be given in the text file as well. The address is of the form:

```
@address_in_hexadecimal
```

In such a case, the system task reads the data into the specified address. Subsequent numbers are loaded from that address onwards.

There are additional system tasks and functions available that can be used to read data from files.

```
$fread     : Reads binary data from file into memory.
$fgetc     : Read a character at a time from a file.
$fgets     : Read a line at a time from a file.
$ungetc    : Insert a character back into a file.
$frewind   : Rewind to beginning of file.
$fseek     : Move to the location specified by
             the offset.
$ftell     : Returns the offset from the beginning
             of the file.
$fscanf    : Read formatted data from file.
$ferror    : To help determine the cause of an error
             after a read task is executed.
```

The **$fread** system function reads binary data from a file into memory or a variable.

```
integer status;
integer fp;
reg [15:0] usb_phl;
reg [31:0] i2c_ram [127:0];

fp = $fopen ("usb_test.dat", "r");
status = $fread (usb_phl, fp); // Reads 16 bits of binary
   // data into reg variable usb_phl.

status = $fread (i2c_ram, fp);
status = $fread (i2c_ram, fp, 63, 10); // Read from file
   // into memory starting from address 63 and read
   // into 10 locations of memory.
```

Annotating from a SDF file

Timing data in a SDF file can be read in using the **$sdf_annotate** system task. The timing annotation can be applied to a module at any level of the hierarchy.

SDF: Standard Delay Format, IEEE Std 1497.

```
$sdf_annotate ("uart.sdf", uart_tb.uart);
// Apply the SDF file "uart.sdf" to the
// submodule uart_tb.uart.
```

10.3.3 Timescale Tasks

The system task:

```
$printtimescale
```

displays the time unit and time precision for the specified module. The **$printtimescale** task with no arguments specified prints the time unit and time precision for the module that contains this task call. If a hierarchical path name to a module is specified as its argument, this system task prints the time unit and precision for the specified module.

```
$printtimescale;

$printtimescale ( hier_path_to_module );
```

Here is a sample output of what appears when these tasks are called.

```
Time scale of (u10) is  100ps / 100ps
Time scale of (u10.u2nand) is  1us / 100ps
```

The system task:

```
$timeformat
```

specifies how the `%t` format specification must report time information. The task is of the form:

```
$timeformat ( units_number , precision ,
              suffix , numeric_field_width );
```

where a *units_number* is:

```
0   for 1 s
-1  for 100 ms
-2  for 10 ms
-3  for 1 ms
-4  for 100 us
-5  for 10us
-6  for 1 us
-7  for 100 ns
-8  for 10 ns
```

```
-9  for 1 ns
-10 for 100 ps
-11 for 10 ps
-12 for 1 ps
-13 for 100 fs
-14 for 10 fs
-15 for 1 fs
```

The system task call:

```
$timeformat (-12, 3, " ps", 5);
$display ("Current simulation time is %t", $time);
```

will display the `%t` specifier value in the **$display** task as:

```
Current simulation time is 0.051 ps
```

If no **$timeformat** is specified, `%t` prints in the smallest precision of all timescales in source.

10.3.4 Simulation Control Tasks

The system task:

```
$finish;
```

makes the simulator exit and return control back to the operating system.

The system task:

```
$stop;
```

causes the simulation to suspend. At this stage, interactive commands may be issued to the simulator. Here is an example of its use.

```
initial
  #500 $stop;
```

After 500 time units, the simulation stops.

10.3.5 Simulation Time Functions

- The following system functions return the simulation time.
    - **$time** : Returns the time as an integer in 64 bits scaled to the time unit of the module that invoked it.
    - **$stime** : Returns time in 32 bits.
    - **$realtime** : Returns time as a real number scaled to the time unit of the module that invokes it.

Here is an example.

```
 `timescale 10ns/1ns
module sync_tb;

 initial
   $monitor ("put_a=%d put_b=%d", put_a, put_b,
                 " get_o=%d", get_o, " at time %t", $time);
endmodule
```

Here is the output it produces.

```
put_a=0 put_b=0 get_o=0 at time 0
put_a=0 put_b=1 get_o=0 at time 5
put_a=0 put_b=0 get_o=0 at time 16
```

The value returned by **$time** is scaled to the time unit of the module `sync_tb` and then rounded. Note that **$timeformat** decides how the time value is to be printed. Here is another example.

```
 initial
   $monitor ("put_a=%d put_b=%d", put_a, put_b,
               " get_o=%d", get_o, " at time %t", $realtime);
```

The output produced looks like this.

```
put_a=0 put_b=1 get_o=0 at time 5.2
put_a=0 put_b=0 get_o=0 at time 15.6
```

10.3.6 Conversion Functions

The following system functions are utility functions that convert between number types.

- **$rtoi** (*real_value*) : Converts a real number to an integer by truncating the decimal value.
- **$itor** (*integer_value*) : Converts integer to real.
- **$realtobits** (*real_value*) : Converts a real into 64-bit vector representation of the real number (IEEE 754 representation of the real number).
- **$bitstoreal** (*bit_value*) : Converts a bit pattern into a real number (opposite of **$realtobits**).
- **$signed** (*value*) : Provides interpretation of the value as signed.
- **$unsigned** (*value*) : Provides interpretation of the value as unsigned.

10.3.7 Probabilistic Distribution Functions

The function:

```
$random [ ( seed ) ]
```

returns a random number as a 32-bit signed integer based on the value of the seed. The seed (must be a reg, integer or a time variable) controls the number that the function returns, that is, a different seed will generate a different random number. If no seed is specified, a random number is generated every time **$random** function is called based on a default seed.

Here is an example.

```
integer seed, random_num;
wire rclk;

initial
  seed = 12;
```

```
always
  @(rclk) random_num = $random (seed);
```

On every edge of `rclk`, **$random** is called which returns a 32-bit signed integer random number.

If a number within a range, say –10 to +10 is desired, the modulus operator can be used to generate such a number as shown in the following example.

```
random_num = $random (seed) % 11;
```

Here is an example where the seed is not explicitly specified.

```
random_num = $random / 2;          // Seed is optional.
```

Note that the sequence of numbers generated is a pseudo-random sequence, that is, the same sequence of numbers is generated for a starting seed value.

The following expression:

```
{$random} % 11
```

returns a random number in the range 0 to 10. The concatenation ({}) operator interprets the signed integer returned by the **$random** function as an unsigned number.

The following functions generate pseudo-random numbers according to the probabilistic function specified in the function name.

```
$dist_uniform ( seed , start , end )

$dist_normal ( seed , mean , standard_deviation )

$dist_exponential ( seed , mean )

$dist_poisson ( seed , mean )

$dist_chi_square ( seed , degree_of_freedom )
```

```
$dist_t ( seed , degree_of_freedom )

$dist_erlang ( seed , k_stage , mean )
```

All parameters to these functions must be integer values.

10.3.8 String Formatting

The following tasks support reading from a string and writing to a string.

```
$swrite      $swriteo    $swriteb  $swriteh
$sformat
$sscanf
```

The **$swrite** tasks are similar to the file **$fwrite** tasks; instead of writing to a file, the **$swrite** tasks write to a string (which is a reg variable). Here are some examples.

```
integer index;
reg [1024:1] name_buf;

$swrite (name_buf, "rx[%d]", index);
// If index is 6, after task execution, name_buf has
// the string "rx[6]".

reg [100:1] string_buffer;

$swrite (string_buffer, "At time %t", $time,
                ", fifo_empty is %d.", fifo_empty);
```

The **$sformat** task is similar to the **$swrite** except that the format must be specified only as its second argument.

```
$sformat (string_buffer, "Time = %t, fifo_empty = %d",
                $time, fifo_empty);
```

The second argument is the format and the rest are variables to be formatted and assigned to string `string_buffer`.

The **$sscanf** system function reads a line from a string (similar to a **$fscanf** that reads from a file), and the values that it reads are stored in the specified arguments.

```
integer status;

status = $sscanf (string_buffer, "%s %d %d",
                  signal_name, lower_bnd, upper_bnd);
// If string_buffer has a string of form "qcm_wr 5 2",
// then after the function call, signal_name has
// "qcm_wr", lower_bnd has 5 and upper_bnd has 2.
```

The **$sscanf** function returns a status of 0 if there is any error in reading the string.

Here is an example that compares signal values with its strengths.

```
reg [3*8-1 : 0] tail_str, head_str;

$swrite (tail_str, "%v", tail_wdata);
$swrite (head_str, "%v", head_wdata);

if (tail_str != head_str)
  $display ("Strengths of tail_str (=%v) and ",
           tail_str, "head_str (=%v) are different.",
           head_str);
```

10.4 Disable Statement

A disable statement is a procedural statement (hence it can only appear within an always or an initial statement). A disable statement can be used to terminate a task or a block (sequential or parallel) before it completes executing all its statements. It can be used to model hardware interrupts and global resets. It is of the form:

```
disable task_id;

disable block_id;
```

After a disable statement is executed, execution continues with the next statement following the task call or the block being disabled.

```
begin: blk_a
  // Stmt 1.
  // Stmt 2.
  disable blk_a;
  // Stmt 3.
  // Stmt 4.
end
// Stmt 5.
```

Statements 3 and 4 are never executed. After the disable statement is executed, statement 5 is executed. Here is another example.

```
task bit_task;
  begin
    // Stmt 6.
    disable bit_task;
    // Stmt 7.
  end
endtask

// Stmt 8.
bit_task;         // Task call.
// Stmt 9.
```

When the disable statement is executed, the task is aborted, that is, statement 7 is never executed. Execution continues with the next statement following the task call which in this example is statement 9.

Disabling a task is not recommended, especially if the task returns output values. This is because the language specifies that the values of the output and inout arguments are indeterminate when a task is disabled. A better approach is to disable the sequential block, if any, within the task. For example,

```
task sample_uart;
  output [0:3] count;
  begin: local_blk
    // Stmt 10.
    count = 10;
    disable local_blk;
    // Stmt 11.
```

```
    end
  endtask
```

When the disable statement gets executed, it causes the sequential block `local_blk` to exit. Since this is the only statement in the task, the task exits gracefully and `count` has its assigned value of 10. If the disable statement were replaced with:

```
disable sample_uart;
```

then after the disable statement gets executed, the value of `count` is indeterminate.

10.5 *Named Events*

Consider the following two always statements.

```
reg ready, done;

// Get the always statements interacting:
initial
  begin
    done = 0;
    #0 done = 1;
  end

always
  @(done) begin
    . . .
    // Finished processing this always statement.
    // Trigger the next always statement.
    // Create an event on ready:
    ready = 0;
    #0 ready = 1;
  end

always
  @(ready) begin
    . . .
    // Finished processing this always statement.
    // Create event to trigger previous always statement:
    done = 0;
```

```
    #0 done = 1;
  end
```

The two assignments in each always statement are needed to ensure that an event is created on `ready` and `done`. It appears that the purpose of `ready` and `done` are to act only as handshake signals between the two always statements.

Verilog HDL provides an alternate mechanism to achieve this - using *named events*. A named event is yet another data type (the two other data types in the language are the variable and the net data types). A named event must be declared before it is used. An example of its declaration is:

```
event ready, done;
```

The event declaration declares two named events, `ready` and `done`. Having declared a named event, an event can be created using the event trigger statement. Examples of such statements are:

```
-> ready;
-> done;
```

Events on named events can be monitored just like events on variables, that is, using the `@` mechanism, such as:

```
@(done) <do_something>
```

So whenever the event trigger statement for `done` is executed, an event is said to occur on `done`, which causes `<do_something>` to execute.

Our simple example of the two always statements can be rewritten using named events as follows.

```
event ready, done;

initial
  -> done;
```

```
always
  @(done) begin
    . . .
    // Trigger the next always statement.
    // Create an event on ready:
    -> ready;
  end

always
  @(ready) begin
    . . .
    // Create event to trigger previous always statement:
    -> done;
  end
```

A state machine can also be described using events. Here is an example of an asynchronous state machine.

```
event state1, state2, state3;

// Reset state:
initial
  begin
    // Reset state logic here.
    -> state1;
  end

always
  @(state1) begin
    // state1 logic here.
    -> state2;            // Create event on state2.
  end

always
  @(state2) begin
    // state2 logic here.
    -> state3;            // Create event on state3.
  end
```

```
always
  @(state3) begin
    // state3 logic here. It can have statements such as:
    if (input_a)
      -> state2;          // Create event on state2.
    else
      -> state1;          // Create event on state1.
  end
```

The initial statement describes the reset logic. Upon completion, it triggers the second always statement. The execution of the last statement in this always statement causes an event to occur on `state2`; this causes the third always statement to execute and subsequently the fourth always statement executes. In the last always statement, an event is made to occur either on `state2` or on `state1` depending on the value of `input_a`.

10.6 Mixing Structure with Behavior

In previous chapters, we discussed the various forms of modeling. Verilog HDL allows all these modeling styles to be combined in a single module. The syntax of a module is:

```
module module_name ( port_list );
  Declarations:
    Input, output and inout declarations.
    Net declarations.
    Variable declarations.
    Parameter declarations.
    Task and function declarations.

  Initial statement.
  Gate instantiation statement.
  Module instantiation statement.
  UDP instantiation statement.
  Always statement.
  Continuous assignment.
endmodule
```

Here is an example of a mixed style description.

```
module mux2x1 (ctrl, a, b, enable, y);
  // Input declaration:
  input ctrl, a, b, enable;
  // Output declaration:
  output y;
  // Wire declaration:
  wire or_ab, not_ctrl;
  // Net declaration assignment:
  wire y = enable == 1 ? or_ab : 'bz;

  // Gate instantiations:
  not (not_ctrl, ctrl);
  or (or_ab, ta, tb);

  // Continuous assignments:
  assign ta = a & ctrl;
  assign tb = b & not_ctrl;
endmodule
```

The module contains a mix of built-in logic gates (structural components) and continuous assignments (dataflow behavior).

10.7 Hierarchical Path Name

Every identifier in Verilog HDL has a unique hierarchical path name. This hierarchical path name is formed by using names separated by a period (.) character. A new hierarchy is defined by:

i. Module instantiation.
ii. Task definition.
iii. Function definition.
iv. Named block.

The complete path name of any identifier starts with the top-level module (a module that is not instantiated by anybody else). This path name can be used in any level in a description. Here is an example. Figure 10-1 shows the hierarchy.

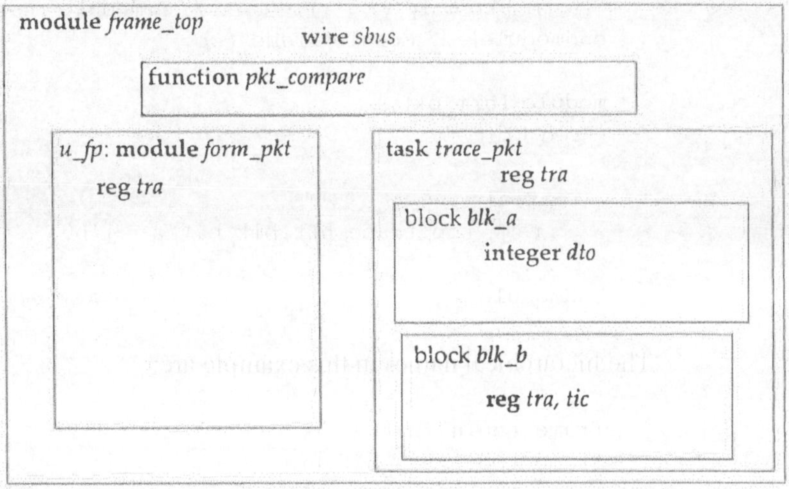

Figure 10-1 Module hierarchy.

```
module frame_top;
  wire sbus;

  function pkt_compare . . .
    . . .
  endfunction

  task trace_pkt;
    . . .
    reg tra;
    begin
      begin: blk_a
        integer dto;
        . . .
      end

      begin: blk_b
        reg tra, tic;
        . . .
        tic = form_pkt.tra;
        . . .
      end
    end
  endtask
```

```
  form_pkt u_fp (. . .);          // A module instantiation.
endmodule  // Module frame_top.

module form_pkt;
  reg tra;

  initial
    frame_top.trace_pkt.blk_b.tra = 1'b0;
  . . .
endmodule
```

The hierarchical names in this example are:

```
frame_top.u_fp.tra
frame_top.trace_pkt.tra
frame_top.trace_pkt.blk_b.tra
frame_top.trace_pkt.blk_a.dto
frame_top.trace_pkt.blk_b.tic
frame_top.sbus
form_pkt.tra
```

These hierarchical names allow free data access to any item from any level in the hierarchy. The value can not only be read, but can also be updated from any level of the hierarchy. An example of such an assignment is shown in module `form_pkt`.

A lower level module can reference an item in a module above it (called upward referencing) or below it (downward referencing) in its hierarchy by qualifying the variable with the module instance name. This is of the form:

```
module_instance_name . variable_name
```

For downward path referencing, the model instance must be at the same level as the lower-level module. Here is an example.

```
module frame_top;
  wire sbus;

  form_pkt_a u_fp (. . .);     // A module instantiation.
```

```
  always @*
    $display (u_fp.tra);              // Downward referencing.
endmodule

module form_pkt_a;
  reg tra;
  . . .
endmodule
```

10.8 Sharing Tasks and Functions

One approach to share tasks and functions among different modules is to write the definitions of the shared tasks and functions in a text file, and then include these in the required module using the `` `include`` compiler directive. Assume that we have the following function and task definitions in a file `package.h`.

```
// File: package.h
function signed_plus (
    input [0:3] a, b
  );
  . . .
endfunction

function signed_minus (
    input [0:3] a, b
  );
  . . .
endfunction

task preset_clear;
  . . .
endtask
```

Here is how the file can be used in a module.

```
module signed_alu (
    input [0:3] a, b,
    input operation,
    output reg [0:3] y
  );
```

```
    // Include the definitions of the shared functions.
    `include "package.h"

    always
      @(a or b or operation)
        y = (operation) ? signed_plus (a, b) :
             signed_minus (a, b);
  endmodule
```

Note that the **`include** directive must be present within the module declaration since the task and function definitions in the file `package.h` are not bounded by a module declaration.

An alternate way to share functions and tasks is to define the shared tasks and functions within a module. And then refer to the required task or function in a different module using a hierarchical name. Here is the same example as above, but this time the task and function definitions appear within a module declaration.

```
module package;
  function signed_plus;
    . . .
  endfunction

  function signed_minus;
    . . .
  endfunction

  task preset_clear;
    . . .
  endtask
endmodule
```

Here is how the shared functions can be referenced in a different module.

```
module signed_alu2 (
   input [0:3] a, b,
   input operation,
   output reg [0:3] y
  );
```

```
always
  @(a or b or operation)
    y = (operation) ? package.signed_plus (a, b) :
        package.signed_minus (a, b);
endmodule
```

10.9 *Attributes*

An attribute provides a mechanism for annotating information about an object or a statement. It provides a standard way to specify non-Verilog or tool-specific information in a Verilog HDL source model. Such information may be used by different tools that read the Verilog HDL source. An attribute can be attached to almost any statement in Verilog HDL. The value of the attribute itself cannot be used anywhere else in the Verilog description. The attribute and its value is attached as a prefix to a statement or an object, and as a suffix to an operator or a function name in an expression. There are no predefined standard attributes. Here are some examples.

IEEE Std 1364.1 defines a standard set of attributes that can be used when writing synthesizable RTL models.

```
(* fsm_register *) reg [SIZE-1:0] current_state;
  // Value of attribute fsm_register is by default 1.

(* dont_touch *) module my_multiplier (
    multiplier, multiplicand, acc
  );

(* full_case = 0, parallel_case = 1 *) case . . . endcase
```

An attribute can even be attached to an operator.

```
total = num_rx + (* implementation = RIPPLE *) num_tx;
```

The language does not define any pre-specified meaning to the attributes. However, tool readers may. For example, a synthesis tool may most probably understand the semantics of the attributes `dont_touch`, `full_case` and `parallel_case`.

10.10 Value Change Dump (VCD) File

A value change dump (VCD) file contains information about value changes on specified variables in design. Its main purpose is to provide information for other post-processing tools.

There are two types of VCD files.

i. *Four-state VCD*: The four values 0, 1, x, and z are stored with no strength information.
ii. *Extended VCD*: The four values 0, 1, x, and z with strength information are stored.

10.10.1 Four-state VCD File

The following system tasks are provided to create and direct information into a four-state VCD file.

i. **$dumpfile** : This system task specifies the name of the dump file. For example,

```
$dumpfile ("uart.dump");
```

ii. **$dumpvars** : This system task specifies the variables whose value changes are to be dumped into the dump file.

```
$dumpvars;
  // With no arguments, it specifies to dump all
  // variables in the design.

$dumpvars (level, module_name);
  // Dumps variables in specified module and in all
  // modules the specified number of levels below.

$dumpvars (1, uart);
  // Dumps variables only in uart module.

$dumpvars (2, uart);
  // All variables in uart and in all modules one
  // level below.
```

```
$dumpvars (0, uart);
  // Level 0 causes all variables in uart and all
  // variables in all module instances below uart.

$dumpvars (0, p_state, n_state);
  // Dumps info about p_state and n_state
  // variables. The level number is not relevant
  // in this case, but must be given.

$dumpvars (3, udiv.clk, uart);
  // The level number applies only to modules, in
  // this case, only to uart, that is, all variables
  // in uart and two levels below. Also dumps value
  // changes on variable udiv.clk.
```

iii. **$dumpoff** : This system task causes the dumping tasks to be suspended.

```
$dumpoff;
```

iv. **$dumpon** : This system task causes all dumping tasks to resume. The syntax is:

```
$dumpon;
```

v. **$dumpall** : This system tasks dumps the values of all specified variables at that time, that is at the time it is executed. The syntax is:

```
$dumpall;
```

vi. **$dumplimit** : This system task specifies the maximum size (in bytes) of a VCD file. Dumping stops when this limit is reached. For example,

```
$dumplimit (1024);      // VCD file is of maximum
                        // 1024 bytes.
```

vii. **$dumpflush** : This system task flushes data in the operating system VCD file buffer to be stored in the VCD file. After the execution of the system task, dumping resumes as before.

```
$dumpflush;
```

10.10.2 Extended VCD File

The following system tasks are provided to create and direct information into an extended VCD file.

i. **$dumpports** : This system task causes the ports of the listed modules to be dumped in the specified file.

```
$dumpports (uart, "dport.dump");
```

ii. **$dumpportsall** : Forces values of all selected ports to be dumped even though they may not have changed values.

```
$dumpportsall ("dport.dump");
```

iii. **$dumpportsoff** : Turns off dumping of port values.

```
$dumpportsoff ("dport.dump");
// Stops dumping to the specified file.
```

iv. **$dumpportson** : Turns on dumping of port values.

```
$dumpportson ("dport.dump");
```

v. **$dumpportslimit** : Limits the size of the VCD file.

```
$dumpportslimit (1024, "dport.dump");
```

vi. **$dumpportsflush** : Flushes the internal buffer of the system to the file.

```
$dumpportsflush ("dport.dump");
```

10.10.3 An Example

Here is an example of an up-down counter that counts between 5 and 12.

```
module count_updown (clk, count, up_down);
  input clk, up_down;
  output reg [0:3] count;

  initial
    count = 'd5;

  always
    @(posedge clk) begin
      if (up_down)
        begin
          count = count + 1;

          if (count > 12)
            count = 12;
        end
      else
        begin
          count = count - 1;

          if (count < 5)
            count = 5;
        end
    end
endmodule

module test_counter;
  reg clock, up_dn;
  wire [0:3] cnt_out;
  parameter ON_DELAY = 1, OFF_DELAY = 2;
  localparam DUMP_FILE = "count.vcd";
  localparam COUNT_DOWN = 50, DUMP_DONE = 200;

  count_updown ucud (clock, cnt_out, up_dn);
```

```
    always
      begin
        clock = 1;
        #ON_DELAY;
        clock = 0;
        #OFF_DELAY;
      end

    initial
      begin
        up_dn = 0;
        #COUNT_DOWN up_dn = 1;
        #DUMP_DONE $dumpflush;
        $stop;                          // Stops the simulation.
      end

    initial
      begin
        $dumpfile (DUMP_FILE);
        $dumplimit (4096);
        $dumpvars (0, test_counter);
        $dumpvars (0, ucud.count, ucud.clk, ucud.up_down);
      end

    initial
      begin
        $dumpportslimit (10000, "count.evcd");
        #10;
        $dumpports (ucud, "count.evcd");
        #40;
        $dumpportsall ("count.evcd");
        #30;
        $dumpportsoff ("count.evcd");
        #20;
        $dumpportson ("count.evcd");
        $dumpportsall ("count.evcd");
        $dumpportsflush ("count.evcd");
      end
  endmodule
```

10.10.4 Format of VCD File

The VCD file is an ASCII file. It has the following information:

- Header information: Gives date, simulator version and timescale unit.
- Node information: Definition of the scope and type of variables being dumped.
- Value changes: Actual value changes with time. Absolute simulation times are recorded.

The four-state VCD file `count.vcd` produced is shown in Figure 10-2. The extended VCD file `count.evcd` produced is shown in Figure 10-3.

10.11 Specify Block

The delays that we have discussed so far such as gate delays and net delays are distributed delays. Delays for paths in a module, called module path delays, can be specified using a specify block. In general, a specify block can be used for the following.

i. To declare paths between a source and a destination.
ii. To assign delay to these paths.
iii. To perform timing checks for the module.

A specify block appears within a module declaration. It is of the form:

```
specify
  spec_param_declarations
  path_declarations
  system_timing_checks
endspecify
```

A specparam (or a specify parameter) declaration declares a parameter for use within the specify block. Here is an example.

```
specparam tSETUP = 20, tHOLD = 25;
```

```
$date
Fri Sep 27 16:23:58 1996
$end
$version
Verilog HDL Simulator 1.0
$end
$timescale
100ps
$end
$scope module Test $end
$var parameter 32 ! ON_DELAY
$end
$var parameter 32 " OFF_DELAY
$end
$var reg 1 # Clock $end
$var reg 1 $ UpDn $end
$var wire 1 % Cnt_Out [0] $end
$var wire 1 & Cnt_Out [1] $end
$var wire 1 ' Cnt_Out [2] $end
$var wire 1 ( Cnt_Out [3] $end
$scope module C1 $end
$var wire 1 ) Clk $end
$var wire 1 * Up_Down $end
$var reg 4 + Count [0:3] $end
$var wire 1 ) Clk $end
$var wire 1 * Up_Down $end
$upscope $end
$upscope $end
$enddefinitions $end
#0
(continued next column)
$dumpvars
1#
0$
b1 !
b10 "
b101 +
1(
0'
1&
1)
0*
$end
#10
0#
0)
#30
1#
1)
b100 +
b101 +
#40
0#
0)
#60
1#
1)
b100 +
b101 +
#70
0#
. . .
```

Figure 10-2 A VCD file.

A specify parameter can also be declared outside of a specify block, but within a module. It can be assigned constant values that could be composed of other specify parameters and module parameters. However, a specparam's value can only be modified via SDF backannotation.

```
$comment
File created using the following
command:
vcd file count.evcd -dumpports
$end
$date
Thu Mar  4 08:44:00 2004
$end
$version
dumpports ModelSim Version 5.8a
$end
$timescale
1ns
$end
$scope module test_counter $end
$scope module ucud $end
$var port 1 <0 clk $end
$var port 1 <1 count [0] $end
$var port 1 <2 count [1] $end
$var port 1 <3 count [2] $end
$var port 1 <4 count [3] $end
$var port 1 <5 up_down $end
$upscope $end
$upscope $end
$enddefinitions $end
#10
$dumpports
pH 0 6 <4
pL 6 0 <3
pH 0 6 <2
pL 6 0 <1
pD 6 0 <0
pD 6 0 <5
$end
(continued next column)
#12
pU 0 6 <0
#13
pD 6 0 <0
#15
pU 0 6 <0
. . .
#49
pD 6 0 <0
#50
$dumpportsall
pH 0 6 <4
pL 6 0 <3
pH 0 6 <2
pL 6 0 <1
pD 6 0 <0
pD 6 0 <5
$end
pU 0 6 <5
#51
pU 0 6 <0
pL 6 0 <4
pH 0 6 <3
#52
pD 6 0 <0
#54
pU 0 6 <0
pH 0 6 <4
#55
pD 6 0 <0
#57
pU 0 6 <0
pL 6 0 <4
pL 6 0 <3
pL 6 0 <2
pH 0 6 <1
. . .
```

Figure 10-3 An extended VCD file.

Three kinds of module paths can be described within a specify block. These are:

- Simple path.
- Edge-sensitive path.
- State-dependent path.

A simple path is declared using one of the following two forms.

```
source *> destination
  // Specifies a full connection: each bit in source
  // connects to all bits in destination.

source => destination
  // Specifies a parallel connection: every bit in source
  // connects to exactly one bit in destination.
```

Here are some examples.

```
input clock;
input [7:4] d;
output [4:1] q;

(clock => q[1]) = 5;
  // Delay from input clock to q[1] is 5.

(d *> q) = (tRISE, tFALL);
  /* Paths are:
      d[7] to q[4]
      d[7] to q[3]
      d[7] to q[2]
      d[7] to q[1]
      d[6] to q[4]
      . . .
      d[4] to q[1]
  */
```

In an edge-sensitive path, the path is described with respect to an edge on the source. For example,

```
(posedge clock => (qb +: da)) = (2:3:2);
  /* The path delay is from the positive edge of
     clock to qb.
     The data path is from da to qb and da does not get
     inverted as it propagates to qb. */
```

A state-dependent path specifies a path delay under some condition when it is true. For example,

```
if (clear)
  (d => q) = (2.1, 4.2);
    // Only if clear is true, use the delay for the
    // specified path.
```

Here is a list of timing checks that can be used within a specify block (a timing check is not a system task even though it contains a leading $ character). Timing checks can appear only within a specify block. No system task can appear in a specify block.

```
$setup         $hold
$setuphold     $period
$skew          $recovery
$width         $nochange
$removal       $recrem
$timeskew      $fullskew
```

The timing check:

```
$setup ( data_event , reference_event , limit );
```

reports a timing violation if:

```
( time_of_reference_event - time_of_data_event ) < limit
```

An example of this check is:

```
$setup (d, posedge ck, 1.0);
```

The timing check:

```
$hold ( reference_event , data_event , limit );
```

reports a violation if:

```
(time_of_data_event - time_of_reference_event) < limit
```

Here is an example.

```
$hold (posedge ck, d, 0.1);
```

The following timing check is a combination of the **$setup** and **$hold** checks.

```
$setuphold ( reference_event , data_event , setup_limit ,
             hold_limit );
```

Here is an example.

```
$setuphold (posedge clk, data, tSETUP, tHOLD);
// Checks for setup and hold times. "posedge clk" is the
// reference event and a change on data is the data event.
```

The above timing check is equivalent to performing the following two separate checks.

```
$setup (data, posedge clk, tSETUP);
$hold (posedge clk, data, tHOLD);
```

The timing check:

```
$width ( reference_event , limit , threshold );
```

reports a violation if:

```
threshold < ( time_of_data_event -
               time_of_reference_event ) < limit
```

The data event is derived from the reference event: it is the reference event with the opposite edge. Here is an example.

```
$width (negedge tclk, 0.0, 0);
```

The timing check:

```
$period ( reference_event , limit );
```

reports a violation if:

```
( time_of_data_event - time_of_reference_event ) < limit
```

The reference event must be an edge-triggered event. The data event is derived from the reference event: it is the reference event with the same edge.

The timing check:

```
$skew ( reference_event , data_event , limit );
```

reports a violation if:

```
time_of_data_event - time_of_reference_event > limit
```

If time of *data_event* is equal to the time of *reference_event*, no violation is reported.

The timing check:

```
$recovery ( reference_event , data_event , limit );
```

reports a timing violation if:

```
( time_of_data_event - time_of_reference_event ) < limit
```

The reference event must be an edge-triggered event. This check records the new reference event time before performing the timing check; therefore if the data event and the reference event both occur at the same simulation time, a violation is reported.

The timing check:

```
$nochange ( reference_event , data_event ,
            start_edge_offset ,end_edge_offset );
```

reports a timing violation if the data event occurs during the specified width of the reference event. The reference event must be an edge-triggered event. The start and stop offsets are relative to the reference event edge. For example,

```
$nochange (negedge clear, preset, 0, 0);
```

will report a violation if `preset` changes while `clear` is low.

The timing check:

```
$removal ( reference_event , data_event , limit );
```

reports a violation if:

```
( time_of_reference_event - time_of_data_event ) < limit
```

The reference event is typically a control signal such as reset or set.

The following timing check is a combination of **$removal** and **$recovery** system tasks.

```
$recrem ( reference_event , data_event , recovery_limit ,
          removal_limit );
```

The timing check:

```
$timeskew ( reference_event , data_event , limit );
```

reports a violation if:

```
( time_of_data_event - time_of_reference_event ) > limit
```

The timing check:

```
$fullskew ( reference_event , data_event ,
            limit_1 , limit_2 );
```

reports a violation if:

```
{ time_of_data_event - time_of_reference_event } >
  limit_1
```

in the case data event follows reference event, and reports a violation if:

```
{ time_of_reference_event - time_of_data_event } >
  limit_2
```

in the case when reference event follows data event.

Each of the above timing checks may optionally have a last argument which is a *notifier*. A timing check updates a notifier, when there is a timing violation, by changing its value according to the following case statement.

```
case ( notifier )
  'bx : notifier = 'b0;
  'b0 : notifier = 'b1;
  'b1 : notifier = 'b0;
  'bz : notifier = 'bz;
endcase
```

A notifier can be used to provide information about the violation or propagate an x to the output that reported the violation. Here is an example of a notifier.

```
reg notify_din;
. . .
$setuphold (negedge clock, din, tSETUP, tHOLD,
                notify_din);
```

In this example, `notify_din` is the notifier. If a timing violation occurs, the variable `notify_din` changes value according to the case statement described earlier for a notifier.

Here is an example of a specify block.

```
specify
  // Specify parameters:
  specparam tCLK_Q = (5:4:6);
  specparam tSETUP = 2.8, tHOLD = 4.4;
```

```
    // Path delays with path specifications:
    (clock *> q) = tCLK_Q;
    (data *> q) = 12;
    (clear, preset *> q) = (4, 5);

    // Timing check:
    $setuphold (negedge clock, data, tSETUP, tHOLD);
  endspecify
```

Along a module path, only pulses that are longer than the path delay propagate to the output. However, this can additionally be controlled by using a special specify block parameter called **PATHPULSE$**. In addition to specifying the pulse width range for which a pulse is rejected, it can also be used to specify a pulse width range that will cause an x to appear at the end of the path. A simple form of this parameter specification is:

```
PATHPULSE$ = ( reject_limit , [ , error_limit ] );
```

If a pulse width is less than the *reject_limit*, the pulse does not propagate to output. If a pulse width is less than the *error_limit* (same as *reject_limit* if not specified) but greater than the *reject_limit*, an x is generated at the target of the path.

A pulse limit can be specified for a specific path as well by using a modified **PATHPULSE$** parameter of the form:

```
PATHPULSE$input_terminal$output_terminal
```

Here is an example of a specify block.

```
specify
  specparam PATHPULSE$ = (1, 2);
    // Reject limit = 1, Error limit = 2.

  specparam PATHPULSE$data$q = 6;
    // Reject limit = Error limit = 6, on path
    // from data to q.
endspecify
```

10.12 Strengths

In addition to the four basic values in Verilog HDL, 0, 1, x and z, additional attributes to these values such as drive strength and charge strength can be specified.

10.12.1 Drive Strength

A drive strength can be specified for the following:

i. A net in a net declaration assignment.
ii. Output terminal of a primitive gate instance.
iii. In a continuous assignment.

A drive strength specification has two values, one is the strength value when the net is assigned a value 1, the second is the strength value when the net is assigned a value 0. It is of the form:

```
( strength_for_1 , strength_for_0 )
```

The order of the values is not important. For an assignment of value 1, only the following strengths are allowed.

- **supply1**
- **strong1**
- **pull1**
- **weak1**
- **highz1**

For an assignment of value 0, the following strengths are allowed.

- **supply0**
- **strong0**
- **pull0**
- **weak0**
- **highz0**

The default strength specification is **(strong0, strong1)**.

Here are some examples.

```
// Strength for a net:
wire (pull1, weak0) #(2, 4) rx_busy = wlen && rx_wr;
  // Strengths can be specified only for scalar
  // nets of type:
  // wire, wand, wor, tri, triand, trior, trireg,
  // tri0, tri1.

// Strength for an output terminal of a gate primitive:
nand (pull1, strong0) #(3:4:4) u0nand (
    par_shift, shift_en[0], shift_en[1], shift_en[2]
);
  // Drive strengths can only be specified for the
  // following gate primitives: and, or, xor, nand, nor,
  // xnor, buf, bufif0, bufif1, not, notif0, notif1,
  // pulldown, pullup.

// Strength in a continuous assignment:
assign (weak1, pull0) #2.56 fe_sync = wr_ctrl;
```

The strength of a net can be printed using the `%v` format specification in a display task. For example,

```
$display ("prq_done is %v", prq_done);
```

produces:

```
prq_done is We1
```

10.12.2 Charge Strength

A trireg net can optionally have a charge strength specified as well. This charge strength specifies the relative size of the capacitance associated with the net. It is one of:

- **small**
- **medium** (default, if not specified)
- **large**

In addition, a charge decay time can be specified for a trireg net. Here is an example.

```
trireg (small) #(5, 4, 20) parity_select;
```

The trireg net `parity_select` has a **small** capacitance. The rise delay is 5 time units, the fall delay is 4 time units and the charge decay time (the charge decays when the net is in high-impedance) is 20 time units.

10.13 Race Condition

If a delay is not used in a continuous assignment or in an always statement, a race condition can occur due to zero delay. This is because Verilog HDL does not define how events, which occur at the same time, are ordered for simulation.

Here is a simple example that illustrates this fact about zero delays using nonblocking assignments.

```
initial
  tx_start <= 0;

initial
  tx_start <= 1;
```

Both values 0 and 1 get scheduled to be assigned to `tx_start` at the end of the time step. Depending on how the events are ordered (internal to a simulator), the result on `tx_start` may be a 0 or a 1.

Here is another example that shows a race condition due to event ordering.

```
initial
  begin
    data_stop = 0;
    dma_ctrl = 1;
    #5 data_stop = 1;
    dma_ctrl = 0;
  end
```

```
always
  @(mode_en or dma_ctrl)
    $display ("The value of mode_en at time", $time,
              " is ", mode_en);

assign mode_en = data_stop;
```

When data_stop and dma_ctrl are assigned values in the initial statement at time 0, the continuous assignment and the always statement are both ready for execution. Which one should be executed first? The Verilog language does not define this order. If the continuous assignment executes first, mode_en will get 0, which in turn will trigger the always statement. But since it is already ready for execution, nothing is done. The always statement gets executed which displays the value of 0 for mode_en.

If we assume that the always statement executes first, the current value of mode_en is printed (the continuous assignment has not yet been executed), and then the continuous assignment gets executed which updates the value of mode_en.

Guideline: Write race-independent models, that is, the behavior should not depend on the order of execution of the always or the initial statements.

Therefore be careful when dealing with zero delay assignments. Here is another example of a race condition.

```
always
  @(posedge master_clk)
    tx_count = tx_load;

always
  @(posedge master_clk)
    next_state = tx_count;
```

The language does not define which always statement is to be executed first when there is a positive edge on master_clk. If the first always statement is executed, tx_count will get the value of tx_load immediately. Subsequently when the second always statement executes, next_state will get the latest value of tx_count (the one assigned in the first always statement).

If the second always statement executes first, next_state will get the old value of tx_count (tx_count has not yet been assigned), and subsequently tx_count will be assigned the value of tx_load. So depending on which always statement executes first, next_state will have a different value. The problem occurs because the procedural assignment occurs instantaneously, that is, without any delay. One way to avoid the problem is to insert intra-statement delays. A better approach is to use nonblocking assignment statements. This is shown next.

```
always
  @(posedge master_clk)
    tx_count <= tx_load;

always
  @(posedge master_clk)
    next_state <= tx_count;
```

When communicating information via variables from one always statement to another, use nonblocking assignments when assigning to the variables to avoid race conditions.

10.14 Command Line Arguments

The two system functions, **$test$plusargs** and **$value$plusargs**, allow access to arguments and their values that are passed in on a simulation invocation line. Quite often, these arguments are passed as plusargs (options with a leading + character), such as:

A plusarg is an option specified with a leading + character.

```
+DEBUG=3
```

The **$test$plusargs** system function allows you to test the existence of a plusarg argument name.

```
$test$plusargs ("DEBUG")
// Returns 1 as it matches the plusarg argument name.

$test$plusargs ("DEB")
// Also returns 1 since the function returns a 1 if the
// prefix of any plusarg argument matches the string
// specified in the function call.
```

The **$value$plusargs** provides the value of a specified plusarg. The function returns a 1 if the specified plusarg has been specified. A format string is used to access the values in plusargs, much like a **$display** statement.

```
$value$plusarg ("DEBUG=%d", debug_value)
// Returns 1 and has the value 3 in debug_value.

$value$plusarg ("STOP_TIME=%s", stop_time)
// Returns 0 if no +STOP_TIME plusarg is specified.

// Use %f format to read a real value argument.
```

10.15 Exercises

1. Can a function call a task?
2. Can a task have delays?
3. Can a function have zero input parameters?
4. What is the difference between **$display** and **$write** system tasks?
5. What is the difference between **$strobe** and **$monitor** system tasks?
6. Write a function that performs a BCD (binary coded decimal) to 7-segment decoding.
7. Write a function that converts a four-character string that contains only decimal digits to an integer value. For example, if *my_buffer* contains the string "4298", convert it to an integer *my_int* that has the value 4298.
8. Does Verilog HDL have a capability to read files other than using the **$readmemb** and **$readmemh** system tasks?
9. What is the difference between **$stop** and **$finish** system tasks?
10. Write a task that dumps the contents of a memory starting from a specified begin and end locations.
11. What is a notifier? Give an example of its use.
12. How would you load a memory from locations 0 through 15. Hexadecimai values are read from a text file `ram.txt`.

13. Write a task that models the behavior of an asynchronous preset clear positive edge triggered N-bit counter.

14. What statement can be used to return from a task?

15. What system task impacts how the **$time** value is to be printed?

16. What mechanism is used to specify a pulse rejection limit?

17. Write a function that performs an arithmetic shift of a 10-bit vector.

18. Show how a disable statement can be used to emulate the behavior of the `continue` and `break` statements of the C programming language.

19. Given an absolute UNIX path name of a file, say of form `/d1/d2/d3/file_a`, write the following functions:
    - *get_directory_name*: returns the directory of file (i.e. `/d1/d2/d3`)
    - *get_base_name*: returns the name of file (i.e. `file_a`)

    Assume that the maximum number of characters in the path name can be at most 512 characters.

❑

11

Verification

This chapter describes techniques for writing test benches. A test bench is a program used for exercising and verifying the correctness of a design. Verilog HDL provides powerful constructs that can be used to describe test benches.

11.1 Writing a Test Bench

A test bench has three main purposes.

i. To generate stimulus for simulation (waveforms).

ii. To apply this stimulus to the module under test and collect output responses.

iii To compare output responses with expected values.

Verilog HDL provides a large number of ways to write a test bench. In this chapter, we explore some of these. A typical test bench is of the form:

```
module test_bench;
  // A test bench typically has no inputs and outputs.
  Local_reg_and_net_declarations
  Generate_waveforms_using_initial_&
    _always_statements
```

```
    Instantiate_module_under_test
    Monitor_output_and_compare_with_expected_values
endmodule
```

Stimulus is automatically applied to the module under test by instantiating it in the testbench module.

11.2 Waveform Generation

There are two main approaches to generate stimulus values.

i. Create waveforms and apply stimulus at certain discrete time intervals.

ii. Generate stimulus based on the state of the module, that is, based on the output response of the module.

Two types of waveforms are typically needed. One is a repetitive pattern, for example, a clock, and the other is a specified set of values.

11.2.1 A Sequence of Values

The best way to generate a sequence of values is to use an initial statement. Here is an example.

```
initial
  begin
    reset = 0;
    #100 reset = 1;
    #80 reset = 0;
    #30 reset = 1;
  end
```

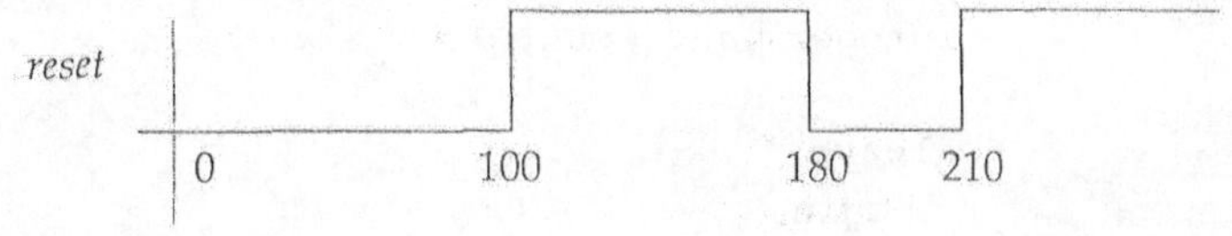

Figure 11-1 Waveform generated using initial statement.

The waveform generated is shown in Figure 11-1. The assignment statements in the initial statement use delay controls to generate a waveform. Alternately, intra-statement delays can also be used to generate a waveform as shown in the following example.

```
initial
  begin
    reset = 0;
    reset = #100 1;
    reset = #80 0;
    reset = #30 1;
  end
```

Since blocking procedural assignments are used, the delays in the above statements are relative delays. If absolute delays are preferred to be used, nonblocking procedural assignments can be used with intra-statement delays, as shown in the following example.

```
initial
  begin
    reset <= 0;
    reset <= #100 1;
    reset <= #180 0;
    reset <= #210 1;
  end
```

The waveforms produced for all the three initial statements are identical to the one shown in Figure 11-1.

To repeat a sequence of values, use an always statement instead of an initial statement; this is because an initial statement executes only once while an always statement executes repeatedly. Figure 11-2 shows the waveform created for the following example with an always statement.

```
parameter REPEAT_DELAY = 35;
integer baud_counter;

always
  begin
    baud_counter = 0;
    #7 baud_counter = 25;
    #2 baud_counter = 5;
```

```
    #8 baud_counter = 10;
    #6 baud_counter = 5;
    #REPEAT_DELAY;
end
```

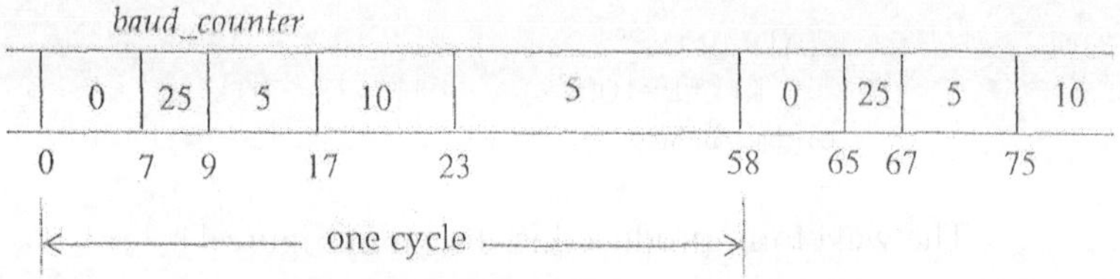

Figure 11-2 A repetitive sequence generated using an always statement.

11.2.2 Repetitive Patterns

It appears that a repetitive pattern can simply be created by having a continuous assignment of the form:

```
assign #(PERIOD/2)   clk_iol = ~clk_iol;
```

But this is not completely correct. The problem is that since `clk_iol` is a net (only a net can be assigned in a continuous assignment), its initial value is a z and ~z is x and ~x is x. Therefore the `clk_iol` gets stuck at the value x forever.

What is needed is a way to initialize the `clk_iol`. This can be done using an initial statement.

```
initial
  clk_iol = 0;
```

But now `clk_iol` has to be a variable data type (since only variable data types can be assigned values in an initial statement), and therefore the continuous assignment needs to be changed to an always statement. Here is a complete clock generator module.

```
module gen_clk_a (clk_a);
  output reg clk_a;
  parameter tPERIOD = 10;

  initial
    clk_a = 0;

  always
    #(tPERIOD/2)    clk_a = ~clk_a;
endmodule
```

The waveform produced is shown in Figure 11-3.

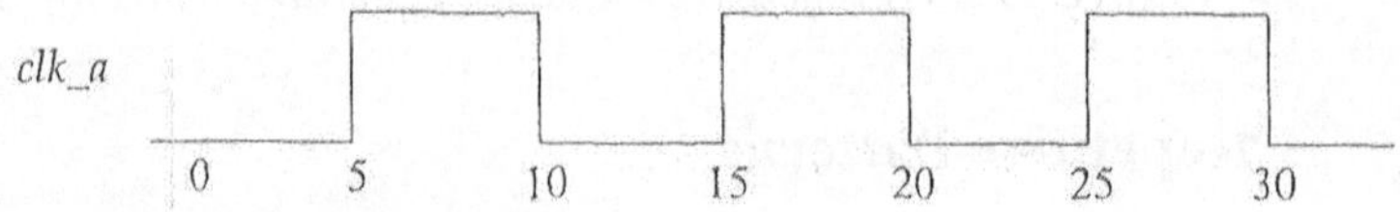

Figure 11-3 Periodic clock.

An alternate way of generating a clock is shown next.

```
module gen_clk_b (clk_b);
  output clk_b;
  reg start;

  initial
    begin
      start = 1;
      #5 start = 0;
    end

  nor #2 (clk_b, start, clk_b);
endmodule
// Generates a clock with on-off width of 2.
```

The initial statement sets `start` to 1, which forces the output of the nor gate to be a 0 (gets out of x value). After 5 time units, when `start` goes to 0, the inversion of the nor gate produces the clock with an on-off period of 4 time units. The waveform produced is shown in Figure 11-4.

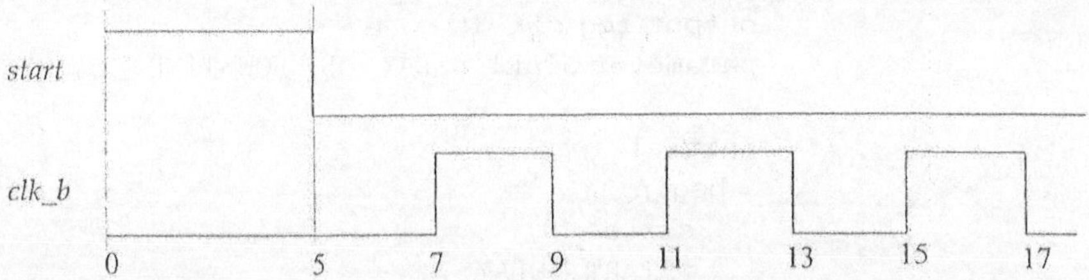

Figure 11-4 A controlled clock.

If a clock with different on-off duration is required, this can be modeled using an always statement as shown in the next model.

```
module gen_clk_c (clk_c);
  parameter tON = 5, tOFF = 10;
  output reg clk_c;

  always
    begin
      #tON    clk_c = 0;
      #tOFF   clk_c = 1;
    end
endmodule
```

No initialization is necessary in this case since the values 0 and 1 are being explicitly assigned. Figure 11-5 shows the waveform generated for this module.

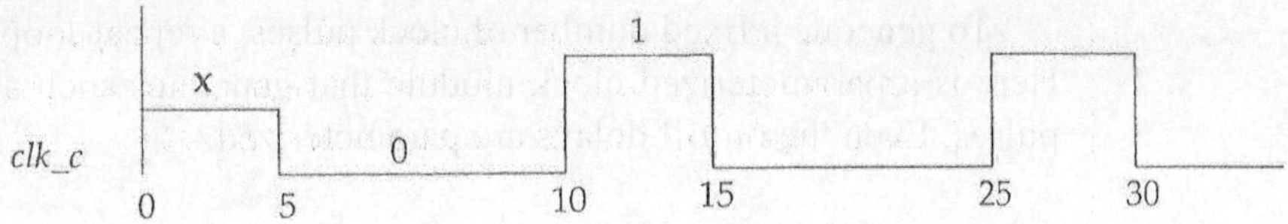

Figure 11-5 Varying on-off period.

To generate a varying on-off period clock after a start-up delay, a forever loop in an initial statement can be used.

```
module gen_clk_d (clk_d);
  output reg clk_d;
  parameter START_DELAY = 5, LOW_TIME = 3, HIGH_TIME = 2;

  initial
    begin
      clk_d = 0;
      #START_DELAY;

      forever
        begin
          clk_d = 1;
          #HIGH_TIME;
          clk_d = 0;
          #LOW_TIME;
        end
    end
endmodule
```

Figure 11-6 shows the waveforms produced.

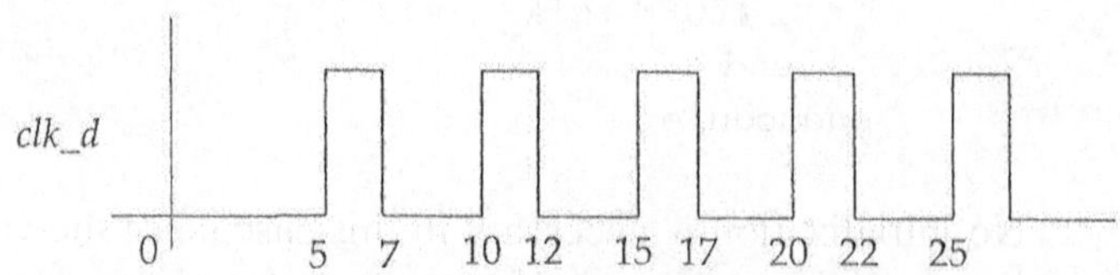

Figure 11-6 Clock with start-up delay.

To generate a fixed number of clock pulses, a repeat-loop can be used. Here is a parameterized clock module that generates such a sequence of pulses. Even the on-off delays are parameterized.

```
module gen_clk_e (clk_e);
  output reg clk_e;
  parameter Tburst = 10, Ton = 2, Toff = 5;

  initial
    begin
      clk_e = 1'b0;
```

```
            repeat (Tburst)
              begin
                #Toff  clk_e = 1'b1;
                #Ton   clk_e = 1'b0;
              end
          end
      endmodule
```

Module `gen_clk_e` can be instantiated with different parameter values for `Tburst`, `Ton` and `Toff`.

```
module test_e_clock;
  wire clk_ea, clk_eb, clk_ec;

  gen_clk_e ua_gen_clk_e (clk_ea);
    // Burst of 10 pulses, on-time of 2 and off-time of 5.

  gen_clk_e #(.Tburst(5), .Ton(1), .Toff(3))
    ub_gen_clk_e ( .clk_e(clk_eb)
  );
    // Burst of 5 pulses, on-time of 1 and off-time of 3.
    // Named parameter association and named port
    // association used.

  gen_clk_e #(25, 8, 10) uc_gen_clk_e (clk_ec);
    // Burst of 25 pulses, on-time of 8 and
    // off-time of 10.
endmodule
```

The waveforms on `clk_eb` is shown in Figure 11-7.

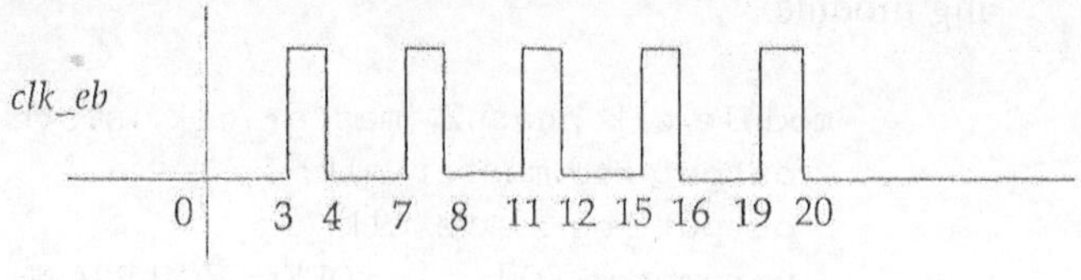

Figure 11-7 Fixed number of clock pulses.

A clock that is phase-delayed from another clock can be generated by using a continuous assignment. Figure 11-8 shows the generated waveforms for the following module that generates two clocks, one of which is phase-delayed from the other.

```
module clk_phase (master_clk, slave_clk);
  output reg master_clk;
  output wire slave_clk;
  parameter tON = 2, tOFF = 3, tPHASE_DELAY = 1;

  always
    begin
      #tON    master_clk = 0;
      #tOFF   master_clk = 1;
    end

  assign #tPHASE_DELAY   slave_clk = master_clk;
endmodule
```

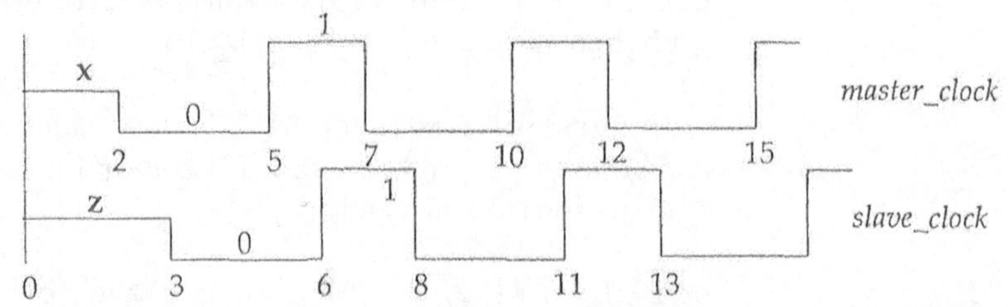

Figure 11-8 Phase-delayed clocks.

A caveat of this approach is that the phase delay has to be less than either the on period or the off period. If a larger phase delay is required, use an always statement with an intra-assignment delay as shown in the following module.

```
module clk_phase2 (master_clk, slave_clk);
  output reg master_clk;
  output reg slave_clk;
  parameter tON = 2, tOFF = 3, tPHASE_DELAY = 10;

  always
    begin
      #tON    master_clk = 0;
      #tOFF   master_clk = 1;
```

```
    end

  always
    @(master_clk)
      slave_clk <= #tPHASE_DELAY master_clk;
endmodule
```

To generate a clock which is double the frequency of another clock, phase-delay the clock by half a cycle and exclusive-or the result with the clock to generate the faster clock.

```
module clk_doubler (
    output double_clk
  );
  parameter tHALF_PERIOD = 2;
  reg clk;
  wire delayed_clk;

  always
    begin
      #tHALF_PERIOD clk = 0;
      #tHALF_PERIOD clk = 1;
    end

  assign #(tHALF_PERIOD/2) delayed_clk = clk;
  assign double_clock = delayed_clk ^ clk;
endmodule
```

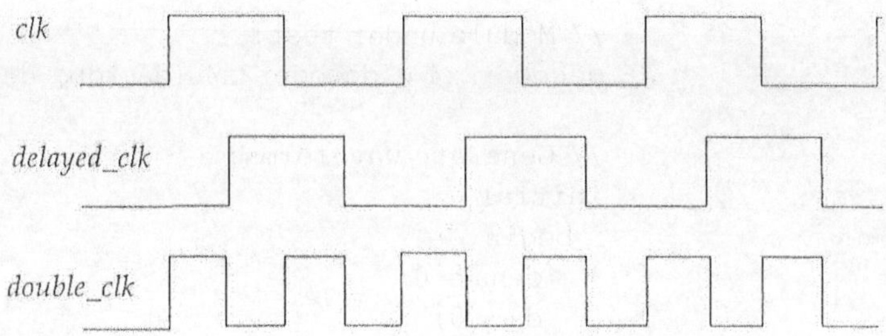

Figure 11-9 Clock doubler.

11.3 Testbench Examples

11.3.1 A Decoder

Here is a description of a 2-to-4 decoder and its test bench. Output is printed any time there is a change of value on either the input or the output.

```
`timescale 1ns/1ns
module decoder2x4 (a, b, enable, y);
  input a, b, enable;
  output [0:3] y;
  wire abar, bbar;

  not #(1, 2)
    u0not (abar, a),
    u1not (bbar, b);

  nand #(4, 3)
    u0nand (y[0], enable, abar, bbar),
    u1nand (y[1], enable, abar, b),
    u2nand (y[2], enable, a, bbar),
    u3nand (y[3], enable, a, b);
endmodule

module decoder_test;
  reg da, db, dena;
  wire [0:3] dy;

  // Module under test:
  decoder2x4 u_decoder2x4 (da, db, dena, dy);

  // Generate waveforms:
  initial
    begin
      dena = 0;
      da = 0;
      db = 0;
      #10 dena = 1;
      #10 da = 1;
      #10 db = 1;
      #10 da = 0;
```

```
      #10 db = 0;
      #10 $stop;
    end

  // Print results:
  always
    @(dena or da or db or dy)
      $display ("At time %t, input is %b%b%b, ",
          "output is %b", $time, da, db, dena, dy);
endmodule
```

Here is the output produced when this test bench is executed.

```
At time        4, input is 000, output is 1111
At time       10, input is 001, output is 1111
At time       13, input is 001, output is 0111
At time       20, input is 101, output is 0111
At time       23, input is 101, output is 0101
At time       26, input is 101, output is 1101
At time       30, input is 111, output is 1101
At time       33, input is 111, output is 1100
At time       36, input is 111, output is 1110
At time       40, input is 011, output is 1110
At time       44, input is 011, output is 1011
At time       50, input is 001, output is 1011
At time       54, input is 001, output is 0111
```

11.3.2 A Flip-flop

Here is a description of a master-slave D-type flip-flop and a test-bench that exercises it.

```
module ms_dflipflop (d, c, q, qbar);
  input d, c;
  output q, qbar;

  not
    u1not (notd, d),
    u2not (notc, c),
    u3not (noty, y);
```

```
  nand
    u1nand (d1, d, c),
    u2nand (d2, c, notd),
    u3nand (y, d1, ybar),
    u4nand (ybar, y, d2),
    u5nand (y1, y, notc),
    u6nand (y2, noty, notc),
    u7nand (q, qbar, y1),
    u8nand (qbar, y2, q);
endmodule

module msdff_test;
  reg d, c;
  wire q, qb;

  ms_dflipflop u_ms_dflipflop (d, c, q, qb);

  always
    #5 c = ~ c;

  initial
    begin
      d = 0;
      c = 0;
      #40 d = 1;
      #40 d = 0;
      #40 d = 1;
      #40 d = 0;
      $stop;
    end

  initial
    $monitor ("Time=%t ::", $time,
              " c=%b, d=%b, q=%b, qb=%b", c, d, q, qb);
endmodule
```

In this testbench, a monitor is set on the two inputs and the two outputs of the flip-flop. Thus, anytime a value changes, the specified argument string is printed out. Here is the output produced upon execution.

```
Time=     0 :: c=0, d=0, q=x, qb=x
Time=     5 :: c=1, d=0, q=x, qb=x
Time=    10 :: c=0, d=0, q=0, qb=1
```

```
Time=       15 :: c=1, d=0, q=0, qb=1
Time=       20 :: c=0, d=0, q=0, qb=1
Time=       25 :: c=1, d=0, q=0, qb=1
Time=       30 :: c=0, d=0, q=0, qb=1
Time=       35 :: c=1, d=0, q=0, qb=1
Time=       40 :: c=0, d=1, q=0, qb=1
Time=       45 :: c=1, d=1, q=0, qb=1
Time=       50 :: c=0, d=1, q=1, qb=0
Time=       55 :: c=1, d=1, q=1, qb=0
Time=       60 :: c=0, d=1, q=1, qb=0
Time=       65 :: c=1, d=1, q=1, qb=0
Time=       70 :: c=0, d=1, q=1, qb=0
Time=       75 :: c=1, d=1, q=1, qb=0
Time=       80 :: c=0, d=0, q=1, qb=0
Time=       85 :: c=1, d=0, q=1, qb=0
Time=       90 :: c=0, d=0, q=0, qb=1
Time=       95 :: c=1, d=0, q=0, qb=1
Time=      100 :: c=0, d=0, q=0, qb=1
Time=      105 :: c=1, d=0, q=0, qb=1
Time=      110 :: c=0, d=0, q=0, qb=1
Time=      115 :: c=1, d=0, q=0, qb=1
Time=      120 :: c=0, d=1, q=0, qb=1
Time=      125 :: c=1, d=1, q=0, qb=1
Time=      130 :: c=0, d=1, q=1, qb=0
Time=      135 :: c=1, d=1, q=1, qb=0
Time=      140 :: c=0, d=1, q=1, qb=0
Time=      145 :: c=1, d=1, q=1, qb=0
Time=      150 :: c=0, d=1, q=1, qb=0
Time=      155 :: c=1, d=1, q=1, qb=0
```

11.4 Reading Vectors from a Text File

It is possible to read vectors (could contain stimulus and expected values) from a text file using the **$readmemb** system task. Here is such an example of testing a 3-bit full-adder circuit. Assume that file `test.vec` contains the following two vectors.

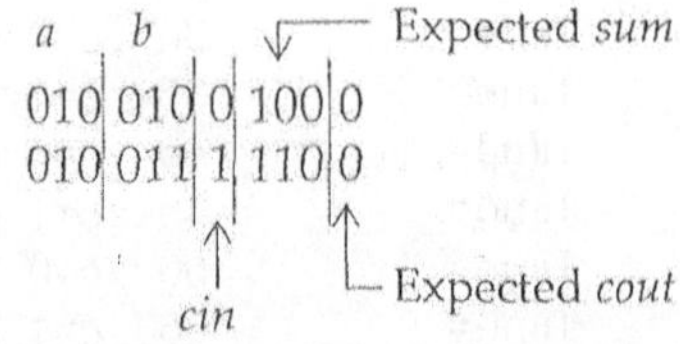

The first three bits correspond to input a, next three bits are for input b, next bit is the carry-in bit, eight to tenth bits are the expected sum result and the last bit is the expected carry-out. Here is the full-adder module and its testbench.

```
module adder1bit (a, b, cin, sum, cout);
  input a, b, cin;
  output sum, cout;

  assign sum = (a ^ b) ^ cin;
  assign cout = (a & b) | (a & cin) | (b & cin);
endmodule

module adder3bit (
    first, second, carry_in, sum_out, carry_out
  );
  input [0:2] first, second;
  input carry_in;
  output [0:2] sum_out;
  output carry_out;
  wire [0:1] car;

  adder1bit
    u1adder1bit (
      .a(first[2]), .b(second[2]), .cin(carry_in),
      .sum(sum_out[2]), .cout(car[1])
    ),
    u2adder1bit (
      .a(first[1]), .b(second[1]), .cin(car[1]),
      .sum(sum_out[1]), .cout(car[0])
    ),
    u3adder1bit (
      .a(first[0]), .b(second[0]), .cin(car[0]),
```

```
    .sum(sum_out[0]), .cout(carry_out)
  );
endmodule

module adder3_testbench1;
  parameter BITS = 11, WORDS = 2;
  reg [1:BITS] vmem [1:WORDS];
  reg [0:2] a, b, sum_ex;
  reg cin, cout_cx;
  integer j;
  wire [0:2] sum;
  wire cout;

  // Instantiate the module under test.
  adder3bit u_adder3bit (
    .first(a), .second(b), .carry_in(cin),
    .sum_out(sum), .carry_out(cout)
  );

  initial
    begin
      $readmemb ("test.vec", vmem);

      for (j = 1; j <= WORDS; j = j + 1)
        begin
            {a, b, cin, sum_ex, cout_ex} <= vmem[j];
            #5;       // Wait for 5 time units for
                      // circuit to settle.

          if ((sum !== sum_ex) || (cout !== cout_ex))
            $display ("****Mismatch on vector %b *****",
                      vmem[j]);
          else
            $display ("No mismatch on vector %b",
                      vmem[j]);
        end
    end
endmodule
```

A memory vmem is first defined; the word size corresponds to the number of bits in each vector and the number of words in memory corresponds to the number of vectors in the file. The **$readmemb** system task reads the vectors in the file test.vec into the memory vmem. The for-loop goes through each of the memory words, that is, each vector, applies these to the module under test, waits for the module to be stable and probes the module outputs. A conditional statement is used to compare expected output values and the monitored output values. If any mismatch occurs, a message is printed to the output. Here is the output produced when the above test bench is executed. Since there are no errors in the model, no mismatches are reported.

```
No mismatch on vector 01001001000
No mismatch on vector 01001111100
```

11.5 Writing Vectors to a Text File

In the previous section on testbench examples, we saw how values are printed to output. Values of signals in a design can be printed to a file as well by using the display system tasks that write to a file such as **$fdisplay, $fmonitor** and **$fstrobe**. Here is the same testbench example as is the previous section, but in this case, the testbench prints out all the input vectors and observed output vectors to a file `mon.out`.

```
module adder3_testbench2;
  parameter BITS = 11, WORDS = 2;
  reg [1:BITS] vmem [1:WORDS];
  reg [0:2] a, b, sum_ex;
  reg cin, cout_ex;
  integer j;
  wire [0:2] sum;
  wire cout;

  // Instantiate the module under test.
  adder3bit u_adder3bit (
    .first(a), .second(b), .carry_in(cin),
    .sum_out(sum), .carry_out(cout)
  );

  initial
    begin: init_blk
      integer mon_out_file;

      mon_out_file = $fopen ("mon.out", "w");
      $readmemb ("test.vec", vmem);
```

```
        for (j = 1; j <= WORDS; j = j + 1)
          begin
            {a, b, cin, sum_ex, cout_ex} = vmem[j];
            #5; // Wait for 5 time units for
                // circuit to settle.

            if ((sum !== sum_ex) || (cout !== cout_ex))
              $display ("****Mismatch on vector %b *****",
                        vmem[j]);
            else
              $display ("No mismatch on vector %b",
                        vmem[j]);

            // Write the input and output vectors to a file:
            $fdisplay (mon_out_file,
                       "Input = %b%b%b, Output = %b%b",
                       a, b, cin, sum, cout);
          end

        $fclose (mon_out_file);
      end
    endmodule
```

Here is what is contained in the file `mon.out` after simulation.

```
Input = 0100100, Output = 1000
Input = 0100111, Output = 1100
```

11.6 Some More Examples

11.6.1 A Clock Divider

A complete testbench that uses the waveform application method is shown next. The module under test is called `divider`. The output responses are written into a file for later comparison.

```
module divider (div_clk, reset, testn, ena);
  input div_clk, reset, testn;
  output ena;
  reg [3:0] counter;

  always
    @(posedge div_clk) begin
      if (~ reset)
        counter <= 0;
      else
        begin
          if (~ testn)
            counter <= 15;
          else
            counter <= counter + 1;
        end
    end

  assign ena = (counter == 15) ? 1 : 0;
endmodule

module divider_tb;
  integer out_file;
  reg clock, reset, testn;
  wire enable;

  initial
    out_file = $fopen ("out.vec", "w");

  always
    begin
      #5 clock = 0;
      #3 clock = 1;
    end

  divider u_divider (
    .div_clk(clock), .reset(reset),
    .testn(testn), .ena(enable)
  );

  initial
    begin
      reset = 0;
```

```
      #50 reset = 1;
    end

  initial
    begin
      testn = 0;
      #100 testn = 1;
      #50 testn = 0;
      #50 $fclose (out_file);
      $finish;                    // Terminate simulation.
    end

  // For every event on the enable output signal,
  // write to file.
  initial
    $fmonitor (out_file,
      "Enable changed to %b at time %t", enable, $time);
endmodule
```

Here is the output contained in the `out.vec` file.

```
Enable changed to x at time      0
Enable changed to 0 at time      8
Enable changed to 1 at time     56
Enable changed to 0 at time    104
Enable changed to 1 at time    152
```

11.6.2 A Factorial Design

This example illustrates a different approach to stimulus generation; in this case the stimulus value is generated based on the state of the module under test. This approach is useful in testing a finite-state machine for which different input stimulus is applied based on the machine's state. Consider a design in which the objective is to compute the factorial of an input number. The handshake mechanism between the module under test and the test bench model is shown in Figure 11-10.

The `reset` input to the module resets the factorial model to an initial state. The `start` signal is set after the `data` input is applied. When computation is complete, the output `done` is set to indicate that the computed result appears on the `fac_out` and `exp_out` outputs. The resulting facto-

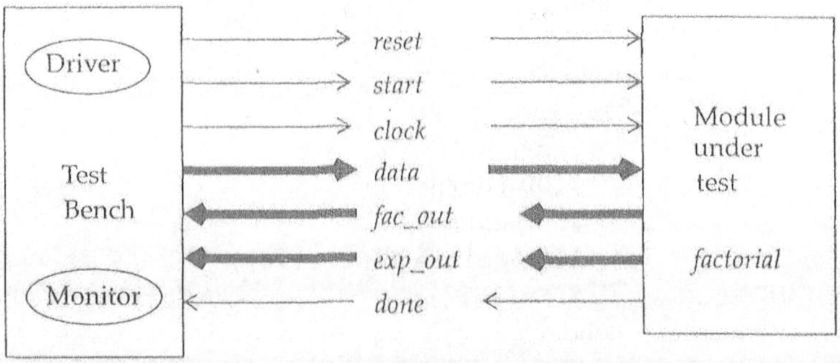

Figure 11-10 Handshake between test bench and entity under test.

rial value is `fac_out*2`$^{exp\_out}$. The test bench model provides input data on `data` starting from values 1 to 20 in increments of one. It applies the data, sets the `start` signal, waits for the `done` signal, and then applies the next input data. Error messages are printed out if the values appearing at the output are not correct. The descriptions for the module and the test bench follows.

```
`timescale 1ns/1ns
module factorial (
    reset, start, clk, data, done, fac_out, exp_out
  );
  input reset, start, clk;
  input [4:0] data;
  output done;
  output [7:0] fac_out, exp_out;

  reg stop;
  reg [4:0] in_latch;
  reg [7:0] exponent, result;
  integer i;

  initial
    stop = 1;

  always
    @(posedge clk) begin
      if ((start == 1) && (stop == 1) && (reset == 1))
        begin
          result = 1;
```

```
                exponent = 0;
                in_latch = data;
                stop = 0;
              end
            else
              begin
                if ((in_latch > 1) && (stop == 0))
                  begin
                    result = result * in_latch;
                    in_latch = in_latch - 1;
                  end

                if (in_latch < 1)
                  stop = 1;

                // Normalization:
                for (i = 1; i <= 5; i = i + 1)
                  if (result > 256)
                    begin
                      result = result / 2;
                      exponent = exponent + 1;
                    end
              end
          end

          assign done = stop;
          assign fac_out = result;
          assign exp_out = exponent;
endmodule


module factorial_testbench;
  parameter IN_MAX = 5, OUT_MAX = 8;
  parameter RESET_ST = 0, START_ST = 1, APPL_DATA_ST = 2,
        WAIT_RESULT_ST = 3;
  reg clk, reset, start;
  wire done;
  reg [IN_MAX-1 : 0] data;
  wire [OUT_MAX-1 : 0] fac_out, exp_out;
  integer next_state;
  parameter MAX_APPLY = 20;
  integer num_applied;
```

```
initial
  num_applied = 1;

always
  begin: clk_blk
    #6 clk = 1;
    #4 clk = 0;
  end

always
  @(negedge clk)    // Falling edge transition.
    case (next_state)
      RESET_ST:
        begin
          reset <= 1;
          start <= 0;
          next_state <= APPL_DATA_ST;
        end
      APPL_DATA_ST:
        begin
          data <= num_applied;
          next_state <= START_ST;
        end
      START_ST:
        begin
          start <= 1;
          next_state <= WAIT_RESULT_ST;
        end
      WAIT_RESULT_ST:
        begin
          reset <= 0;
          start <= 0;
          wait (done == 1);

          if (num_applied ==
                      fac_out * ('h0001 << exp_out))
          $display ("Incorrect result from factorial",
                    " model for input value %d", data);
```

Blocking assignment used on `num_applied` since its value is used in the following statement.

```
          num_applied = num_applied + 1;

          if (num_applied < MAX_APPLY)
            next_state <= APPL_DATA_ST;
          else
            begin
              $display ("Test completed successfully");
              $finish;  // Terminate simulation.
            end
        end
      default:
        next_state <= START_ST;
    endcase

  // Apply to module under test:
  factorial u_factorial (
    .reset(reset), .start(start),
    .clk(clk), .data(data), .done(done),
    .fac_out(fac_out), .exp_out(exp_out)
  );
endmodule
```

11.6.3 A Sequence Detector

Here is a model for a sequence detector. The model checks for a sequence of three consecutive one's on the data line. Data is checked on every falling edge of clock. Figure 11-11 shows the state diagram. A test bench is also provided.

```
module count3_1s (data, clock, detect3_1s);
  input data, clock;
  output reg detect3_1s;
  integer count;

  initial
    begin
      count <= 0;
      detect3_1s <= 0;
    end
```

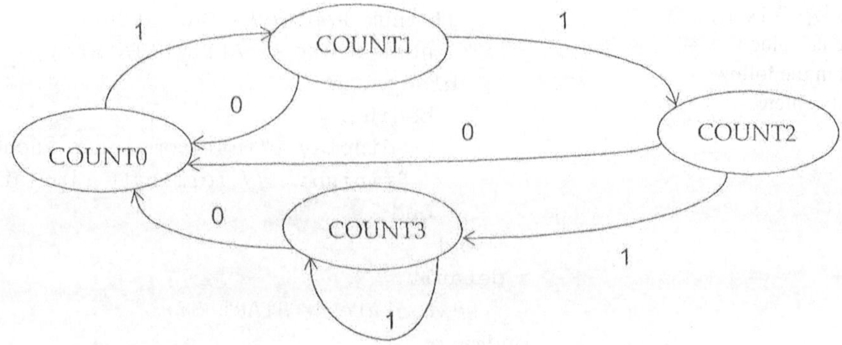

Figure 11-11 A sequence detector.

Used blocking assignment for `count` as its value is used later in a conditional.

```
  always
    @(negedge clock) begin
      if (data == 1)
        count = count + 1;
      else
        count = 0;

      if (count >= 3)
        detect3_1s <= 1;
      else
        detect3_1s <= 0;
    end
endmodule

module count3_1s_top;
  reg data, clock;
  integer out_file;

  // Instantiate module under test;
  count3_1s u_count3_1s (
    .data(data), .clock(clock), .detect3_1s(detect)
  );

  initial
    begin
      clock = 0;
```

```
        forever
          #5 clock = ~ clock;
      end

    initial
      begin
        data = 0;
        #5 data = 1;
        #40 data = 0;
        #10 data = 1;
        #40 data = 0;
        #20 $stop;          // Stop simulation.
      end

    initial
      begin
        // Save monitor information in file.
        out_file = $fopen ("results.vectors", "w");
        $fmonitor (out_file,
                   "clock = %b, data = %b, detect = %b",
                   clock, data, detect);
      end
    endmodule
```

11.6.4 A LED Sequencer

Here is a model for a LED sequencer. This sequencer lights up the LEDs in the following fashion (shown for an 8-bit sequence):

```
00000000
10000000
11000000
11100000
11110000
11111000
11111100
11111110
11111111
00000000
```

The model is a generic model - the number of LEDs can be specified via a generic parameter. This model has been implemented using a shift register. A test bench also accompanies the model.

```
module led_sequencer_tb;
  parameter MAX_LEN = 8;
  wire [MAX_LEN-1:0] led;
  reg clk, rst;

  always
    begin
      #1 clk = 1'b0;
      #2 clk = 1'b1;

      if ($time > 200)
        $finish;
    end

  initial
    begin
      rst = 1'b1;
      #11 rst = 1'b0;
    end

  led_sequencer #(.MAX_LENGTH(MAX_LEN)) u_led (
      .clk(clk), .rst(rst), .led_out(led)
  );

  always
    @(led)
      $display ("At time ", $time, ", LEDS = ", led);
endmodule

module led_sequencer
  # ( parameter MAX_LENGTH = 8 )
    ( input clk, rst,
      output reg [MAX_LENGTH-1:0] led_out
    );

  always
    @(posedge clk, posedge rst)
      if (rst)
        led_out <= {MAX_LENGTH{1'b0}};
```

```
        else
          if (led_out == {MAX_LENGTH{1'b1}})
            led_out <= {MAX_LENGTH{1'b0}};
          else
            led_out <= {1'b1, led_out[MAX_LENGTH-1:1]};
endmodule
```

Here is the output of the simulation run.

```
At time 0, LEDS = 00000000
At time 11, LEDS = 10000000
At time 14, LEDS = 11000000
At time 17, LEDS = 11100000
At time 20, LEDS = 11110000
At time 23, LEDS = 11111000
At time 26, LEDS = 11111100
At time 29, LEDS = 11111110
At time 32, LEDS = 11111111
At time 35, LEDS = 00000000
At time 38, LEDS = 10000000
. . .
```

11.7 *Utilities*

11.7.1 Checking for x

To check if at least one bit of a vector is an x, you can use the reduction xor operator and the case equality operator as shown in the following example.

```
wire [7:0] my_vector;
reg reduced_bit;
. . .
always
  @(my_vector) begin
    reduced_bit = ^ my_vector;

    if (reduced_bit === 1'bx)
      $display ("Found at least one x in the vector.");
  end
```

Yet another way to check the presence of an **x** or a **z** in a vector is to compare the vector with itself using the logical comparison operator. The logical comparison will fail if either operand has an **x** or a **z** in it.

```
if (my_vector == my_vector)
  ;
else
  $display ("Vector %b has at least one x or a z.",
              my_vector);
```

11.7.2 Passing a File to a Task

A file can be passed as an argument to a task by passing its file pointer. The file pointer obtained by using the **$fopen** system task is passed to the task as an integer variable. The file display system tasks can be used to write to the file using the specified file pointer. Here is an example of such use.

```
module pass_file2task;
  task write_messages2file (
      input [31:0] channel_id
    );
    begin
      $fdisplay (channel_id, "Printing this message ",
                 "from task write_messages2file");
      // Do other things you want with the file using the
      // channel identifier.
      $fdisplay (channel_id, "Some more messages ****");
    end
  endtask

  integer ch_id;

  initial
    begin
      ch_id = $fopen ("mydebug.out", "w");
      write_messages2file (ch_id);
      #10 $fclose (ch_id);
    end
endmodule
```

11.7.3 Debugging Opcodes

Since Verilog HDL has no notion of enumeration types, constants that are used to define certain things simply appear as bits during simulation, making debugging difficult. One way to work around this is to define the constants as strings. Here is an example that shows this.

```
module arith_logic_unit
  # ( parameter ADD = 2'b00, SUB = 2'b01, MUL = 2'b11,
              NOP = 2'b10 )
    ( input [0:3] opd1, opd2,
      input [0:1] opcode,
      output reg [0:7] result
    );
  reg [3*8:1] opcode_str;

  always
    @(opd1, opd2, opcode)
      case (opcode)
        ADD: result = opd1 + opd2;
        SUB: result = opd1 - opd2;
        MUL: result = opd1 * opd2;
        NOP: result = 'bx;
      endcase

  always
    @(opcode)
      case (opcode)
        ADD: opcode_str = "ADD";
        SUB: opcode_str = "SUB";
        MUL: opcode_str = "MUL";
        NOP: opcode_str = "NOP";
      endcase
endmodule
```

11.7.4 Check No Missing Clock

Here is an example of a model that checks to see if there is a missing clock pulse.

```
module check_clock
  # ( parameter tPERIOD = 3 )
  ( input clock
  );
 time curr_time, last_time;

 always
   @(posedge clock) begin
     curr_time = $time;

     if ((curr_time - last_time) > tPERIOD)
       $display ("Assertion fail: Clock not periodic");

     last_time = curr_time;
   end
endmodule
```

11.7.5 Clock Burst Generator

Here is a model of a clock generator that is controlled by a signal. In the example, the signal `clock_control` is declared within the model, but it could very well be an input to the model. Clock bursts are generated only when `clock_control` is high, else clock is off.

```
module controlled_clock
  # ( parameter ON_DELAY = 1, OFF_DELAY = 2 )
    ( output reg clock
    );
  reg clock_control;

  initial
    begin
      clock_control = 0;
      #5 clock_control = 1;
      #50 clock_control = 0;
      #25 clock_control = 1;
      #60 clock_control = 0;
      #40 clock_control = 1;
      #20 clock_control = 0;
      #10 $finish;
    end
  // Alternatively clock_control could also be an input
```

```
      // that controls the clock generation.

    always
      begin
        wait (clock_control);
        #OFF_DELAY clock = 1;
        #ON_DELAY clock = 0;
      end
  endmodule
```

11.8 Exercises

1. Generate a clock with an on-period and an off-period of 3ns and 10ns respectively.
2. Write a Verilog HDL model that generates the waveform shown in Figure 11-12.

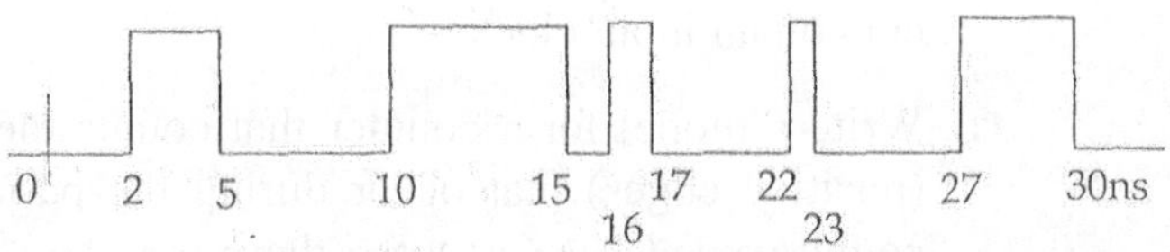

Figure 11-12 A waveform.

3. Generate a clock `clk_v` that is phase-delayed from the clock `clk_d` described in module `gen_clk_d` (Figure 11-6). The phase-delay is 15ns. [Hint: Using a continuous assignment statement may not be appropriate].
4. Write a test bench that tests a sequence detector. The detector checks an input data stream on every positive clock edge for a pattern 10010. If such a pattern is found, the output is set to a 1, else it is set to a 0.
5. Write a module that generates two clocks, `clock_a` and `clock_b`. `clock_a` starts with a delay of 10ns while `clock_b` starts with a delay of 40ns. Both clocks have the same on-off period, on-period is 1ns while the off-period is 2ns. `clock_b` is synchronized with the edges of `clock_a` but has opposite polarity.

6. Describe a behavioral model for a 4-bit adder / subtracter. Exercise this model with a test bench. All input values and expected values are described within the test bench itself. Dump the input values, expected values and monitored output values to a text file.

7. Describe an ALU that performs all the relational operations (<, <=, >, >=) on two 4-bit operands. Write a test bench that reads the test patterns and the expected result from a text file.

8. Write a module that performs an arithmetic shift of an input vector. Specify the size of the input as a parameter with a default value of 32. Also specify the amount of shift as a parameter with a default value of 1. Write a test bench that tests such a module which performs an arithmetic shift on a 12-bit vector and shifts 8 times.

9. Write a model for an `N` times clock multiplier. The input is a reference clock of an unknown frequency. The output should be synchronized with every positive edge of the reference clock. [Hint: Determine the clock period of the reference clock].

10. Write a model that displays the time whenever a 0 to 1 transition occurs on an input clock.

11. Write a model for a counter that counts the number of clock pulses (positive edges) that occur during the period `count_flag` is 1. If count exceeds `MAX_COUNT`, the `overflow` output is set and counter stays at the `MAX_COUNT` limit. The rising edge of `count_flag` causes the counter to reset to 0 and start counting again. Write a test bench to test this model.

12. Write a model for a parameterized Gray code counter. Default it to a size of 3. The counter gets asynchronously reset when the variable `reset` is 0. The counter transitions on every negative edge of a clock. Then instantiate a 4-bit Gray code counter in a test bench and test the model.

13. Write a behavioral model for an asynchronous reset toggle flip-flop. If toggle is 1, the output toggles between 0 and 1. If toggle is 0, output stays in previous state. Then, using the specify block, specify a setup time of 2ns and a hold time of 3ns. Verify the model using a test bench.

14. Write a test master for a system-on-chip (SOC) that takes in a sequence of instructions and performs the appropriate transaction on the SOC bus. There are two kinds of instructions (in this exercise):

```
read_memory <memory_location>
write_memory <memory_location> <data>
```

Assume a 32-bit address bus and two 32-bit data buses, one for the read data and one for the write data. There is also a signal `read_write` that indicates whether a read cycle or a write cycle is going on. You may choose any input format to represent the sequence of instructions.

❑

12

Modeling Examples

This chapter provides a number of hardware modeling examples using Verilog HDL.

12.1 Modeling Simple Elements

A basic hardware element is a wire. A wire can be modeled in Verilog HDL as a net data type. Consider a 4-bit and gate, the behavior of which is described next.

```
`timescale 1ns/1ns
module and4 (a, b, y);
  input [3:0] a, b;
  output [3:0] y;

  assign #5 y = a & b;
endmodule
```

The delay for the & (and) logic is specified to be 5ns. The hardware represented by this model is shown in Figure 12-1.

This example and the one following show that Boolean equations can be modeled as expressions in continuous assignment statements. Wires can be modeled as net data types. For example, in the following descrip-

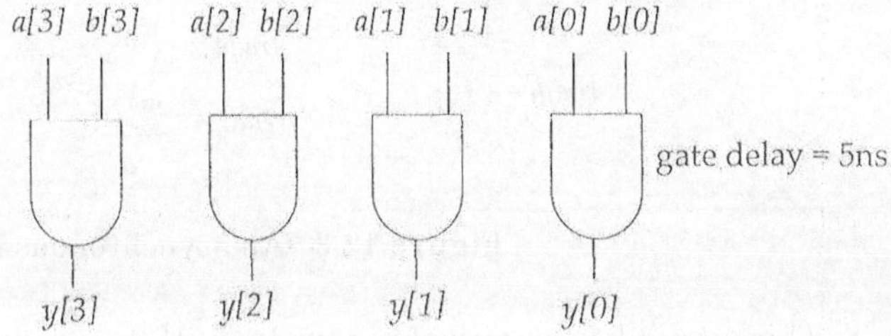

Figure 12-1 A 4-bit and gate.

tion, irda represents a wire that connects the output of the ~ (not) operator to the input of the ^ (xor) operator. Figure 12-2 shows the circuit represented by the module.

```
module boolean_ex (sync, eoc, tag);
  input sync, eoc;
  output tag;
  wire irda;

  assign irda = ~ eoc;
  assign tag = irda ^ sync;
endmodule
```

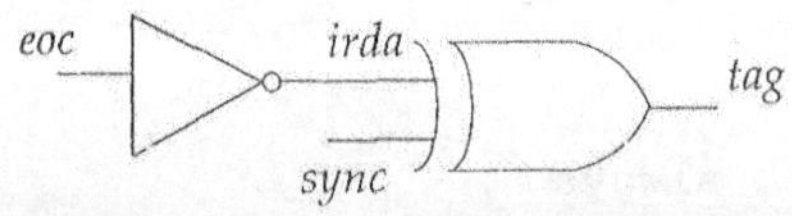

Figure 12-2 A combinational circuit.

Consider the following behavior and its corresponding hardware representation as shown in Figure 12-3.

```
module asynchronous;
  wire treqa, treqb, tic, tread;

  assign tic = treqa | tread;
  assign treqa = ~ (treqb & tic);
endmodule
```

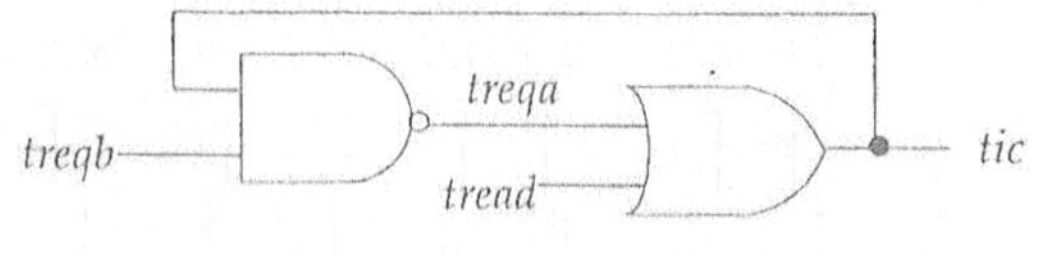

Figure 12-3 An asynchronous loop.

This circuit has an asynchronous loop. If the model were simulated with a certain set of values (`treqb` = 1, `tread` = 0), simulation time would never advance because the simulator would always be iterating between the two assignments. The iteration time would be two zero delays. Therefore, extra caution must be exercised when values are assigned to nets using continuous assignment that have zero delay and when these same net values are used in expressions.

In certain cases, it is desirable to have such an asynchronous loop. An example of such an asynchronous loop is shown next; the statement represents a periodic waveform with a cycle of 20ns. Its hardware representation is shown in Figure 12-4. Note that such an always statement needs an initial statement that initializes the variable to either a 0 or a 1, else the variable will be stuck at the value x.

```
reg rcen;

initial
  rcen = 0;

always
  #10 rcen = ~ rcen;
```

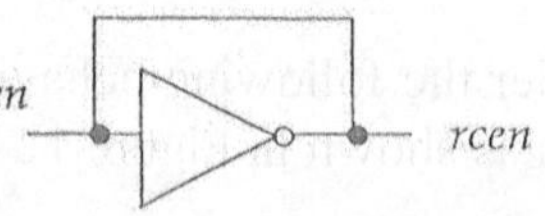

Figure 12-4 A clock generator.

Elements of a vector net or a variable can be accessed, as either a single element called bit-select, or a slice called part-select. For example,

```
reg addr_drive;
reg [0:4] curr_gnt;
reg [5:0] bound, data_drive;

always
  begin
    . . .
    data_drive[4:0] = bound[5:1] | curr_gnt;
    // data_drive[4:0] and bound[5:1] are part-selects.
    data_drive[5] = addr_drive & bound[5];
    // data_drive[5] and bound[5] are bit-selects.
  end
```

The first procedural assignment implies:

```
data_drive[4] = bound[5] | curr_gnt[0];
data_drive[3] = bound[4] | curr_gnt[1];
. . .
```

Bit-selects, part-selects and vectors can be concatenated to form larger vectors. For example,

```
wire [7:0] next_ctrl, ctrl_word;
wire parity;
. . .
assign next_ctrl = {parity, ctrl_word[6:0]};
```

It is also possible to refer to an element of a vector whose index value is computable only at runtime. For example,

```
next_vector = pb_selector[vec_addr];
```

implies a decoder whose output is `next_vector`, and `vec_addr` specifies the selection address. `pb_selector` is a vector; it models the behavior of the decoder.

Shift operations can be performed using the predefined shift operators. Alternately, shift operations can be modeled using the concatenation operator. For example,

```
wire [0:7] rsp_state, trn_state;
. . .
```

```
assign trn_state = {rsp_state[1:7], rsp_state[0]};
  // A left-rotate operation.
assign trn_state = {rsp_state[7], rsp_state[0:6]};
  // A right-rotate operation.
assign trn_state = {rsp_state[1:7], 1'b0};
  // A left-shift operation.
```

Subfields of a vector, called part-select, can also be used in expressions. For example, consider a 32-bit instruction register, `instr_reg`, in which the first 16 bits denote the address, next 8 bits represent the opcode, and the remaining 8 bits represent the index. Given the following declarations,

```
reg [31:0] memory [0:1023];
wire [31:0] instr_reg;
wire [15:0] address;
wire [7:0] op_code, index;
wire [0:9] prog_ctr;
wire read_ctl;
```

one way to read the subfield information from the `instr_reg` is to use three continuous assignment statements. The part-selects of the instruction register are assigned to specific wires.

```
assign instr_reg = memory[prog_ctr];

assign address = instr_reg[31:16];
assign op_code = instr_reg[15:8];
assign index = instr_reg[7:0];
. . .

always
  @(posedge read_ctl)
    task_call (address, op_code, index);
```

A tristate gate can be modeled behaviorally using a continuous assignment statement. An example is:

```
wire tri_out = enable ? tri_in : 1'bz;
```

When `enable` is 1, `tri_out` gets the value of `tri_in`. When `enable` is 0, `tri_out` has a high impedance value.

12.2 Different Styles of Modeling

This section gives examples of the three different modeling styles provided by the language: dataflow, behavioral, and structural. Consider the circuit shown in Figure 12-5, which saves the value of the input `sm_rdata` into a register and then multiplies it with input `selreg`.

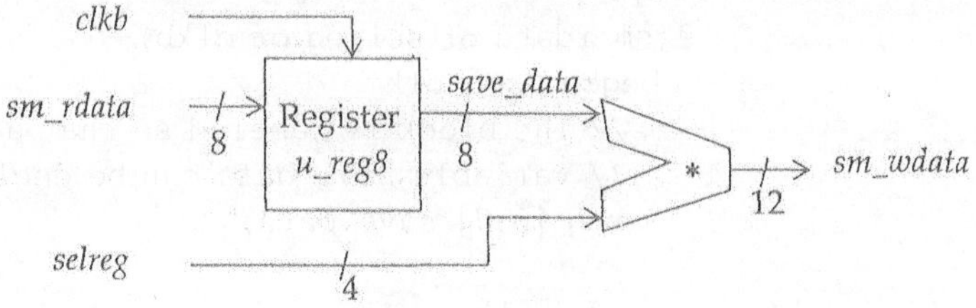

Figure 12-5 A buffered multiplier.

The first modeling style is the dataflow style in which continuous assignment statements are used to model the circuit.

```
module save_multiplier_dataflow (
    sm_rdata, selreg, clkb, sm_wdata
  );
  input [0:7] sm_rdata;
  input [0:3] selreg;
  input clkb;
  output [0:11] sm_wdata;
  wire save_data;

  assign sm_wdata = save_data * selreg;
  assign save_data = clkb ? sm_rdata : save_data;
endmodule
```

This representation does not directly imply any structure, but implicitly describes it. However, its functionality is very clear. The register has been modeled using a clock control.

The second way to describe the circuit is to model it as a sequential program using an always statement with a sequential block.

```
module save_multiplier_sequential (
    sm_rdata, selreg, clkb, sm_wdata
  );
  input [0:7] sm_rdata;
  input [0:3] selreg;
  input clkb;
  output reg [0:11] sm_wdata;

  always
    @(sm_rdata or selreg or clkb)
      begin: seq_blk
        // The block is labeled so that a local
        // variable save_data can be declared.
        reg [0:7] save_data;

        if (clkb)
          save_data = sm_rdata;

        sm_wdata = save_data * selreg;
      end
endmodule
```

This model also describes the behavior, but does not imply any structure, either explicitly or implicitly. In this case, the register has been modeled using an `if` statement.

The third way to describe the `save_multiplier` circuit is to model it as a netlist assuming the existence of an 8-bit register and an 8-bit multiplier.

```
module save_multiplier_netlist (
    sm_rdata, selreg, clkb, sm_wdata
  );
  input [0:7] sm_rdata;
  input [0:3] selreg;
  input clkb;
  output [0:11] sm_wdata;
  wire [0:7] save_data, s1;
  wire [0:15] s2;
```

```
    reg8 u_reg8 (
      .din(sm_rdata), .clk(clkb), .dout(save_data)
    );
    mult8 u_mult8 (
      .a(save_data), .b({4'b0000, selreg}), .z(sm_wdata)
    );
  endmodule
```

This description explicitly describes the structure, but the behavior is unknown. This is because the reg8 and mult8 module names are arbitrary, and they could have any behavior associated with them.

Of these three different modeling styles, the behavioral style of modeling is generally the fastest to simulate.

12.3 Modeling Delays

Consider a 3-input nor gate. Its behavior can be modeled using a continuous assignment, such as shown in the following example.

```
assign #12 gate_out = ~(a | b | c);
```

This statement models the nor gate with a delay of 12 time units. This delay represents the time from an event on signal a, b, or c until the result value appears on signal gate_out. An event could be any value change, for example, x->z, x-> 0, or 1 -> 0.

If the rise time and the fall time were to be explicitly modeled, use two delays in the assignment, such as:

```
assign #(12, 14) zoom = ~(a | b | c);
  /* 12 is the rise delay, 14 is the fall delay and
    min(12, 14) = 12 is the transition to x delay */
```

In case of logic that can be assigned the value z, a third delay value, which is the turn-off delay, can also be specified, such as:

```
assign #(12, 14, 10) zoom = a > b ? c : 'bz;
  // Rise delay is 12, fall delay is 14, transition to x
  // delay is min(12, 14, 10), and turn-off delay is 10.
```

Each of the delay values can also be represented using *min:typ:max* notation, such as in the following example.

```
assign #(9:10:11, 11:12:13, 13:14:15)
   zoom = a > b ? c : 'bz;
```

A delay value could in general be an expression.

Delays in primitive gate instances and UDPs can be modeled by specifying the delay values in the instantiation. Here is an example of a 5-input primitive and gate.

```
and #(2, 3) uland (aout, in1, in2, in3, in4, in5);
```

The output rise delay has been specified as 2 time units and the output fall delay has been specified as 3 time units.

Delays in a module at port boundaries can be specified using a specify block. For example, here is an example of a half-adder module.

```
module half_adder (a, b, s, c);
  input a, b;
  output s, c;

  specify
    (a => s) = (1.2, 0.8);
    (b => s) = (1.0, 0.6);
    (a => c) = (1.2, 1.0);
    (b => c) = (1.2, 0.6);
  endspecify

  assign s = a ^ b;
  assign c = a | b;
endmodule
```

Instead of modeling the delays in the continuous assignments, the delays have been modeled using a specify block. Is there a way to specify the delays external to the module? One option is to use the SDF[1] (Standard Delay Format) and the backannotation mechanism possibly provided by a

1. See Bibliography.

Verilog simulator. If this information needs to be specified in the Verilog HDL model explicitly, one approach is to create two dummy modules on top of the `half_adder` module each with a different set of delays.

```
module half_adder2 (a, b, s, c);
  input a, b;
  output s, c;

  assign s = a ^ b;
  assign c = a | b;
endmodule

module half_adder_optimistic (a, b, s, c);
  input a, b;
  output s, c;

  specify
    (a => s) = (1.2, 0.8);
    (b => s) = (1.0, 0.6);
    (a => c) = (1.2, 1.0);
    (b => c) = (1.2, 0.6);
  endspecify

  half_adder2 u_half_adder2 (
    .a(a), .b(b), .s(s), .c(c)
  );
endmodule

module half_adder_pessimistic (a, b, s, c);
  input a, b;
  output s, c;

  specify
    (a => s) = (0.6, 0.4);
    (b => s) = (0.5, 0.3);
    (a => c) = (0.6, 0.5);
    (b => c) = (0.6, 0.3);
  endspecify

  half_adder2 u_half_adder2 (
    .a(a), .b(b), .s(s), .c(c)
  );
endmodule
```

With these modules, the module `half_adder2` is independent of any delays, and depending on which delay mode that you would like to use, simulate the appropriate top-level module `half_adder_optimistic` or `half_adder_pessimistic`.

Transport Delays

Delays specified in continuous assignments and gate-level primitives model inertial delay. Transport delay can be modeled using a nonblocking assignment with an intra-statement delay. Here is an example.

```
module transport (wave_a, delayed_wave);
  parameter TRANSPORT_DELAY = 500;
  input wave_a;
  output reg delayed_wave;

  always
    @(wave_a) delayed_wave <= #TRANSPORT_DELAY wave_a;
endmodule
```

The always statement contains a nonblocking assignment with an intra-statement delay. Any change on `wave_a` gets scheduled on `delayed_wave` `TRANSPORT_DELAY` in the future. Consequently, a waveform that appears on `wave_a` appears on `delayed_wave` delayed by `TRANSPORT_DELAY`; an example of such a delayed waveform is shown in Figure 12-6.

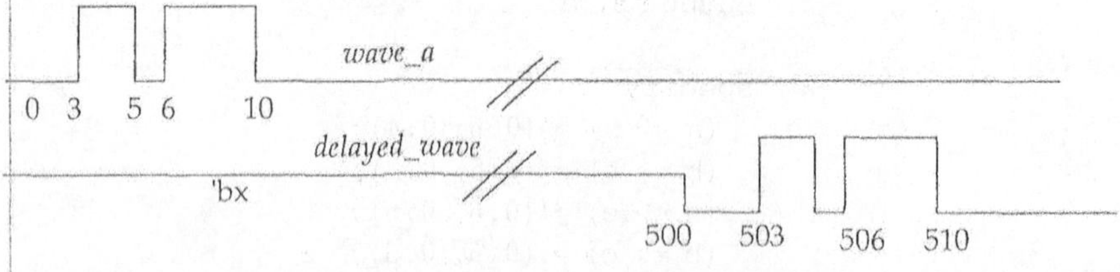

Figure 12-6 Transport delay example.

12.4 Modeling a Truth Table

A truth table can be modeled in a number of ways, including the following.

i. Using an UDP
ii. Using a function and a case statement
iii. Using a **$readmem** system task
iv. Using an initial statement

Here is an example truth table that we model.

a	*b*	*c*	*y*
0	0	0	1
0	0	1	1
0	1	0	1
0	1	1	0
1	0	0	1
1	0	1	0
1	1	0	0
1	1	1	0

Here is the truth table described using an UDP.

```
primitive majority0_udp (
   output y,
   input a, b, c
  );

  table
   // a     b     c     : y
      0     0     0     : 1   ;
      0     0     1     : 1   ;
      0     1     0     : 1   ;
      0     1     1     : 0   ;
      1     0     0     : 1   ;
      1     0     1     : 0   ;
      1     1     0     : 0   ;
      1     1     1     : 0   ;
  endtable
endprimitive
```

Here is the same truth table described using a function and case statement.

```
function majority0_func (
   input [2:0] data
  );

  case (data)
    3'b000: majority0_func = 1'b1;
    3'b001: majority0_func = 1'b1;
    3'b010: majority0_func = 1'b1;
    3'b011: majority0_func = 1'b0;
    3'b100: majority0_func = 1'b1;
    3'b101: majority0_func = 1'b0;
    3'b110: majority0_func = 1'b0;
    3'b111: majority0_func = 1'b0;
  endcase
endfunction
```

The truth table can be written in a text file and read in using a **$readmem** system task. The text file `majority0.dat` contains the following (first three bits are the inputs and the last bit is the output):

```
0001
0011
0101
0110
1001
1010
1100
1110
```

Here is the source code that reads in the text file into the table `majority0_table`.

```
reg [3:0] majority0_table [0:7];

initial
  $readmemb ("majority0.dat", majority0_table);
```

The truth table can also be explicitly setup using an initial statement.

```
reg [2:0] majority0_table [0:7];

initial
 begin
   majority0_table[3'b000] = 1'b1;
   majority0_table[3'b001] = 1'b1;
   majority0_table[3'b010] = 1'b1;
   majority0_table[3'b011] = 1'b0;
   majority0_table[3'b100] = 1'b1;
   majority0_table[3'b101] = 1'b0;
   majority0_table[3'b110] = 1'b0;
   majority0_table[3'b111] = 1'b0;
 end
```

12.5 Modeling Conditional Operations

Operations that occur under certain conditions can be modeled using either a continuous assignment with a conditional operator, or using an `if` statement or a case statement in an always statement. Let us consider an arithmetic logic circuit. Its behavior can be modeled using a continuous assignment as shown below.

```
module simple_alu (a, b, c, selop, alu);
  input [3:0] a, b, c;
  input selop;
  output [3:0] alu;

  assign alu = selop ? a + b : a - b;
endmodule
```

A multiplexer can also be modeled using an always statement. The value of the select lines are first determined and, based on this value, a case statement selects the appropriate input that is to be assigned to the output.

```
`timescale 1ns/1ns
module multiplexer (sel_input, a, b, c, d, mux_out);
  input [0:1] sel_input;
  input a, b, c, d;
```

```
  output reg mux_out;
  reg temp;
  parameter MUX_DELAY = 15;

  always
    @(sel_input or a or b or c or d) begin: p1_blk
      case (sel_input)
        0: temp = a;
        1: temp = b;
        2: temp = c;
        3: temp = d;
      endcase

      mux_out = #MUX_DELAY temp;
    end
endmodule
```

The multiplexer could also have been modeled using a continuous assignment of the form:

```
assign #MUX_DELAY mux_out =
    (sel_input == 0) ? a :
    (sel_input == 1) ? b :
    (sel_input == 2) ? c :
    (sel_input == 3) ? d :
    1'bx;
```

Here is a model for a N-bit even parity checker.

```
module even_parity_checker
  # ( parameter N = 16 )
    ( input [N-1:0] bus_in,
      output parity_out
    );

  assign parity_out = ^ bus_in;
endmodule
```

12.6 Modeling Synchronous Logic

So far in this chapter, most of the examples that we have seen are combinational logic. For modeling synchronous logic, the variable data type has been provided in the language to model registers and memories. However not every variable data type infers synchronous logic. A common way to model synchronous logic is by controlling the assignment.

Consider the following example, which shows how controlling a reg variable can model a synchronous edge-triggered D-type flip-flop.

```
`timescale 1ns/1ns
module d_flip_flop (d, clock, q);
  input d, clock;
  output reg q;

  always
    @(posedge clock)
      q <= #5 d;
endmodule
```

The semantics of the always statement indicates that when there is a rising edge on `clock`, `q` will get the value of `d` after 5ns, else the value of `q` does not change (a variable retains its value until it is assigned a new value). The behavior in the always statement expresses the semantics of a D-type flip-flop. Given this module, an 8-bit register can be modeled as follows.

An array of instances.

```
module register8 (d, q, clock);
  parameter START = 0, STOP = 7;
  input [START : STOP] d;
  input clock;
  output [START : STOP] q;
  wire [START : STOP] fan_clk;

  d_flip_flop u_d_flip_flop [START : STOP] (
    .d(d), .clock (fan_clk), .q(q)
  );

  buf ulbuf (
    fan_clk[0], fan_clk[1], fan_clk[2], fan_clk[3],
    fan_clk[4], fan_clk[5], fan_clk[6], fan_clk[7],
    clock
```

```
  );
endmodule
```

Consider a gated cross-coupled latch circuit, as shown in Figure 12-7, and its dataflow model.

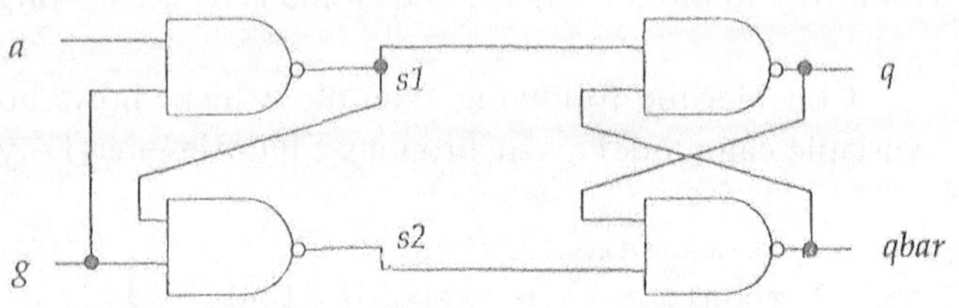

Figure 12-7 A gated latch.

```
module gated_ff (a, g, q, qbar);
  input a, g;
  output q, qbar;
  wire s1, s2;

  assign s1 = ~ (a & g);
  assign s2 = ~ (s1 & g);
  assign q = ~ (qbar & s1);
  assign qbar = ~ (q & s2);
endmodule
```

In this example, the semantics of the continuous assignments implies a latch.

A memory can be modeled as an array of registers. Here is an example. `ASIZE` is the number of bits on the address port, and `DSIZE` is the number of bits on the data port of the RAM.

```
module ram_generic (address, data_in, data_out, rw);
  parameter ASIZE = 6, DSIZE = 4;
  input [ASIZE-1:0] address;
  input [DSIZE-1:0] data_in;
  input rw;
  output reg [DSIZE-1:0] data_out;
  reg [DSIZE-1:0] mem_ff [0:2**ASIZE-1];
```

```
    always
      @(rw)
        if (rw)          // Read
          data_out <= mem_ff[address];
        else
          mem_ff[address] <= data_in;
  endmodule
```

Synchronous logic can also be modeled using level-sensitive or edge-triggered controls. For example, a level-sensitive D flip-flop can be modeled as follows.

```
module level_sens_flipflop (strobe, d, q, qbar);
  input strobe, d;
  output reg q, qbar;

  always
    begin
      wait (strobe == 1);
      q = d;
      qbar = ~ d;
    end
endmodule
```

When strobe is 1, any events on d are transferred to q, but when strobe becomes 0, the values in q and qbar are retained, and any change in input d no longer affects the values of q and qbar.

It is important to understand the semantics of a procedural assignment to determine the inference of synchronous logic. Consider the difference between the following two modules, proc_assign1 and proc_assign2.

```
module proc_assign1;
  reg sm_oe;

  initial
    sm_oe = 0;
```

```
  always
    sm_oe = ~ sm_oe;
endmodule

module proc_assign2;
  wire sclk;
  reg sm_oe;

  initial
    sm_oe = 0;

  always
    @(sclk)
      if (~ sclk)
         sm_oe = ~ sm_oe;
endmodule
```

Module proc_assign1 implies the circuit shown in Figure 12-8, while module proc_assign2 implies the circuit shown in Figure 12-9.

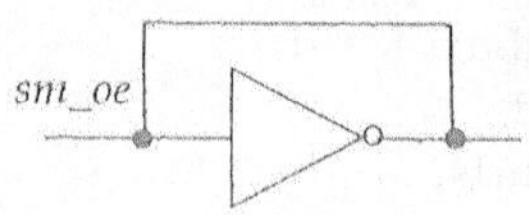

Figure 12-8 No flip-flop implied.

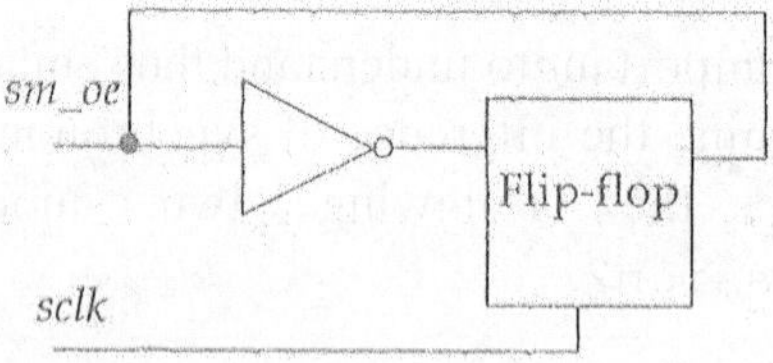

Figure 12-9 A flip-flop implied.

If proc_assign1 were simulated as is, simulation would go into an endless loop due to the zero delay asynchronous loop (simulation time does not advance). In module proc_assign2, the value of sm_oe is latched only on the falling edge of the sclk signal, and thereafter, any changes on sm_oe (input of flip-flop) do not affect the output of flip-flop.

12.7 A Generic Shift Register

A generic serial-in, serial-out shift register can be modeled using a for-loop with an always statement. The number of registers is specified as a parameter so that it can be modified when the generic shift register is instantiated in another design.

```
module shift_register (d, srclk, y);
  input d, srclk;
  output y;
  parameter NUM_REG = 6;
  reg [1:NUM_REG] q;
  integer p;

  always
    @(negedge srclk) begin
      // Shift register one bit right:
      for (p = 1; p < NUM_REG; p = p + 1)
        q[p + 1] <= q[p];

      // Push in the serial data:
      q[1] <= d;
    end

  // Get the output from the rightmost register:
  assign y = q[NUM_REG];
endmodule
```

Shift registers of varying sizes can be obtained by instantiating module shift_register using different parameter values.

```
module multi_srs;
  wire data, clk, ya, yb, yc;

  // 6-bit shift register:
  shift_register u0shift_register (
    data, clk, ya
  );
```

Named association used for parameters and ports.

```
  // 4-bit shift register:
  shift_register #(.NUM_REG(4)) u1shift_register (
    .d(data), .srclk(clk), .y(yb)
  );

  // 10-bit shift register:
  shift_register #10 u2shift_register (
    data, clk, yc
  );
endmodule
```

12.8 A Gray Counter

Here is a model for a generic N-bit Gray counter with an asynchronous reset.

```
module gray_counter
  # ( parameter NBITS = 4 )
    ( input ck, preclear,
      output reg [0:NBITS-1] q
    );
  reg [0:NBITS-1] gray_cnt;
  integer k;

  always
    @(posedge ck, negedge preclear) begin
      if (!preclear)
        q <= 0;
      else begin
        // Store in temporary variable:
        gray_cnt = q;

        // Convert from Gray to binary:
        for (k = 1; k < NBITS; k = k + 1)
          if (gray_cnt[k-1])
            gray_cnt[k] = !gray_cnt[k];

        gray_cnt = gray_cnt + 1;
```

```
        // Convert back to Gray:
        for (k = NBITS-1; k > 0; k = k - 1)
          if (gray_cnt[k-1])
            gray_cnt[k] = !gray_cnt[k];

      q <= gray_cnt;
    end
  end
endmodule
```

12.9 *A Decade Counter*

Here is a model for a decade counter.

Guideline: Use _n as a suffix or n_ as a prefix for active low signals.

```
module decade_counter
  # ( parameter SIZE = 4 )
    ( input clock, load_n, clear_n, updown,
      input [SIZE-1:0] load_data,
      output reg [SIZE-1:0] q
    );

  always
    @(negedge load_n, negedge clear_n, posedge clock)
      if (!load_n)
        q <= load_data;
      else if (!clear_n)
        q <= 0;
      else // posedge clock
        if (updown)
          q <= (q + 1) % 10;
        else
          begin
            if (q == 0)
              q <= 9;
            else
              q <= q - 1;
          end
endmodule
```

12.10 Parallel to Serial Converter

Here is a model for a parallel to serial converter. When reset is active, the shift register is reset to all zeros. When load is active, the parallel load data gets stored in the shift register. When both load and reset are inactive, data is shifted out of shift register on every positive clock edge. Both reset and load are also synchronous to the positive edge of the clock.

Guideline: Use `rst_` as a prefix or `_rst` as a suffix for reset signals.

```
module parallel2serial
  # ( parameter BUS_WIDTH = 8 )
    ( input [BUS_WIDTH-1:0] parallel_load,
      input clock, ps_rst, load,
      output reg serial_out
    );
  reg [BUS_WIDTH-1:0] shift_register;

  always
    @(posedge clock)
      if (ps_rst)
        shift_register <= 0;
      else if (load)
        shift_register <= parallel_load;
      else
        {serial_out, shift_register} <=
          {shift_register, 1'b0};
endmodule
```

12.11 State Machine Modeling

State machines can usually be modeled using a case statement with an always statement. The state information is stored in a register. The multiple branches of the case statement contain the behavior for each state. Here is an example of a simple multiplication algorithm represented as a state machine. When the `reset` signal is high, the accumulator `acc` and the counter `count` are initialized. When `reset` goes low, multiplication starts. If the bit of the multiplier `mplr` in position `count` is 1, the multiplicand `mcnd` is added to the accumulator. Next, the multiplicand is left-shifted by one bit, and the counter is incremented. If `count` is 16, multiplication is complete and the `done` signal is set high. If not, the `count` bit of the multiplier `mplr` is checked and the always statement repeated. The state diagram is shown in Figure 12-10 and the corresponding state machine model is shown next.

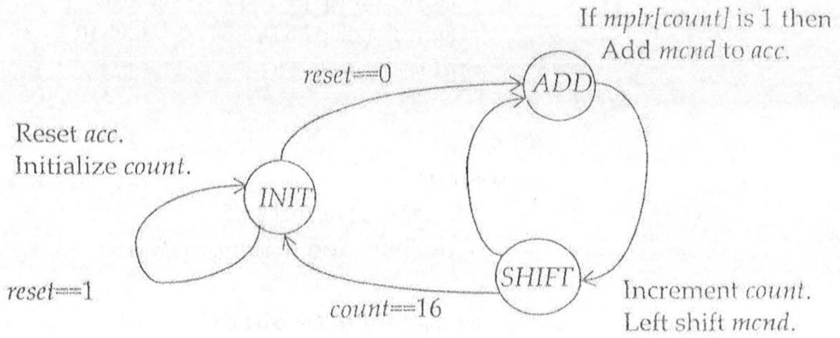

Figure 12-10 State diagram for multiplier.

```
module multiply (mplr, mcnd, clock, reset, done, acc);
      // mplr is multiplier, mcnd is multiplicand.
  input [15:0] mplr, mcnd;
  input clock, reset;
  output reg done;
  output reg [31:0] acc;

  parameter INIT = 0, ADD = 1, SHIFT = 2;
  reg [0:1] mpy_state;
  reg [31:0] mcnd_temp;

  initial
    mpy_state <= INIT;           // Initial state is INIT.

  always
    @(negedge clock) begin: process
      integer count;

      case (mpy_state)
        INIT :
          if (reset)
            mpy_state <= INIT;
            /* The above statement is not really necessary
              since mpy_state will retain its old value */
          else
```

```
            begin
              acc <= 0;
              count <= 0;
              mpy_state <= ADD;
              done <= 0;
              mcnd_temp[15:0] <= mcnd;
              mcnd_temp[31:16] <= 16'd0;
            end

        ADD :
          begin
            if (mplr[count])
              acc <= acc + mcnd_temp;

            mpy_state <= SHIFT;
          end

        SHIFT :
          begin
            // Left-shift mcnd_temp:
            mcnd_temp <= {mcnd_temp[30:0], 1'b0};
            count = count + 1;

            if (count == 16)
              begin
                mpy_state <= INIT;
                done <= 1;
              end
            else
              mpy_state <= ADD;
          end
        endcase          // case mpy_state
    end                  // sequential block process
endmodule
```

Used blocking assignment for count since its value is used in the following condition.

The variable mpy_state holds the state of the model. Initially, the model is in state INIT and it stays in this state as long as reset is true. When reset is false, the accumulator acc is cleared, the counter count is reset, the multiplicand mcnd is loaded into a temporary variable mcnd_temp, and the model advances to state ADD. When model is in the ADD state, the multiplicand in mcnd_temp is added to acc only if the bit at the count position of the multiplier is a 1 and then the model advances to state SHIFT. In this state, the multiplier is left-shifted once, the counter is incremented, and if the counter value is 16, `done` is set to true and the model returns to state `INIT`. At this time, `acc` contains the result of the multiplication. If the counter value was less than 16, the model repeats itself going through states `ADD` and `SHIFT` until the counter value becomes 16.

State transitions occur at every falling edge of the clock; this is specified using the `@(negedge clock)` timing control.

12.12 *Interacting State Machines*

Interacting state machines can be described as separate always statements communicating via common variables. Consider the state diagram shown in Figure 12-11 for two interacting processes, `tx`, a transmitter, and `mp`, a microprocessor. If process `tx` is not busy, process `mp` sets the data to be transmitted on a data bus and sends a signal `load_tx` to process `tx` to load the data and begin transmitting. `tx_busy` is set by process `tx` during transmission to indicate that it is busy and cannot receive any further data from process `mp`.

A skeleton model for these two interacting processes is shown. Only the control signals and state transitions are shown. Data manipulation code is not described.

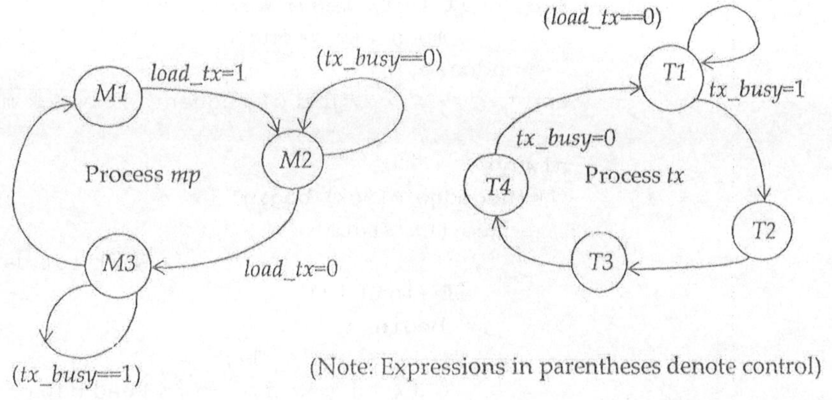

Figure 12-11 State diagram of two interacting processes.

```
module interacting_fsm (clock);
  input clock;

  parameter M1 = 0, M2 = 1, M3 = 2;
  parameter T1 = 0, T2 = 1, T3 = 2, T4 = 3;
  reg [0:1] mp_state;
  reg [0:1] tx_state;
  reg load_tx, tx_busy;

  always
    @(negedge clock) begin: mp
     case (mp_state)

       M1 :         // Load data on data bus.
        begin
          load_tx <= 1;
          mp_state <= M2;
        end

       M2 :       // Wait for acknowledgment.
         if (tx_busy)
           begin
             mp_state <= M3;
             load_tx <= 0;
           end

       M3 :       // Wait for tx to finish.
         if (~ tx busy)
           mp_state <= M1;
     endcase
   end              // End of sequential block mp

   always
     @(negedge clock) begin: tx
      case (tx_state)
       T1 :                          // Wait for data to load.
         if (load_tx)
           begin
             tx_state <= T2;
             tx_busy <= 1;       // Read data from data bus.
           end
```

```
            T2 :                        // Sending leading flag.
              tx_state <= T3;

            T3 :
              tx_state <= T4;           // Transmitting data.

            T4 :     // Send trailing flag to end transmission.
              begin
                tx_busy <= 0;
                tx_state <= T1;
              end
          endcase
        end             // End of sequential block tx.
    endmodule
```

The sequence of actions for this interacting finite-state machine is shown in Figure 12-12.

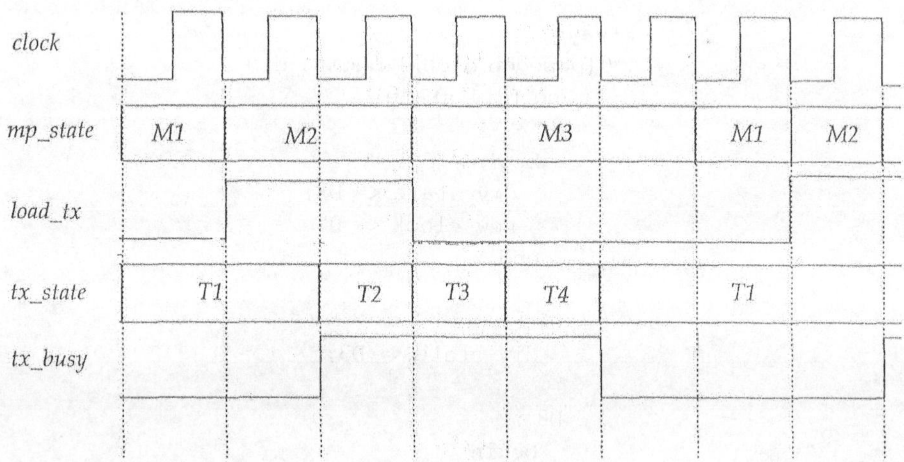

Figure 12-12 Sequence of actions for the two interacting processes.

Consider another example of two interacting processes, `div`, a clock divider, and `rx`, a receiver. In this case, process `div` generates a new clock and process `rx` goes through its sequence of states synchronized to this new clock. The state diagram is shown in Figure 12-13.

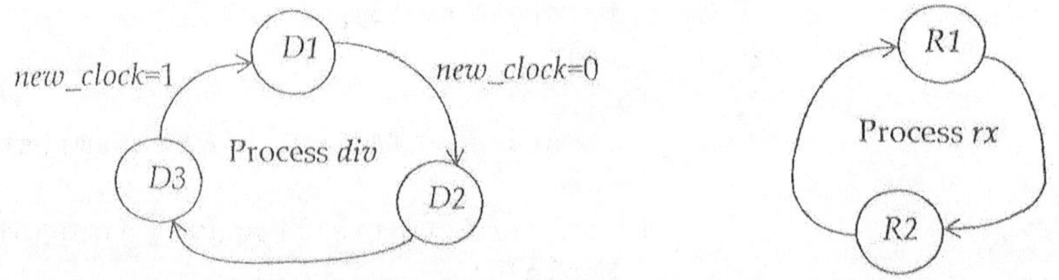

Figure 12-13 div generates clock for rx.

```
module another_example_fsm2 (clock);
  input clock;

  parameter D1 = 1, D2 = 2, D3 = 3;
  parameter R1 = 1, R2 = 2;
  reg [0:1] div_state, rx_state;
  reg new_clock;

  always
    @(posedge clock) begin: div
      case (div_state)
        D1 :
          begin
            div_state <= D2;
            new_clock <= 0;
          end

        D2 :
          div_state <= D3;

        D3 :
          begin
            new_clock <= 1;
            div_state <= D1;
          end
      endcase
    end              // Sequential block div
```

```
always
  @(negedge new_clock) begin: rx
    case (rx_state)
      R1 : rx_state <= R2;
      R2 : rx_state <= R1;
    endcase
  end          // Sequential block rx
endmodule
```

Sequential block `div` generates a new clock `new_clock` as it goes through its sequence of states. The state transitions in this process occur on the rising edge of `clock`. Sequential block `rx` is executed every time a falling edge on `new_clock` occurs. The sequence of waveforms for these interacting state machines is shown in Figure 12-14.

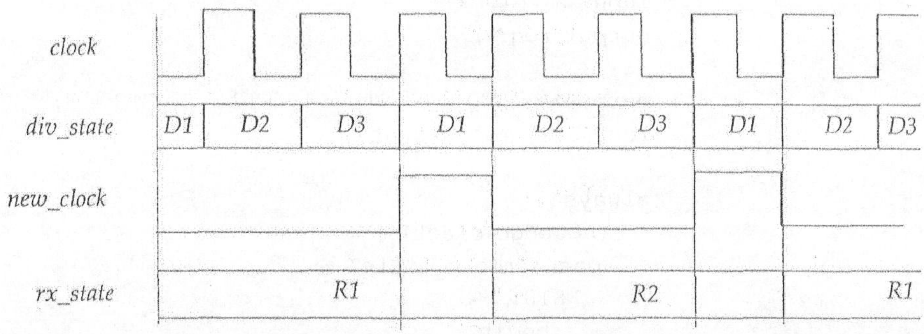

Figure 12-14 Interaction between processes `rx` and `div`.

12.13 Modeling a Moore FSM

The output of a Moore finite state machine (FSM) depends only on the state and not on its inputs. This type of behavior can be modeled using an always statement with a case statement that switches on the state value. An example of a state transition diagram for a Moore finite state machine is shown in Figure 12-15 and its corresponding behavior model appears next.

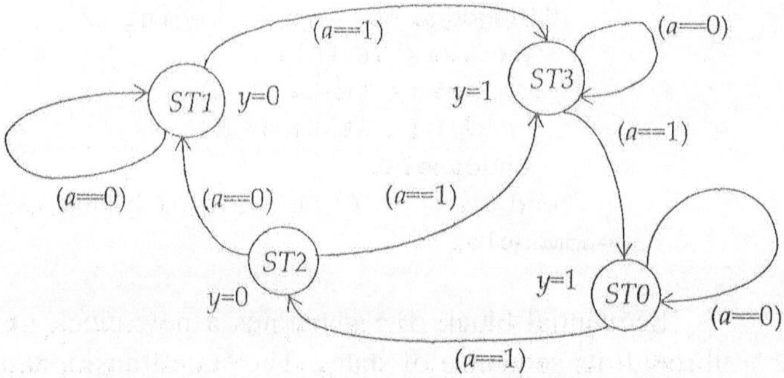

Figure 12-15 State diagram of a Moore machine.

```
module moore_fsm (a, clock, y);
  input a, clock;
  output reg y;

  parameter ST0 = 0, ST1 = 1, ST2 = 2, ST3 = 3;
  reg [0:1] moore_state;

  always
    @(negedge clock)
      case (moore_state)
        ST0:
          begin
            y <= 1;
            moore_state <= a ? ST2 : ST0;
          end

        ST1 :
          begin
            y <= 0;
            moore_state <= a ? ST3 : ST1;
          end

        ST2:
          begin
            y <= 0;
            moore_state <= a ? ST3 : ST1;
          end
```

```
        ST3:
          begin
            y <= 1;
            moore_state <= a ? ST0 : ST3;
          end
      endcase
    endmodule
```

12.14 *Modeling a Mealy FSM*

In a Mealy finite state machine, the outputs not only depend on the state of the machine but also on its inputs. This type of finite state machine can be modeled in a style similar to that of the Moore FSM, that is, using a single always statement. To show the variety of the language, a different style is used to model a Mealy machine. In this case we use two always statements, one that models the synchronous aspect of the finite state machine and one that models the combinational part of the finite state machine. Here is an example of a state transition table shown in Figure 12-16 and its corresponding behavior model.

Present state	Input *a* = 0	Input *a* = 1
ST0	*ST0* / 0	*ST3* / 1
ST1	*ST1* / 1	*ST0* / 0
ST2	*ST2* / 0	*ST1* / 1
ST3	*ST2* / 0	*ST1* / 0

(Entries in table are next state and output *y*)

Figure 12-16 State transition table for a Mealy machine.

```
module mealy_fsm (a, clock, y);
  input a, clock;
  output reg y;

    parameter ST0 = 0, ST1 = 1, ST2 = 2, ST3 = 3;
    reg [1:2] p_state, n_state;
```

```
always
  @(negedge clock)    // Synchronous part.
    p_state <= n_state;

always
  @(p_state or a) begin: comb_part
    case (p_state)
      ST0:
        begin
          y <= a ? 1 : 0;
          n_state <= a ? ST3 : ST0;
        end

      ST1 :
        begin
          y <= a ? 0 : 1;
          n_state <= a ? ST0 : ST1;
        end

      ST2 :
        begin
          y <= a ? 1 : 0;
          n_state <= a ? ST1 : ST2;
        end

      ST3 :
        begin
          y <= 0;
          n_state <= a ? ST1 : ST2;
        end
    endcase
  end           // Sequential block comb_part
endmodule
```

In this type of finite state machine, it is important to put the input signals in the event list for the combinational part sequential block since the outputs may directly depend on the inputs independent of the clock. Such a condition does not occur in a Moore finite state machine since outputs depend only on states and state changes occur synchronously on clock.

12.15 *A Simplified Blackjack Program*

This section presents a state machine description of a simplified blackjack program. The blackjack program is played with a deck of cards. Cards 2 to 10 have values equal to their face value, and an ace has a value of either 1 or 11. The object of the game is to accept a number of random cards such that the total score (sum of values of all cards) is as close as possible to 21 without exceeding 21.

When a new card is inserted, `card_rdy` is true and `card_value` has the value of the card. `request_card` indicates when the program is ready to accept a new card. If a sequence of cards is accepted such that the total exceeds 21, `lost` is set to true indicating that it has lost; otherwise `won` is set to true indicating that the game has been won. The state sequencing is controlled by `clock`. The input and outputs of the blackjack program are shown in Figure 12-17.

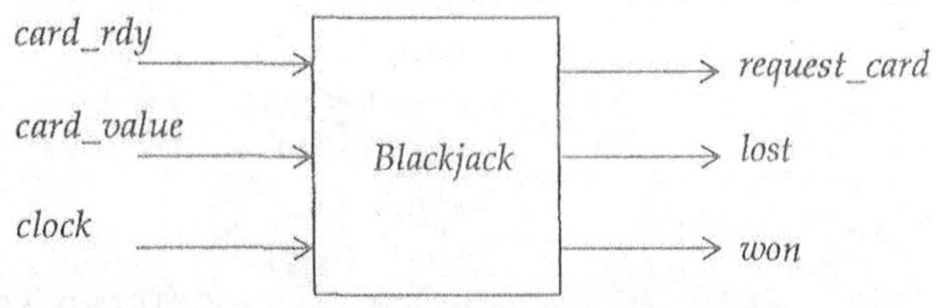

Figure 12-17 External view of blackjack program.

The behavior of the program is described in the following module declaration. The program accepts cards until its score is at least 17. The first ace is counted as a 11 unless the score exceeds 21, in which case 10 is subtracted so that the value of 1 is used for an ace. Three variables are used to store the values of the program: `total` to hold the sum, `current_card_value` to hold the value of the card read (which could be 1 through 10), and `ace_as_11` to remember whether an ace was counted as a 11 instead of a 1. The state of the blackjack program is stored in variable `bj_state`.

```
module blackjack (
   card_rdy, card_value, request_card, won, lost,
   clock
  );
  input card_rdy, clock;
  input [0:3] card_value;
  output reg request_card, lost, won;

  parameter INITIAL_ST = 0, GETCARD_ST = 1,
            REMCARD_ST = 2, ADD_ST = 3, CHECK_ST = 4,
            WIN_ST = 5, BACKUP_ST = 6, LOSE_ST = 7;
  reg [0:2] bj_state;
  reg [0:3] current_card_value;
  reg [0:4] total;
  reg ace_as_11;

  always
    @(negedge clock)
      case (bj_state)
        INITIAL_ST :
          begin
            total <= 0;
            ace_as_11 <= 0;
            won <= 0;
            lost <= 0;
            bj_state <= GETCARD_ST;
          end

        GETCARD_ST :
          begin
            request_card <= 1;

            if (card_rdy)
              begin
                current_card_value <= card_value;
                bj_state <= REMCARD_ST;
              end       // Else stay in GETCARD_ST state.
          end
```

```
REMCARD_ST :      // Wait for card to be removed.
  if (card_rdy)
    request_card <= 0;
  else
    bj_state <= ADD_ST;

ADD_ST :
  begin
    if (~ ace_as_11 && current_card_value)
      begin
        current_card_value = 11;
        ace_as_11 <= 1;
      end

    total <= total + current_card_value;
    bj_state <= CHECK_ST;
  end

CHECK_ST :
  if (total < 17)
    bj_state <= GETCARD_ST;
  else
    if (total < 22)
      bj_state <= WIN_ST;
    else
      bj_state <= BACKUP_ST;

BACKUP_ST :
  if (ace_as_11)
    begin
      total <= total - 10;
      ace_as_11 <= 0;
      bj_state <= CHECK_ST;
    end
  else
    bj_state <= LOSE_ST;

LOSE_ST :
  begin
    lost <= 1;
    request_card <= 1;
```

Blocking assignment used for `current_card_value` as its value is used in the following statement.

```
          if (card_rdy)
            bj_state <= INITIAL_ST;
          // Else stay in this state.
        end

      WIN_ST :
        begin
          won <= 1;
          request_card <= 1;

          if (card_rdy)
            bj_state <= INITIAL_ST;
          // Else stay in this state.
        end
      endcase
endmodule     // blackjack
```

12.16 A Scan Cell

Here is a model for a scan cell. When select_enable is high, serial_in is shifted into the scan cell and the rest of the data shifts right. When select_enable is low, it behaves like a normal D-flipflop.

```
module scan_cell
  # ( parameter WIDTH = 4 )
    ( input clock, serial_in, select_enable,
      input [0:WIDTH-1] data,
      output reg [0:WIDTH-1] q
  );
  integer j;

  task basic_cell (
      input si, d, se,
      output q
    );

    q = se ? si : d;
  endtask
```

```
    always
      @(posedge clock) begin
        basic_cell (serial_in, data[0],
                     select_enable, q[0]);

        for (j = 1; j < WIDTH; j = j + 1)
          basic_cell (q[j-1], data[j],
                     select_enable, q[j]);
      end
  endmodule
```

12.17 A BCD to 7-segment Decoder

Here is a model for a BCD to seven-segment decoder. The decode information is stored in a two-dimensional variable. A latch enable signal latches the input BCD value. An output polarity control signal is also provided.

```
module bcd_2_7segment (
    input latch_enable, output_polarity,
    input [3:0] bcd_in,
    output [6:0] abcdefg
  );
  reg [6:0] bcd_table [10:0], output_buf;
  reg [3:0] latched_bcd;

  initial
    begin
      bcd_table[0] = 7'b1111110;
      bcd_table[1] = 7'b0110000;
      bcd_table[2] = 7'b1101101;
      bcd_table[3] = 7'b1111001;
      bcd_table[4] = 7'b0110011;
      bcd_table[5] = 7'b1011011;
      bcd_table[6] = 7'b1011111;
      bcd_table[7] = 7'b1110000;
      bcd_table[8] = 7'b1111111;
      bcd_table[9] = 7'b1111011;
      bcd_table[10] = 7'b1011010; // Illegal BCD value.
    end
```

```
always
  @(latch_enable)
    if (latch_enable)
      latched_bcd <= bcd_in;

always
  @(latched_bcd)
    if (latched_bcd <= 9)
      output_buf <= bcd_table[latched_bcd];
    else
      output_buf <= bcd_table[10];

assign abcdefg = output_polarity ?
                        output_buf : ~ output_buf;
endmodule
```

12.18 *Utilities*

12.18.1 Default Value on a Bus

When all drivers to a bus are turned off, that is, they are in high-impedance state, it is possible to assign a default value to the bus using the pullup and pulldown primitive components. Here is a skeleton example that shows how.

```
module default_bus;
  wire bus_bit;

  pulldown u1 (bus_bit);
  cpu u2cpu (bus_bit);
  controller u3controller (bus_bit);
endmodule

module cpu (
    output hrbus_bit
  );

  assign hrbus_bit = is_cpu_master ? cpu_bus_bit: 1'bz;
endmodule
```

```
module controller (
    output hrbus_bit
  );

    assign hrbus_bit = is_ctrler_master ?
                            ctrler_bus_bit : 1'bz;

endmodule
```

If the bus_bit signal from both modules cpu and controller are off, bus_bit takes on the value 0 since it is connected to a pulldown primitive component.

12.19 *Exercises*

1. Write a Verilog HDL model for a mango juice drink machine. The machine dispenses a can of mango juice that costs 15 cents. Only nickels and dimes are accepted. Any change must be returned. Test the model using a test bench.

2. Write a model that describes the behavior of a flip-flop with synchronous preset and clear.

3. Write a model for a 4-bit shift register with serial-in data, parallel-in data, a clock and parallel-out data. Test the model using a test bench.

4. Describe a D-type flip-flop using behavioral constructs. Then using this module, write a model for a 8-bit register.

5. Write a test bench that tests the blackjack model described in Section 12.15.

6. Using the shift operator, describe a decoder module and then test it with a test bench. The number of inputs to the decoder is specified as:

   ```
   define NUM_INPUTS 4
   [ Hint: Use the shift operator to figure out the number of
   outputs of decoder]
   ```

7. Write a model for a 8-bit parallel to serial converter. The input is a 8-bit vector. Send the bits out, one bit at a time, starting from the most significant bit on the rising edge of a clock. Read the next input only after all the bits of the previous input vector have been sent out.

8. Write a model for a 8-bit serial to parallel converter that does the opposite of Exercise 7. Sample the input stream after a small delay from the positive edge of clock to account for transmission delay. Connect the models written in this exercise and the one in Exercise 7 using a top level module and test it out using a test bench.

9. Write a model for a N-bit counter with a hold control. If the hold is a 1, the counter holds its value, when hold goes to 0, the counter is reset to 0 and starts counting again. Write a test bench to test this model.

10. Write a model for a generic queue, size of word in queue is `N` and number of words in queue in `M`. `input_data` is the word that gets written into the queue; the word is added to the queue when input `add_word` is a 1. A word that is read from the queue is stored in `output_data`; the word is read from the queue when input `read_word` is a 1. Flags `empty` and `full` are set appropriately. All transactions occur at the falling edge of clock `clkq`. Write a test bench to test out the model.

11. Write a model for a parameterizable clock divider. The period of the output clock is `2*N` times that of the input clock. The output clock is synchronized to the rising edge of the input clock. Write a test bench and test the model.

A

Syntax Reference

This appendix presents the complete syntax[1] of the Verilog HDL language.

A.1 Keywords

Following are the keywords of the Verilog HDL language. Note that only lower case names are keywords.

always	**and**	**assign**	**automatic**
begin	**buf**	**bufif0**	**bufif1**
case	**casex**	**casez**	**cell**
cmos	**config**		
deassign	**default**	**defparam**	**design**
disable			
edge	**else**	**end**	**endcase**
endconfig	**endfunction**	**endgenerate**	**endmodule**

1. Reprinted here with permission from IEEE Std 1364-2001, Copyright © 2001, IEEE, All rights reserved.

endprimitive	endspecify	endtable	endtask
event			
for •	force	forever	fork
function			
generate	genvar		
highz0	highz1		
if	ifnone	incdir	include
initial	inout	input	instance
integer			
join			
large	liblist	library	localparam
macromodule	medium	module	
nand	negedge	nmos	nor
noshowcancelled		not	notif0
notif1			
or	output		
parameter	pmos	posedge	primitive
pull0	pull1	pulldown	pullup
pulsestyle_onevent		pulsestyle_ondetect	
rcmos	real	realtime	reg
release	repeat	rnmos	rpmos
rtran	rtranif0	rtranif1	
scalared	showcancelled	signed	small
specify	specparam	strong0	strong1
supply0	supply1		
table	task	time	tran
tranif0	tranif1	tri	tri0
tri1	triand	trior	trireg
unsigned	use		
vectored			

wait	wand	weak0	weak1
while	wire	wor	
xnor	xor		

A.2 *Syntax Conventions*

The following conventions are used in describing the syntax, which is described using the Backus-Naur Form (BNF).

i. The syntax rules are organized in an alphabetical order by their left-hand nonterminal name.

ii. Reserved words, operators and punctuation marks that are part of the syntax appear in **boldface.**

iii. A name in *italics* prefixed to a nonterminal name represents the semantic meaning associated with that nonterminal name.

iv. The vertical bar symbol, non-bold, (|) separates alternative items.

v. Square brackets, non-bold, ([. . .]) denote optional items.

vi. Curly braces, non-bold, ({ . . . }) identify an item that is repeated zero or more times.

vii. Square brackets, parentheses, and curly braces and other characters (such as , ;) appearing in bold (**[...]**, **(...)**, **{ ... }**) indicate characters that are part of the syntax.

viii. The starting nonterminal name is `source_text`.

ix. The terminal names used in this grammar appear in upper case.

A.3 *The Syntax*

```
always_construct ::=
    always
      statement

arrayed_identifier ::=
      simple_arrayed_identifier
    | escaped_arrayed_identifier

attribute_instance ::=
    (* attr_spec { , attr_spec } *)
```

```
attr_name ::=
    identifier

attr_spec ::=
      attr_name = constant_expression
    | attr_name

base_expression ::=
    expression

binary_base ::=
    '[s|S]b | '[s|S]B

binary_digit ::=
    x_digit | z_digit | 0 | 1

binary_module_path_operator ::=
    == | != | && | || | & | | | ^ | ^~ | ~^

binary_number ::=
    [ size ] binary_base binary_value

binary_operator ::=
      + | - | * | / | %
    | == | != | === | !== | && | || | ** | < | <= | > | >=
    | & | | | ^ | ^~ | ~^ | >> | << | >>> | <<<

binary_value ::=
    binary_digit { _ | binary_digit }

block_comment ::=
    /* comment_text */

block_identifier ::= identifier

block_item_declaration ::=
      { attribute_instance } block_reg_declaration
    | { attribute_instance } event_declaration
    | { attribute_instance } integer_declaration
    | { attribute_instance } local_parameter_declaration
    | { attribute_instance } parameter_declaration
    | { attribute_instance } real_declaration
    | { attribute_instance } realtime_declaration
    | { attribute_instance } time_declaration

block_reg_declaration ::=
    reg [ signed ] [ range ] list_of_block_variable_identifiers ;

block_variable_type ::=
      variable_identifier
    | variable_identifier dimension { dimension }

blocking_assignment ::=
    variable_lvalue = [ delay_or_event_control ] expression
```

case_item ::=
  expression { , expression } : statement_or_null
  | **default** [:] statement_or_null

case_statement ::=
  case (expression) case_item { case_item } **endcase**
  | **casez** (expression) case_item { case_item } **endcase**
  | **casex** (expression) case_item { case_item } **endcase**

cell_clause ::=
  cell [library_identifier.]cell_identifier

cell_identifier ::= identifier

charge_strength ::=
  (**small**)
  | (**medium**)
  | (**large**)

checktime_condition ::=
  mintypmax_expression

cmos_switch_instance ::=
  [name_of_gate_instance] (output_terminal , input_terminal ,
  ncontrol_terminal , pcontrol_terminal)

cmos_switchtype ::=
  cmos | **rcmos**

combinational_body ::=
  table
  combinational_entry { combinational_entry }
  endtable

combinational_entry ::=
  level_input_list : output_symbol ;

comment ::=
  one_line_comment
  | block_comment

comment_text ::=
  { ANY_ASCII_CHARACTER }

concatenation ::=
  { expression { , expression } }

conditional_expression ::=
  expression1 ? { attribute_instance } expression2 : expression 3

conditional_statement ::=
  if (expression) statement_or_null [**else** statement_or_null]
  | if_else_if_statement

```
config_declaration ::=
    config config_header ;
      design_statement
      { config_rule_statement }
    endconfig

config_identifier ::= identifier

config_rule_statement ::=
      default_clause liblist_clause
    | inst_clause liblist_clause
    | inst_clause use_clause
    | cell_clause liblist_clause
    | cell_clause use_clause

constant_base_expression ::=
      constant_expression

constant_concatenation ::=
    { constant_expression { , constant_expression } }

constant_function_call ::=
    function_identifier { attribute_instance } ( constant_expression
      { , constant_expression } )

constant_expression ::=
      constant_primary
    | unary_operator { attribute_instance } constant_primary
    | constant_expression binary_operator { attribute_instance }
        constant_expression
    | constant_expression ? { attribute_instance }
        constant_expression : constant_expression
    | string

constant_mintypmax_expression ::=
      constant_expression
    | constant_expression : constant_expression : constant_expression

constant_multiple_concatenation ::=
    { constant_expression constant_concatenation }

constant_primary ::=
      constant_concatenation
    | constant_function_call
    | ( constant_mintypmax_expression )
    | constant_multiple_concatenation
    | genvar_identifier
    | number
    | parameter_identifier
    | specparam_identifier
```

constant_range_expression ::=
    constant_expression
  | msb_constant_expression : lsb_constant_expression
  | constant_base_expression +: width_constant_expression
  | constant_base_expression –: width_constant_expression

continuous_assign ::=
  assign [drive_strength] [delay3] list_of_net_assignments ;

controlled_reference_event ::=
  controlled_timing_check_event

controlled_timing_check_event ::=
  timing_check_event_control specify_terminal_descriptor
    [&&& timing_check_condition]

current_state ::=
  level_symbol

data_event ::=
  timing_check_event

data_source_expression ::=
  expression

decimal_base ::=
  '[s|S]d | '[s|S]D

decimal_digit ::=
  0 | 1 | 2 | 3 | 4 | 5 | 6 | 7 | 8 | 9

decimal_number ::=
    unsigned_number
  | [size] decimal_base unsigned_number
  | [size] decimal_base x_digit { _ }
  | [size] decimal_base z_digit { _ }

default_clause ::=
  default

delayed_data ::=
    terminal_identifier
  | terminal_identifier [constant_mintypmax_expression]

delayed_reference ::=
    terminal_identifier
  | terminal_identifier [constant_mintypmax_expression]

delay2 ::=
    # delay_value
  | # (delay_value [, delay_value])

delay3 ::=
    # delay_value
  | # (delay_value [, delay_value [, delay_value]])

delay_control ::=
    # delay_value
  | # (mintypmax_expression)

delay_or_event_control ::=
    delay_control
  | event_control
  | **repeat** (expression) event_control

delay_value ::=
    unsigned_number
  | parameter_identifier
  | specparam_identifier
  | mintypmax_expression

description ::=
    module_declaration
  | udp_declaration

design_statement ::=
  design { [library_identifier.]cell_identifier } ;

dimension ::=
  [dimension_constant_expression : dimension_constant_expression]

dimension_constant_expression ::=
  constant_expression

disable_statement ::=
    disable hierarchical_task_identifier ;
  | **disable** hierarchical_block_identifier ;

drive_strength ::=
    (strength0 , strength1)
  | (strength1 , strength0)
  | (strength0 , **highz1**)
  | (strength1 , **highz0**)
  | (**highz1** , strength0)
  | (**highz0** , strength1)

edge_control_specifier ::=
  edge [edge_descriptor { , edge_descriptor }]

edge_descriptor ::=
    01
  | **10**
  | z_or_x zero_or_one
  | zero_or_one z_or_x

edge_identifier ::=
  posedge | **negedge**

edge_indicator ::=
    (level_symbol level_symbol)
  | edge_symbol

edge_input_list ::=
{ level_symbol } edge_indicator { level_symbol }

edge_sensitive_path_declaration ::=
parallel_edge_sensitive_path_description = path_delay_value
| full_edge_sensitive_path_description = path_delay_value

edge_symbol ::=
r | R | f | F | p | P | n | N | *

enable_gate_instance ::=
[name_of_gate_instance] (output_terminal , input_terminal ,
enable_terminal)

enable_gate_type ::=
bufif0 | bufif1 | notif0 | notif1

enable_terminal ::=
expression

end_edge_offset ::=
mintypmax_expression

error_limit_value ::=
limit_value

escaped_arrayed_identifier ::=
escaped_identifier [range]

escaped_hierarchical_branch[1] ::=
escaped_identifier [[unsigned_number]]
[{ . escaped_identifier [[unsigned_number]] }]

escaped_hierarchical_identifier ::=
escaped_hierarchical_branch
{ . simple_hierarchical_branch | . escaped_hierarchical_branch }

escaped_identifier ::=
\ { ANY_ASCII_CHARACTER_EXCEPT_WHITE_SPACE } white_space

event_based_flag ::=
constant_expression

event_control ::=
@ hierarchical_event_identifier
| @ (event_expression)
| @*
| @(*)

event_declaration ::=
event list_of_event_identifiers ;

---

1. The period in `escaped_hierarchical_identifier` and `escaped_hierarchical_branch` shall be preceded by `white_space`, but shall not be followed by `white_space`.

```
event_expression ::=
        expression
      | hierarchical_identifier
      | posedge expression
      | negedge expression
      | event_expression or event_expression
      | event_expression , event_expression

event_identifier ::= identifier

event_trigger ::=
      -> hierarchical_event_identifier ;

exp ::=
      e | E

expression ::=
        primary
      | unary_operator { attribute_instance } primary
      | expression binary_operator { attribute_instance } expression
      | conditional_expression
      | string

expression1 ::=
      expression

expression2 ::=
      expression

expression3 ::=
      expression

file_path_spec ::=
      file_path

full_edge_sensitive_path_description ::=
      ( [ edge_identifier ] list_of_path_inputs *> ( list_of_path_outputs
          [ polarity_operator ] : data_source_expression ) )

full_path_description ::=
      ( list_of_path_inputs [ polarity_operator ] *> list_of_path_outputs )

function_blocking_assignment ::=
      variable_lvalue = expression

function_call ::=
      hierarchical_function_identifier { attribute_instance }
          ( expression { , expression } )

function_case_item ::=
        expression { , expression } : function_statement_or_null
      | default [ : ] function_statement_or_null
```

```
function_case_statement ::=
        case ( expression ) function_case_item { function_case_item }
        endcase
      | casez ( expression ) function_case_item { function_case_item }
        endcase
      | casex ( expression ) function_case_item { function_case_item }
        endcase
function_conditional_statement ::=
        if ( expression ) function_statement_or_null
          [ else function_statement_or_null ]
      | function_if_else_if_statement
function_declaration ::=
        function [ automatic ] [ signed ] [ range_or_type ] function_identifier ;
          function_item_declaration { function_item_declaration }
          function_statement
        endfunction
      | function [ automatic ] [ signed ] [ range_or_type ] function_identifier
            ( function_port_list ) ;
          { block_item_declaration }
          function_statement
        endfunction
function_identifier ::= identifier
function_if_else_if_statement ::=
        if ( expression ) function_statement_or_null
          { else if ( expression ) function_statement_or_null }
          [ else function_statement_or_null ]
function_item_declaration ::=
        block_item_declaration
      | { attribute_instance } tf_input_declaration ;
function_loop_statement ::=
        forever function_statement
      | repeat ( expression ) function_statement
      | while ( expression ) function_statement
      | for ( variable_assignment ; expression ; variable_assignment )
          function_statement
function_port_list ::=
        { attribute_instance } tf_input_declaration
          { , { attribute_instance } tf_input_declaration }
function_seq_block ::=
        begin [ : block_identifier { block_item_declaration } ]
          { function_statement } end
```

function_statement ::=
{ attribute_instance } function_blocking_assignment ;
| { attribute_instance } function_case_statement
| { attribute_instance } function_conditional_statement
| { attribute_instance } function_loop_statement
| { attribute_instance } function_seq_block
| { attribute_instance } disable_statement
| { attribute_instance } system_task_enable

function_statement_or_null ::=
function_statement
| { attribute_instance } ;

gate_instance_identifier ::= arrayed_identifier

gate_instantiation ::=
cmos_switchtype [delay3] cmos_switch_instance
{ , cmos_switch_instance } ;
| enable_gatetype [drive_strength] [delay3] enable_gate_instance
{ , enable_gate_instance } ;
| mos_switchtype [delay3] mos_switch_instance
{ , mos_switch_instance } ;
| n_input_gatetype [drive_strength] [delay2] n_input_gate_instance
{ , n_input_gate_instance } ;
| n_output_gatetype [drive_strength] [delay2]
n_output_gate_instance { , n_output_gate_instance } ;
| pass_switchtype pass_switch_instance { , pass_switch_instance } ;
| pass_en_switchtype [delay3] pass_enable_switch_instance
{ , pass_enable_switch_instance } ;
| **pulldown** [pulldown_strength] pull_gate_instance
{ , pull_gate_instance } ;
| **pullup** [pullup_strength] pull_gate_instance { ; pull_gate_instance } ;

generate_block ::=
begin [: generate_block_identifier] { generate_item } **end**

generate_block_identifier ::= identifier

generate_case_statement ::=
case (constant_expression) genvar_case_item
{ genvar_case_item } **endcase**

generate_conditional_statement ::=
if (constant_expression) generate_item_or_null [**else**
generate_item_or_null]

generated_instantiation ::=
generate { generate_item } **endgenerate**

generate_item ::=
    generate_conditional_statement
  | generate_case_statement
  | generate_loop_statement
  | generate_block
  | module_or_generate_item

generate_item_or_null ::=
    generate_item
  | ;

generate_loop_statement ::=
  for (genvar_assignment ; constant_expression ; genvar_assignment)
    begin : generate_block_identifier { generate_item } **end**

genvar_assignment ::=
  genvar_identifier = constant_expression

genvar_case_item ::=
    constant_expression { , constant_expression } : generate_item_or_null
  | **default** [:] generate_item_or_null

genvar_declaration ::=
  genvar list_of_genvar_identifiers ;

genvar_function_call ::=
  genvar_function_identifier { attribute_instance }
    (constant_expression { , constant_expression })

genvar_function_identifier ::= identifier /* Hierarchy disallowed */

genvar_identifier ::= identifier

hex_base ::=
  '[s|S]h | '[s|S]H

hex_digit ::=
    x_digit | z_digit
  | **0 | 1 | 2 | 3 | 4 | 5 | 6 | 7 | 8 | 9**
  | **a | b | c | d | e | f | A | B | C | D | E | F**

hex_number ::=
  [size] hex_base hex_value

hex_value ::=
  hex_digit { _ | hex_digit }

hierarchical_block_identifier ::= hierarchical_identifier

hierarchical_event_identifier ::= hierarchical_identifier

hierarchical_function_identifier ::= hierarchical_identifier

hierarchical_identifier ::=
    simple_hierarchical_identifier
  | escaped_hierarchical_identifier

hierarchical_net_identifier ::= hierarchical_identifier

hierarchical_task_identifier ::= hierarchical_identifier

hierarchical_variable_identifier ::= hierarchical_identifier

identifier ::=
    simple_identifier
  | escaped_identifier

if_else_if_statement ::=
  if (expression) statement_or_null
    { **else if** (expression) statement_or_null }
    [**else** statement_or_null]

include_statement ::=
  include file_path_spec **;**

init_val ::=
  1'b0 | 1'b1 | 1'bx | 1'bX | 1'B0 | 1'B1 | 1'Bx | 1'BX | 1 | 0

initial_construct ::=
  initial
    statement

inout_declaration ::=
  inout [net_type] [**signed**] [range] list_of_port_identifiers

inout_port_identifier ::= identifier

inout_terminal ::=
  net_lvalue

input_declaration ::=
  input [net_type] [**signed**] [range] list_of_port_identifiers

input_identifier ::=
    input_port_identifier
  | inout_port_identifier

input_port_identifier ::= identifier

input_terminal ::=
  expression

inst_clause ::=
  instance inst_name

inst_name ::=
  topmodule_identifier{.instance_identifier}

instance_identifier ::= identifier

integer_declaration ::=
  integer list_of_variable_identifiers **;**

level_input_list ::=
  level_symbol { level_symbol }

level_symbol ::=
  0 | 1 | x | X | ? | b | B

```
liblist_clause ::=
    liblist [ { library_identifier } ]

library_declaration ::=
    library library_identifier file_path_spec [ { , file_path_spec } ]
      [ -incdir file_path_spec [ { , file_path_spec } ] ] ;

library_descriptions ::=
    library_declaration
  | include_statement
  | config_declaration

library_identifier ::= identifier

library_text ::=
    { library_descriptions }

limit_value ::=
    constant_mintypmax_expression

list_of_block_variable_identifiers ::=
    block_variable_type { , block_variable_type }

list_of_event_identifiers ::=
    event_identifier [ dimension { dimension } ]
      { , event_identifier [ dimension { dimension } ] }

list_of_genvar_identifiers ::=
    genvar_identifier { , genvar_identifier }

list_of_module_connections ::=
      ordered_port_connection { , ordered_port_connection }
    | named_port_connection { , named_port_connection }

list_of_net_assignments ::=
    net_assignment { , net_assignment }

list_of_net_decl_assignments ::=
    net_decl_assignment { , net_decl_assignment }

list_of_net_identifiers ::=
    net_identifier [ dimension { dimension } ]
      { , net_identifier [ dimension { dimension } ] }

list_of_parameter_assignments ::=
      ordered_parameter_assignment { , ordered_parameter_assignment }
    | named_parameter_assignment { , named_parameter_assignment }

list_of_path_delay_expressions ::=
      t_path_delay_expression
    | trise_path_delay_expression , tfall_path_delay_expression
    | trise_path_delay_expression , tfall_path_delay_expression ,
        tz_path_delay_expression
    | t01_path_delay_expression , t10_path_delay_expression ,
        t0z_path_delay_expression , tz1_path_delay_expression ,
        t1z_path_delay_expression , tz0_path_delay_expression
```

```
    | t01_path_delay_expression , t10_path_delay_expression ,
        t0z_path_delay_expression , tz1_path_delay_expression ,
        t1z_path_delay_expression , tz0_path_delay_expression ,
        t0x_path_delay_expression , tx1_path_delay_expression ,
        t1x_path_delay_expression , tx0_path_delay_expression ,
        txz_path_delay_expression , tzx_path_delay_expression
list_of_path_inputs ::=
    specify_input_terminal_descriptor { , specify_input_terminal_descriptor }
list_of_path_outputs ::=
    specify_output_terminal_descriptor
      { , specify_output_terminal_descriptor }
list_of_port_connections ::=
      ordered_port_connection { , ordered_port_connection }
    | named_port_connection { , named_port_connection }
list_of_port_declarations ::=
      ( port_declaration { , port_declaration } )
    | ( )
list_of_port_identifiers ::=
    port_identifier { , port_identifier }
list_of_ports ::=
    ( port { , port } )
list_of_real_identifiers ::=
    real_type { , real_type }
list_of_specparam_assignments ::=
    specparam_assignment { , specparam_assignment }
list_of_variable_identifiers ::=
    variable_type { , variable_type }
list_of_variable_port_identifiers ::=
    port_identifier [ = constant_expression ]
      { , port_identifier [ = constant_expression ] }
local_parameter_declaration ::=
      localparam [ signed ] [ range ] list_of_param_assignments ;
    | localparam integer list_of_param_assignments ;
    | localparam real list_of_param_assignments ;
    | localparam realtime list_of_param_assignments ;
    | localparam time list_of_param_assignments ;
long_comment ::=
    /* comment_text */
```

```
loop_statement ::=
      forever statement
    | repeat ( expression ) statement
    | while ( expression ) statement
    | for ( variable_assignment ; expression ; variable_assignment )
        statement
lsb_constant_expression ::=
    constant_expression
memory_identifier ::= identifier
mintypmax_expression ::=
      expression
    | expression : expression : expression
module_declaration ::=
      { attribute_instance } module_keyword module_identifier
        [ module_parameter_port_list ] [ list_of_ports ] ;
          { module_item }
      endmodule
    | {attribute_instance } module_keyword module_identifier
        [ module_parameter_port_list ] [ list_of_port_declarations ] ;
          { non_port_module_item }
      endmodule
module_identifier ::= identifier
module_instance ::=
    name_of_instance ( [ list_of_port_connections ] )
module_instance_identifier ::= arrayed_identifier
module_instantiation ::=
    module_identifier [ parameter_value_assignment ] module_instance
      { , module_instance } ;
module_item ::=
      module_or_generate_item
    | port_declaration ;
    | { attribute_instance } generated_instantiation
    | { attribute_instance } local_parameter_declaration
    | { attribute_instance } parameter_declaration
    | { attribute_instance } specify_block
    | { attribute_instance } specparam_declaration
module_item_declaration ::=
      parameter_declaration
    | input_declaration
    | output_declaration
    | inout_declaration
    | net_declaration
    | reg_declaration
```

| integer_declaration
| real_declaration
| time_declaration
| realtime_declaration
| event_declaration
| task_declaration
| function_declaration

module_keyword ::=
module | **macromodule**

module_or_generate_item ::=
{ attribute_instance } module_or_generate_item_declaration
| { attribute_instance } parameter_override
| { attribute_instance } continuous_assign
| { attribute_instance } gate_instantiation
| { attribute_instance } udp_instantiation
| { attribute_instance } module_instantiation
| { attribute_instance } initial_construct
| { attribute_instance } always_construct

module_or_generate_item_declaration ::=
net_declaration
| reg_declaration
| integer_declaration
| real_declaration
| time_declaration
| realtime_declaration
| event_declaration
| genvar_declaration
| task_declaration
| function_declaration

module_parameter_port_list ::=
(parameter_declaration { , parameter_declaration })

module_path_concatenation ::=
{ module_path_expression { , module_path_expression } }

module_path_conditional_expression ::=
module_path_expression ? { attribute_instance }
module_path_expression : module_path_expression

module_path_expression ::=
module_path_primary
| unary_module_path_operator { attribute_instance }
module_path_primary
| module_path_expression binary_module_path_operator
{ attribute_instance } module_path_expression
| module_path_conditional_expression

module_path_mintypmax_expression ::=
    module_path_expression
  | module_path_expression : module_path_expression
     : module_path_expression

module_path_multiple_concatenation ::=
  { constant_expression module_path_concatenation }

module_path_primary ::=
    number
  | identifier
  | module_path_concatenation
  | module_path_multiple_concatenation
  | function_call
  | system_function_call
  | constant_function_call
  | (module_path_mintypmax_expression)

mos_switch_instance ::=
  [name_of_gate_instance] (output_terminal , input_terminal ,
    enable_terminal)

mos_switchtype ::=
  nmos | **pmos** | **rnmos** | **rpmos**

msb_constant_expression ::=
  constant_expression

multiple_concatenation ::=
  { constant_expression concatenation }

n_input_gate_instance ::=
  [name_of_gate_instance] (output_terminal , input_terminal
    { , input_terminal })

n_input_gatetype ::=
  and | **nand** | **or** | **nor** | **xor** | **xnor**

n_output_gate_instance ::=
  [name_of_gate_instance] (output_terminal { , output_terminal } ,
    input_terminal)

n_output_gatetype ::=
  buf | **not**

name_of_gate_instance ::=
  gate_instance_identifier [range]

name_of_instance ::=
  module_instance_identifier [range]

name_of_system_function ::=
  $identifier

name_of_udp_instance ::=
  udp_instance_identifier [range]

named_parameter_assignment ::=
parameter_identifier ([expression])

named_port_connection ::=
{ attribute_instance } . port_identifier ([expression])

ncontrol_terminal ::=
expression

net_assignment ::=
net_lvalue = expression

net_concatenation ::=
{ net_concatenation_value { , net_concatenation_value } }

net_concatenation_value ::=
hierarchical_net_identifier
| hierarchical_net_identifier [expression] { [expression] }
| hierarchical_net_identifier [expression] { [expression] }
[range_expression]
| hierarchical_net_identifier [range_expression]
| net_concatenation

net_decl_assignment ::=
net_identifier = expression

net_declaration ::=
net_type [**signed**] [delay3] list_of_net_identifiers ;
| net_type [drive_strength] [**signed**] [delay3]
list_of_net_decl_assignments ;
| net_type [**vectored** | **scalared**] [**signed**] range [delay3]
list_of_net_decl_assignments ;
| net_type [drive_strength] [**vectored** | **scalared** } [**signed**] range
[delay3] list_of_net_decl_assignments ;
| **trireg** [charge_strength] [**signed**] [delay3] list_of_net_identifiers ;
| **trireg** [drive_strength] [**signed**] [delay3]
list_of_net_decl_assignments ;
| **trireg** [charge_strength] [**vectored** | **scalared**] [**signed**] range
[delay3] list_of_net_identifiers ;
| **trireg** [drive_strength] [**vectored** | **scalared**] [**signed**] range
[delay3] list_of_net_decl_assignments ;

net_identifier ::= identifier

net_lvalue ::=
hierarchical_net_identifier
| hierarchical_net_identifier [constant_expression]
{ [constant_expression] }
| hierarchical_net_identifier [constant_expression]
{ [constant_expression] } [constant_range_expression]
| hierarchical_net_identifier [constant_range_expression]
| net_concatenation

net_type ::=
    supply0 | supply1 | tri | triand | trior | tri0 | tri1 | wire | wand | wor

next_state ::=
    output_symbol | -

nonblocking_assignment ::=
    variable_lvalue <= [delay_or_event_control] expression

non_port_module_item ::=
    { attribute_instance } generated_instantiation
    | { attribute_instance } local_parameter_declaration
    | { attribute_instance } module_or_generate_item
    | { attribute_instance } parameter_declaration
    | { attribute_instance } specify_block
    | { attribute_instance } specparam_declaration

non_zero_decimal_digit ::=
    1 | 2 | 3 | 4 | 5 | 6 | 7 | 8 | 9

non_zero_unsigned_number ::=
    non_zero_decimal_digit { _ | decimal_digit }

notify_reg ::=
    variable_identifier

number ::=
    decimal_number
    | octal_number
    | binary_number
    | hex_number
    | real_number

octal_base ::=
    '[s|S]o | '[s|S]O

octal_digit ::=
    x_digit | z_digit | **0 | 1 | 2 | 3 | 4 | 5 | 6 | 7**

octal_number ::=
    [size] octal_base octal_value

octal_value ::=
    octal_digit { _ | octal_digit }

one_line_comment ::=
    // comment_text \n

ordered_parameter_assignment ::=
    expression

ordered_port_connection ::=
    { attribute_instance } [expression]

output_declaration ::=
output [net_type] [**signed**] [range] list_of_port_identifiers
| **output** [**reg**] [**signed**] [range] list_of_port_identifiers
| **output reg** [**signed**] [range] list_of_variable_port_identifiers
| **output** [output_variable_type] list_of_port_identifiers
| **output** output_variable_type list_of_variable_port_identifiers

output_identifier ::=
output_port_identifier
| inout_port_identifier

output_port_identifier ::= identifier

output_symbol ::=
0 | **1** | **x** | **X**

output_terminal ::=
net_lvalue

output_variable_type ::=
integer | **time**

par_block ::=
fork
[**:** block_identifier
{ block_item_declaration }]
{ statement }
join

parallel_edge_sensitive_path_description ::=
([edge_identifier] specify_input_terminal_descriptor =>
(specify_output_terminal_descriptor [polarity_operator] :
data_source_expression))

parallel_path_description ::=
(specify_input_terminal_descriptor [polarity_operator] =>
specify_output_terminal_descriptor)

param_assignment ::=
parameter_identifier = constant_expression

parameter_declaration ::=
parameter [**signed**] [range] list_of_param_assignments ;
| **parameter integer** list_of_param_assignments ;
| **parameter real** list_of_param_assignments ;
| **parameter realtime** list_of_param_assignments ;
| **parameter time** list_of_param_assignments ;

parameter_identifier ::= identifier

parameter_override ::=
defparam list_of_param_assignments ;

parameter_value_assignment ::=
(list_of_parameter_assignments)

pass_en_switchtype ::=
    tranif0 | **tranif1** | **rtranif1** | **rtranif0**

pass_enable_switch_instance ::=
    [name_of_gate_instance] (inout_terminal , inout_terminal ,
        enable_terminal)

pass_switch_instance ::=
    [name_of_gate_instance] (inout_terminal , inout_terminal)

pass_switchtype ::=
    tran | **rtran**

path_declaration ::=
        simple_path_declaration ;
    | edge_sensitive_path_declaration ;
    | state_dependent_path_declaration ;

path_delay_expression ::=
    constant_mintypmax_expression

path_delay_value ::=
        list_of_path_delay_expressions
    | (list_of_path_delay_expressions)

pcontrol_terminal ::=
    expression

polarity_operator ::=
    + | −

port ::=
        [port_expression]
    | . port_identifier ([port_expression])

port_declaration ::=
        { attribute_instance } inout_declaration
    | { attribute_instance } input_declaration
    | { attribute_instance } output_declaration

port_expression ::=
        port_reference
    | { port_reference { , port_reference } }

port_identifier ::= identifier

port_reference ::=
        port_identifier
    | port_identifier [constant_expression]
    | port_identifier [constant_range_expression]

```
primary ::=
      number
    | hierarchical_identifier
    | hierarchical_identifier [ expression ] { [ expression ] }
    | hierarchical_identifier [ expression ] { [ expression ] }
        [ range_expression ]
    | hierarchical_identifier [ range_expression ]
    | concatenation
    | multiple_concatenation
    | function_call
    | system_function_call
    | constant_function_call
    | ( mintypmax_expression )
procedural_continuous_assignments ::=
      assign variable_assignment
    | deassign variable_lvalue
    | force variable_assignment
    | force net_assignment
    | release variable_lvalue
    | release net_lvalue
procedural_timing_control_statement ::=
    delay_or_event_control statement_or_null
pull_gate_instance ::=
    [ name_of_gate_instance ] ( output_terminal )
pulldown_strength ::=
      ( strength0 , strength1 )
    | ( strength1 , strength0 )
    | ( strength0 )
pullup_strength ::=
      ( strength0 , strength1 )
    | ( strength1 , strength0 )
    | ( strength1 )
pulse_control_specparam ::=
      PATHPULSE$ = ( reject_limit_value [ , error_limit_value ] ) ;
    | PATHPULSE$specify_input_terminal_descriptor
        /*no space; continue*/ $specify_output_terminal_descriptor =
        ( reject_limit_value [ , error_limit_value ] ) ;[1]
pulse_style_declaration ::=
      pulsestyle_onevent list_of_path_outputs ;
    | pulsestyle_ondetect list_of_path_outputs ;
```

1. For example, PATHPULSECLKQ = (5, 3);

range ::=
  [msb_constant_expression : lsb_constant_expression]

range_or_type ::=
  range | **integer** | **real** | **realtime** | **time**

range_expression ::=
  expression
  | msb_constant_expression : lsb_constant_expression
  | base_expression +: width_constant_expression
  | base_expression –: width_constant_expression

real_declaration ::=
  real list_of_real_identifiers ;

real_identifier ::= identifier

real_number ::=
  unsigned_number . unsigned_number
  | unsigned_number [. unsigned_number] exp [sign]
    unsigned_number

realtime_declaration ::=
  realtime list_of_real_identifiers ;

real_type ::=
  real_identifier [= constant_expression]
  | real_identifier dimension { dimension }

reference_event ::=
  timing_check_event

reg_declaration ::=
  reg [**signed**] [range] list_of_variable_identifiers ;

reject_limit_value ::=
  limit_value

remain_active_flag ::=
  constant_mintypmax_expression

scalar_constant ::=
  1'b0 | 1'b1 | 1'B0 | 1'B1 | 'b0 | 'b1 | 'B0 | 'B1 | 1 | 0

scalar_timing_check_condition ::=
  expression
  | ~ expression
  | expression == scalar_constant
  | expression === scalar_constant
  | expression != scalar_constant
  | expression !== scalar_constant

seq_block ::=
    begin
        [: block_identifier
            { block_item_declaration }]
        { statement }
    end

seq_input_list ::=
    level_input_list | edge_input_list

sequential_body ::=
    [udp_initial_statement]
    table
        sequential_entry
        { sequential_entry }
    endtable

sequential_entry ::=
    seq_input_list : current_state : next_state ;

short_comment ::=
    // comment_text \n

showcancelled_declaration ::=
        showcancelled list_of_path_outputs ;
    | **noshowcancelled** list_of_path_outputs ;

sign ::=
    + | -

simple_arrayed_identifier ::=
    simple_identifier [range]

simple_hierarchical_branch ::=
    simple_identifier [[unsigned_number]]
        [{ . simple_identifier [[unsigned_number]] }]

simple_hierarchical_identifier[1] ::=
    simple_hierarchical_branch [. escaped_identifier]

simple_identifier[2] ::=
    [a-zA-Z_] { [a-zA-Z_$0-9] }

simple_path_declaration ::=
        parallel_path_description = path_delay_value
    | full_path_description = path_delay_value

---

1. The period (.) in `simple_hierarchical_name` and `simple_hierarchical_branch` shall not be preceded or followed by `white_space`.
2. A `simple_identifier` and `arrayed_reference` shall start with an alpha or underscore character, shall have at least one character, and shall not have any spaces.

```
size ::=
    non_zero_unsigned_number

source_text ::=
    { description }

specify_block ::=
    specify
      { specify_item }
    endspecify

specify_input_terminal_descriptor ::=
      input_identifier
    | input_identifier [ constant_expression ]
    | input_identifier [ constant_range_expression ]

specify_item ::=
      specparam_declaration
    | pulsestyle_declaration
    | showcancelled_declaration
    | path_declaration
    | system_timing_check

specify_output_terminal_descriptor ::=
      output_identifier
    | output_identifier [ constant_expression ]
    | output_identifier [ constant_range_expression ]

specify_terminal_descriptor ::=
      specify_input_terminal_descriptor
    | specify_output_terminal_descriptor

specparam_assignment ::=
      specparam_identifier = constant_mintypmax_expression
    | pulse_control_specparam

specparam_declaration ::=
    specparam [ range ] list_of_specparam_assignments ;

specparam_identifier ::= identifier

stamptime_condition ::=
    mintypmax_expression

start_edge_offset ::=
    mintypmax_expression

state_dependent_path_declaration ::=
      if ( module_path_expression ) simple_path_declaration
    | if ( module_path_expression ) edge_sensitive_path_declaration
    | ifnone simple_path_declaration
```

statement ::=
  { attribute_instance } blocking_assignment ;
| { attribute_instance } case_statement
| { attribute_instance } conditional_statement
| { attribute_instance } disable_statement
| { attribute_instance } event_trigger
| { attribute_instance } loop_statement
| { attribute_instance } nonblocking_assignment ;
| { attribute_instance } par_block
| { attribute_instance } procedural_continuous_assignments ;
| { attribute_instance } procedural_timing_control_statement
| { attribute_instance } seq_block
| { attribute_instance } system_task_enable
| { attribute_instance } task_enable
| { attribute_instance } wait_statement

statement_or_null ::=
  statement
| { attribute_instance } ;

strength0 ::=
  supply0 | strong0 | pull0 | weak0

strength1 ::=
  supply1 | strong1 | pull1 | weak1

string ::=
  " { ANY_ASCII_CHARACTERS_EXCEPT_NEWLINE } "

system_function_call ::=
  system_function_identifier [(expression { , expression })]

system_function_identifier[1] ::= $[a-zA-Z0-9_$] { [a-zA-Z0-9_$] }

system_task_enable ::=
  system_task_identifier [(expression { , expression })] ;

system_task_identifier ::= $[a-zA-Z0-9_$] { [a-zA-Z0-9_$] }

system_timing_check ::=
  $setup_timing_check
| $hold_timing_check
| $setuphold_timing_check
| $recovery_timing_check
| $removal_timing_check
| $recrem_timing_check
| $skew_timing_check

1. The $ character in a `system_function_identifier` or `system_task_identifier` shall not be followed by `white_space`. A `system_function_identifier` or `system_task_identifier` shall not be escaped.

```
        | $timeskew_timing_check
        | $fullskew_timing_check
        | $period_timing_check
        | $width_timing_check
        | $nochange_timing_check
task_declaration ::=
          task [ automatic ] task_identifier ;
            { task_item_declaration }
            statement
          endtask
        | task [ automatic ] task_identifier ( task_port_list ) ;
            { block_item_declaration }
            statement
          endtask
task_enable ::=
        hierarchical_task_identifier [ ( expression { , expression } ) ] ;
task_identifier ::= identifier
task_item_declaration ::=
          block_item_declaration
        | { attribute_instance } tf_input_declaration ;
        | { attribute_instance } tf_output_declaration ;
        | { attribute_instance } tf_inout_declaration ;
task_port_item ::=
          { attribute_instance } tf_input_declaration
        | { attribute_instance } tf_output_declaration
        | { attribute_instance } tf_inout_declaration
task_port_list ::=
        task_port_item { , task_port_item }
task_port_type ::=
        time | real | realtime | integer
terminal_identifier ::= identifier
text_macro_identifier ::= simple_identifier
tf_inout_declaration ::=
          inout [ reg ] [ signed ] [ range ] list_of_port_identifiers
        | inout [ task_port_type ] list_of_port_identifiers
tf_input_declaration ::=
          input [ reg ] [ signed ] [ range ] list_of_port_identifiers
        | input [ task_port_type ] list_of_port_identifiers
tf_output_declaration ::=
          output [ reg ] [ signed ] [ range ] list_of_port_identifiers
        | output [ task_port_type ] list_of_port_identifiers
```

threshold ::=
constant_expression

time_declaration ::=
time list_of_variable_identifiers ;

timing_check_condition ::=
scalar_timing_check_condition
| (scalar_timing_check_condition)

timing_check_event ::=
[timing_check_event_control] specify_terminal_descriptor
[&&& timing_check_condition]

timing_check_event_control ::=
posedge
| **negedge**
| edge_control_specifier

timing_check_limit ::=
expression

tfall_path_delay_expression ::=
path_delay_expression

topmodule_identifier ::= identifier

trise_path_delay_expression ::=
path_delay_expression

txz_path_delay_expression ::=
path_delay_expression

tx0_path_delay_expression ::=
path_delay_expression

tx1_path_delay_expression ::=
path_delay_expression

tzx_path_delay_expression ::=
path_delay_expression

tz0_path_delay_expression ::=
path_delay_expression

tz1_path_delay_expression ::=
path_delay_expression

tz_path_delay_expression ::=
path_delay_expression

t0x_path_delay_expression ::=
path_delay_expression

t0z_path_delay_expression ::=
path_delay_expression

t01_path_delay_expression ::=
path_delay_expression

```
t1x_path_delay_expression ::=
    path_delay_expression
t1z_path_delay_expression ::=
    path_delay_expression
t10_path_delay_expression ::=
    path_delay_expression
t_path_delay_expression :=
    path_delay_expression
udp_body ::=
      combinational_body
    | sequential_body
udp_declaration ::=
      { attribute_instance } primitive udp_identifier ( udp_port_list );
        udp_port_declaration { udp_port_declaration }
        udp_body
      endprimitive
    | { attribute_instance } primitive udp_identifier
        ( udp_declaration_port_list );
        udp_body
      endprimitive
udp_declaration_port_list ::=
    udp_output_declaration , udp_input_declaration
      { , udp_input_declaration }
udp_identifier ::= identifier
udp_initial_statement ::=
    initial udp_output_port_identifier = init_val ;
udp_input_declaration ::=
    { attribute_instance } input list_of_port_identifiers
udp_instance ::=
    [ name_of_udp_instance ] ( output_terminal , input_terminal
      { , input_terminal } )
udp_instance_identifier ::= arrayed_identifier
udp_instantiation ::=
    udp_identifier [ drive_strength ] [ delay2 ] udp_instance
      { , udp_instance } ;
udp_output_declaration ::=
      { attribute_instance } output port_identifier
    | { attribute_instance } output reg port_identifier
        [ = constant_expression ]
```

udp_port_declaration ::=
udp_output_declaration ;
| udp_input_declaration ;
| udp_reg_declaration ;

udp_port_list ::=
output_port_identifier , input_port_identifier { , input_port_identifier }

udp_reg_declaration ::=
{ attribute_instance } **reg** variable_identifier

unary_module_path_operator ::=
! | ~ | & | ~& | | | ~| | ^ | ~^ | ^~

unary_operator ::=
+ | - | ! | ~ | & | ~& | | | ~| | ^ | ~^ | ^~

unsigned_number ::=
decimal_digit { _ | decimal_digit }

use_clause ::=
use [library_identifier.]cell_identifier[:**config**]

variable_assignment ::=
variable_lvalue = expression

variable_concatenation ::=
{ variable_concatenation_value { , variable_concatenation_value } }

variable_concatenation_value ::=
hierarchical_variable_identifier
| hierarchical_variable_identifier [expression] { [expression] }
| hierarchical_variable_identifier [expression] { [expression] }
[range_expression]
| hierarchical_variable_identifier [range_expression]
| variable_concatenation

variable_identifier ::= identifier

variable_lvalue ::=
hierarchical_variable_identifier
| hierarchical_variable_identifier [expression] { [expression] }
| hierarchical_variable_identifier [expression] { [expression] }
[range_expression]
| hierarchical_variable_identifier [range_expression]
| variable_concatenation

variable_type ::=
variable_identifier [= constant_expression]
| variable_identifier dimension { dimension }

wait_statement ::=
wait (expression) statement_or_null

white_space ::=
space | tab | newline | eof

x_digit ::= **x** | **X**

z_digit ::= **z** | **Z** | **?**

zero_or_one ::= **0** | **1**

z_or_x ::= **x** | **X** | **z** | **Z**

$fullskew_timing_check ::=
 $fullskew (reference_event **,** data_event **,** timing_check_limit **,**
 timing_check_limit [**,** [notify_reg] [**,** [event_based_flag]
 [**,** [remain_active_flag]]]] **) ;**

$hold_timing_check ::=
 $hold (reference_event **,** data_event **,** timing_check_limit
 [**,** [notify_reg]] **) ;**

$nochange_timing_check ::=
 $nochange (reference_event **,** data_event **,** start_edge_offset **,**
 end_edge_offset [**,** [notify_reg]] **) ;**

$period_timing_check ::=
 $period (controlled_reference_event **,** timing_check_limit
 [**,** [notify_reg]] **) ;**

$recovery_timing_check ::=
 $recovery (reference_event **,** data_event **,**
 timing_check_limit [**,** [notify_reg]] **) ;**

$recrem_timing_check ::=
 $recrem (reference_event **,** data_event **,** timing_check_limit **,**
 timing_check_limit [**,** [notify_reg] [**,** [stamptime_condition]
 [**,** [checktime_condition] [**,** [delayed_reference]
 [**,** [delayed_data]]]]]] **) ;**

$removal_timing_check ::=
 $removal (reference_event **,** data_event **,**
 timing_check_limit [**,** [notify_reg]] **) ;**

$setuphold_timing_check ::=
 $setuphold (reference_event **,** data_event **,**
 timing_check_limit **,** timing_check_limit [**,** [notify_reg]
 [**,** [stamptime_condition] [**,** [checktime_condition]
 [**,** [delayed_reference] [**,** [delayed_data]]]]]] **) ;**

$setup_timing_check ::=
 $setup (data_event **,** reference_event **,** timing_check_limit
 [**,** [notify_reg]] **) ;**

$skew_timing_check ::=
 $skew (reference_event **,** data_event **,** timing_check_limit
 [**,** [notify_reg]] **) ;**

$timeskew_timing_check ::=
 $timeskew (reference_event **,** data_event **,** timing_check_limit
 [**,** [notify_reg] [**,** [event_based_flag] [**,** [remain_active_flag]]]] **) ;**

```
$width_timing_check ::=
    $width ( controlled_reference_event , timing_check_limit ,
      threshold [ , [ notify_reg ] ] ) ;
```

□

Bibliography

1. Arnold M., *Verilog Digital Computer Design: Algorithms to Hardware*, Prentice Hall, NJ, 1998.
2. Bhasker J., *Verilog HDL Synthesis: A Practical Primer*, Star Galaxy Publishing, PA, 1998, ISBN 0-9650391-5-3.
3. Lee J., *Verilog Quickstart*, Kluwer Academic, MA, 1997.
4. Palnitkar S., *Verilog HDL: A Guide to Digital Design and Synthesis*, Prentice Hall, NJ, 1996, ISBN 0-13-451675-3.
5. Sagdeo V., *Complete Verilog Book*, Kluwer Academic, MA, 1998.
6. Smith D., *HDL Chip Design*, Doone Publications, 1996.
7. Sternheim E., R. Singh and Y. Trivedi, *Digital Design and Synthesis with Verilog HDL*, Automata Publishing Company, CA, 1993.
8. Thomas D. and P. Moorby, *The Verilog Hardware Description Language*, Kluwer Academic, MA, 1991, ISBN 0-7923-9126-8.
9. *IEEE Standard Hardware Description Language Based on the Verilog Hardware Description Language*, IEEE Std 1364-1995, IEEE, 1995.
10. *IEEE Standard Hardware Description Language Based on the Verilog Hardware Description Language*, IEEE Std 1364-2001, IEEE, 2001.
11. *IEEE Standard for Standard Delay Format (SDF)*, IEEE Std 1497-2001, IEEE, 2001.

❑

Index

- character 107
- operator 65
! 72
!= 71
!== 71
$bitstoreal 223
$display 19, 129, 211, 258
$displayb 211
$displayh 211
$displayo 211
$dist_chi_square 224
$dist_erlang 225
$dist_exponential 224
$dist_normal 224
$dist_poisson 224
$dist_t 225
$dist_uniform 224
$dumpall 239
$dumpfile 238
$dumpflush 239
$dumplimit 239
$dumpoff 239
$dumpon 239
$dumpports 240
$dumpportsall 240
$dumpportsflush 240
$dumpportslimit 240
$dumpportsoff 240
$dumpportson 240
$dumpvars 238
$fclose 216
$fdisplay 217, 276
$fdisplayb 217
$fdisplayh 217
$fdisplayo 217
$ferror 219
$fgetc 219
$fgets 219
$finish 221, 258
$fmonitor 217, 276
$fmonitorb 217
$fmonitorh 217
$fmonitoro 217
$fopen 215
$fread 219
$frewind 219
$fscanf 219
$fseek 219
$fstrobe 217, 276
$fstrobeb 217
$fstrobeh 217
$fstrobeo 217
$ftell 219
$fwrite 217, 225
$fwriteb 217
$fwriteh 217
$fwriteo 217
$hold 247
$itor 223
$monitor 22, 214, 258

$monitorb 214
$monitorh 214
$monitoro 214
$monitoroff 215
$monitoron 215
$nochange 249
$period 249
$printtimescale 220
$random 223
$readmem 306
$readmemb 47, 218, 258, 273
$readmemh 47, 218, 258
$realtime 222
$realtobits 223
$recovery 249
$recrem 250
$removal 250
$rtoi 223
$sdf_annotate 219
$setup 247
$setuphold 248
$sformat 225
$signed 68, 223
$skew 249
$sscanf 225
$stime 222
$stop 141, 221, 258
$strobe 213, 258
$strobeb 213
$strobeh 213
$strobeo 213
$swrite 225
$swriteb 225
$swriteh 225
$swriteo 225
$test$plusargs 257
$time 27, 222, 259
$timeformat 220, 222
$ungetc 219
$unsigned 68, 223
$value$plusargs 257
$width 248
$write 211, 258
$writeb 211
$writeh 211
$writeo 211
% character 212
% operator 65
%B 211
%b 211
%C 211
%c 211
%D 211
%d 211
%H 211
%h 211
%M 211
%m 211
%O 211
%o 211
%S 211
%s 211
%T 211
%t 211
%V 211
%v 211, 254
& 5, 73, 75
&& 72
(??) 108
(?0) 108
(01) 108
(0x) 108
* operator 65
** operator 65
*> 246
+ operator 65
+: 247
. character 232
/ operator 65
< 69
<< 77
<<< 77
<= 69
<= assignment symbol 145
= assignment symbol 144
== 71
=== 71
=> 246
> 69
>= 69
>> 77
>>> 77
? character 37, 105, 154
@* event list 134
^ 73, 76
^~ 73
`celldefine 33
`default_nettype 30, 43, 97
`define 28, 54
`else 29
`elsif 29
`endcelldefine 33
`endif 29
`ifdef 29

`ifndef 29
`include 30, 235
`line 33
`nounconnected_drive 32
`resetall 30
`timescale 8, 10, 22, 30, 94
`unconnected_drive 32
`undef 28
| 5, 73, 75
|| 72
~ 73
~& 75
~^ 73, 76
~| 75

A
absolute delay 262
algorithmic-level xv, 1, 4
always statement 11, 17, 18, 122, 125, 140, 150, 158, 228, 262, 296, 307, 309
and gate 3, 15, 84
architectural-level 4
arithmetic left-shift 77
arithmetic operator 65
arithmetic right-shift 77
arithmetic shift 259
array 51
array declaration 51
array element 61
array of instances 96, 184
ASCII character 211
assign procedural statement 158
asynchronous clear 109
asynchronous loop 296, 312
asynchronous preset 127
asynchronous reset 314
asynchronous state machine 230
attribute 237
automatic function 207, 209
automatic keyword 200
automatic task 200

B
base format 34
based integer 57
BCD 258
behavior 122
behavioral modeling 122
behavioral style 3, 8, 11, 299
bidirectional switch 93
binary 211
binary and 73
binary coded decimal 258
binary data 219
binary exclusive-nor 73
binary exclusive-or 73
binary minus 65
binary number 35
binary or 73
binary plus 65
binding 193
bit-select 44, 59, 113, 171, 179, 296
bit-wise operator 73
bitwise-and 5
bitwise-or 5
blackjack program 327
block 226
block label 19, 136
block statement 136
blocking procedural assignment 13, 22, 144, 262
BNF xviii
Boolean equation 294
break 259
buf gate 87
bufif0 88
bufif1 88

C
capacitive node 42
case equality 71
case equality operator 76
case expression 152, 191
case inequality 71
case item expression 152
case statement 152, 306, 307, 316, 323
case-sensitive 25, 26
casex statement 154
casez statement 154
cell 192
cell module 33
character 38
charge decay time 255
charge strength 254
clock 155
clock divider 277
clock edge 110
clock generator 290
closing file 215
cmos 90
combinational logic 112, 309
combinational logic primitive 3
combinational UDP 104

command line argument 257
comma-separated event list 134
compiler directive xviii, 8, 10, 27, 235
complete path name 232
complimentary MOS 92
concatenated target 19
concatenation 79, 113, 171, 179
concatenation operator 297
condition 188
conditional compilation 29
conditional operator 78, 307
conditional selection 191
conditional statement 150, 276
configuration 192
constant 34, 57
constant expression 81, 209
constant function 209
constant literal 81
constant part-select 60
constant-valued expression 50
continue 259
continuous assignment 6, 8, 9, 10, 18, 112, 122, 149, 158, 254, 263, 294, 298, 301, 304, 307
conversion function 223
counter 259, 334
cross-coupled nand-gate 20
curly brace xviii

D
data event 248
data type 38, 229
dataflow behavior 6, 8, 10, 112
dataflow modeling 122
dataflow style 3, 8, 9, 299
deassign procedural statement 158
decade counter 182, 315
decimal 35, 211
decimal notation 37
decoder 9, 99, 270, 297, 333
default delay 94
default strength specification 254
defparam statement 53, 173, 209
delay 8, 9, 30, 94, 116, 131, 301
delay control 19, 123, 126, 130, 142
delay specification 94, 117
delayed waveform 304
disable statement 136, 155, 226, 259
display task 211, 254
distributed delay 243
divide 65
don't-care 37, 105, 154
downward referencing 234
drive strength 253
drive strength specification 253
D-type flip-flop 109, 333

E
edge-sensitive path 246
edge-triggered event control 132
edge-triggered flip-flop 107
edge-triggered sequential UDP 107
edge-triggered timing control 127
elaboration time 185, 188, 191, 209
equality operator 71
escape sequence 211
escaped identifier 25
even parity 308
event 113, 229, 301
event control 12, 123, 126, 132, 143
event declaration 229
event trigger statement 229
explicit zero delay 131
expression 56, 113, 141, 171
extended VCD 238
external port 178

F
factorial design 279
fall delay 94, 117
fall time 301
falling edge 319, 323
false 33
file I/O task 215
file name 33
file pointer 216, 288
flip-flop 127, 309, 313, 333
floating point value 59
force procedural statement 160
forever loop 265
forever-loop statement 155
fork 138
for-loop statement 19, 125, 157
format specification 211, 215, 220
four-state VCD 238
free-format 26
FSM 323
full connection 246
full-adder 11, 15, 115, 273
function 204, 258, 306
function call 62, 208
function definition 205, 232

G
gate delay 21, 93, 243
gate instantiation 15, 18, 21, 84, 93, 96, 122, 166, 170, 176
gate primitive 15, 254
gate-level 1, 4, 15
gate-level modeling 122, 166
gate-level primitive 6, 304
generate block label 187
generate statement 185
generate-case 185, 191
generate-conditional 185, 188
generate-loop 185
generic queue 334
genvar declaration 186
genvar variable 186
global variable 202, 209
Gray code 292
Gray code counter 292
Gray counter 314
greater than 69
greater than or equal to 69

H
half-adder 7, 302
handshake signal 229
hexadecimal 35, 211
hierarchical design 3
hierarchical name 211, 236
hierarchical path name 173, 232
hierarchy 15, 169
high-impedance 33
hold control 334
hold time 292

I
identifier 25, 171, 232
IEEE standard 2
IEEE Std 1364.1 237
IEEE Std 1364-1995 xv, 2
IEEE Std 1364-2001 xv, xix, 2
if statement 76, 150, 300, 307
impedance 91
implicit conversion 37
implicit event control 134
implicit net 97
implicit net declaration 29, 43
include statement 192
indeterminate 227
indexed part-select 60
inertial delay 117
initial statement 11, 14, 17, 18, 22, 106, 110, 122, 123, 158, 261, 296, 307
inline argument declaration style 200
inout argument 199
inout port 167
input argument 199
input declaration 205
input parameter 258
input port 167, 171
instance binding 194
instance statement 194
integer 34, 48, 125
integer declaration 48
integer division 65
integer register 48
integer variable 59, 67
interconnection 15
internal port 178
inter-statement delay 13, 22, 142
intra-statement delay 13, 142, 257, 262, 304

J
JK flip-flop 111

K
keywords 26

L
Language Reference Manual xvii
latch 107, 310
LED sequencer 285
left-rotate 298
left-shift 77, 298
less than 69
less than or equal to 69
level-sensitive D flip-flop 311
level-sensitive event control 127, 135
level-sensitive sequential UDP 107
library 192
library declaration 192
library map file 192
line number 33
local parameter 54, 58, 169
local variable 138, 200, 209, 300
localparam 54
logic function 5
logic-0 33
logic-1 33
logical and 72
logical equality 71
logical equality operator 76
logical inequality 71

logical left shift 77
logical library 192
logical operator 72
logical or 72
logical right shift 77
loop statement 155
LRM xvii

M
macro 28
magnitude comparator 120
majority circuit 109
master-slave D-type flip-flop 271
master-slave flip-flop 100, 120
Mealy finite state machine 325
memory 45, 61, 310
memory declaration 61
memory element 61
min:typ:max 95, 302
mixed-design style 17
mixed-level modeling 4
module 6, 166
module declaration 31, 236
module instance 15
module instantiation 17, 19, 53, 166, 232
module parameter 173
module path 252
module path delay 243
module port declaration style 17, 167
module port list style 17, 167
modulus 65
monitor task 214
Moore finite state machine 323
MOS switch 90
multi-dimensional array 51
multiple-input gate 84
multiple-output gate 87
multiplexer 97, 105, 307
multiplication algorithm 316
multiplier 176
multiply 65

N
named association 17, 22, 174
named block 232
named event 229
nand gate 3, 84
n-channel control 92
negative edge 133
negedge 133
net 9, 15, 58, 67, 112, 167, 254, 263
net bit-select 59
net data type 3, 8, 39, 229
net declaration 39, 58, 115, 118, 167
net declaration assignment 115, 119
net delay 118, 243
net part-select 60
net signal strength 211
net type 29, 38
netlist 300
newline 212
nmos 90
nmos gate 3
non-automatic function 209
non-automatic task 203
nonblocking 257
nonblocking assignment 255, 257, 304
nonblocking procedural assignment 13, 145, 262
none default_nettype 30, 43, 97
non-resistive switch 91
nor gate 84
not gate 87
notif0 88
notif1 88
notifier 251, 258
n-type MOS transistor 90

O
octal 35, 211
Open Verilog International 2
opening file 215
operand 56
operator xviii, 56, 63
or gate 3, 15, 84
or-separated event list 134
output argument 199
output port 167
OVI 2

P
parallel block 136, 138
parallel connection 246
parallel to serial converter 316, 333
parameter 53, 58, 168, 209, 313
parameter declaration 29, 53, 58, 81
parameter name 81
parameter port 168
parameter port list 168
parameter specification 252
parameter value 176
parameterizable clock divider 334

parameterized Gray code counter 292
parity checker 308
parity generator 101
part-select 44, 60, 113, 171, 179, 296
path delay 3, 252
path name 259
path specification 252
PATHPULSE$ 252
p-channel control 92
period character 232
phase-delayed 267
pin-to-pin delay 3
PLI xv, 3
plusarg 257
pmos 90
pmos gate 3
port 6, 167
port association 169
port declaration 167
port list 166, 177
posedge 133
positional association 17, 19, 170, 174
positive edge 134
power 65
precedence 63
primitive gate 83, 102
primitive logic gate 3
priority encoder 102, 110
procedural assignment 13, 106, 112, 123, 125, 126, 141, 149, 257, 311
procedural construct 6, 11
procedural continuous assignment 158
procedural statement 123, 126, 130, 132, 201, 226
procedure 198
process-level 4
programming language interface xv, 1, 3
propagation delay 93
pseudo-random 224
p-type MOS transistor 90
pull gate 90
pulldown 90
pullup 90
pulse limit 252
pulse rejection limit 259
pulse width 252
punctuation mark xviii

Q

queuing-level 4

R

race condition 255
random number 223
range specification 39, 96
rcmos 90
real 34, 37
real constant 57
real declaration 51
real variable 51, 59
realtime declaration 51
realtime variable 51, 59
recursive function 207
reduction and 75
reduction nand 75
reduction nor 75
reduction operator 75
reduction or 75
reduction xnor 76
reduction xor 76
reference event 248
reg 12
reg declaration 45
reg register 67, 167
reg variable 45, 59, 106, 201, 206, 225, 309
register 300, 309
register type 38
register-transfer-level 4
reject limit 252
relational operator 69
relative delay 262
release procedural statement 160
remainder 65
repeat event control 143, 156
repeat-loop 266
repeat-loop statement 156
replication 80
reserved identifier 26
reserved word xviii
resistance 91
resistive switch 90, 91, 93
response monitoring 4
right-rotate 298
right-shift 77
rise delay 94, 117
rise time 301
rising edge 309, 323
rnmos 90
rpmos 90
RTL xvi, 4
rtran 93
rtranif0 93

rtranif1 93

S

scalar expression 81
scalar net 58, 113
scalar register 59
scalared keyword 44
scientific notation 37
SDF 219, 302
SDF backannotation 244
SDF file 219
seed 223
selection address 297
sequence detector 283
sequencer 285
sequential behavior 6, 112
sequential block 12, 14, 19, 124, 127, 136, 137, 138, 142, 146, 227, 299, 323
sequential logic primitive 3
sequential UDP 106
serial to parallel converter 334
setup time 292
shift operation 297
shift operator 77, 297, 333
shift register 313, 316, 333
signed division 78
signed keyword 39, 45, 53, 205
signed number 34, 57, 59
signed operand 62, 75
signed qualifier 35, 57, 67
signed value 67
simple decimal 34
simple path 246
simulation 260
simulation control task 221
simulation time 222, 312
simulation time function 222
sized integer constant 57
SOC 293
specify block 96, 243, 292, 302
specify parameter 243
specparam declaration 243
square bracket xviii
Standard Delay Format 302
state machine 230, 316
state transition 319
state transition table 325
state-dependent path 247
static 136
static condition 188
static task 200
stimulus 4, 18, 260
strength 91, 93
strength value 253
string 34, 37, 211
string constant 57
strobe task 213
structural style 3, 8, 15, 182, 299
structural-level 4
structure 6
supply0 43
supply1 43
switch 83, 90, 93
switch-level xv, 1, 4
switch-level modeling 3
switch-level primitive 4, 6, 15
symbolic library 192
synchronous logic 309
synthesizable RTL 237
system function xviii, 27, 209, 210
system function call 62
system task xviii, 19, 27, 209, 210
system-on-chip 293

T

tab 212
table entry 108
target 113
task 198, 226, 258
task call 198
task definition 198, 232
task enable statement 201
terminal 84
test bench 260
test constraint 4
text file 306
text macro 28
text substitution 28
three-state driver 88
time 50
time declaration 50
time format 211
time precision 8, 10, 30, 220
time unit 8, 10, 30, 220, 301
time variable 50, 59
timescale task 220
timing annotation 219
timing check 3, 247
timing control 123, 126, 130
timing violation 247
toggle flip-flop 292
toggle-type flip-flop 110
tran 93

tranif0 93
tranif1 93
transistor-level 15
transport delay 304
tri net 40
tri0 42
tri1 42
triand 41
trior 41
trireg 42
trireg net 254
tristate gate 88, 298
true 33
truth table 305
turn-off delay 94, 106, 117, 301
type conversion 49

U
UDP 3, 103, 305
UDP declaration 103
UDP definition 104
UDP instantiation 103, 106, 122, 166
UDP modeling 166
unary logical negation 72
unary minus 65
unary negation 73
unary plus 65
unconnected module input 172
unconnected module output 172
unconnected port 171
undeclared net 43, 97
underscore 34
unidirectional switch 90
unknown 33,
unsigned number 45, 57, 59
unsigned operand 62, 75
unsigned value 67
unsized decimal number 57
unsized integer constant 57
up-down counter 183, 241
upward referencing 234
user-defined function call 62
user-defined primitive 3, 6, 15, 103

V
value change dump 238
value set 33
variable 59, 136, 309
variable bit-select 59
variable data type 3, 11, 17, 141, 229, 309
variable declaration 59, 167
variable declaration assignment 124
variable part-select 60
variable type 38, 44
VCD 238
VCD file 238
vector net 44, 58, 113, 118
vector register 59
vectored keyword 44
verification 18
violation 248

W
wand 41
waveform 22, 137, 260, 304
while-loop statement 157
white space 25, 26, 47
wildcard 134
wire 294
wire net 40
wor 41
write task 211

X
xnor gate 84
xor gate 15, 84

Z
zero delay 9, 13, 116, 131, 145, 155, 255, 296, 312